From Human Trafficking to Human Rights

Reframing Contemporary Slavery

Edited by

Alison Brysk

and

Austin Choi-Fitzpatrick

PENN

UNIVERSITY OF PENNSYLVANIA PRESS

PHILADELPHIA

Published by
University of Pennsylvania Press
Philadelphia, Pennsylvania 19104-4112
www.upenn.edu/pennpress

10 9 8 7 6 5 4 3 2 1

Library of Congress Cataloging-in-Publication Data

From human trafficking to human rights : reframing
contemporary slavery / edited by Alison Brysk and Austin
Choi-Fitzpatrick. — 1st ed.
        p. cm. — (Pennsylvania studies in human rights)
     Includes bibliographical references and index.
     ISBN 978-0-8122-2276-0 (hardcover : alk. paper)
     1. Slavery.   2. Human trafficking.   3. Forced labor.
4. Human rights.   I. Brysk, Alison, 1960–   II. Choi
Fitzpatrick, Austin.   III. Series: Pennsylvania studies in
human rights.
HT867.F676 2012
306.3'62—dc23

                                                    2011030588

Contents

From Human Trafficking to Human Rights

Rethinking Trafficking

Alison Brysk and Austin Choi-Fitzpatrick

Over the last decade, the problem of modern slavery has moved from being a marginal concern to a mainstream issue, with significant advances in levels of public awareness, official engagement, and specialized research. Trafficking in persons for the purposes of forced prostitution has been the primary focal point of this renewed interest in questions of human bondage. From 1865 through 1990 slavery suffered from issue depletion, only to be rediscovered as human trafficking and successfully adopted as a cause célèbre. Scholars, activists, policy makers, and the general public have found the plight of millions to be a departure point for larger conversations about globalization, prostitution, and a host of other issues. While all of this attention is critical, we believe too much of this conversation has been superficial, incomplete, or distorted—leading to a tragically inadequate response. The contributions in this volume stem from a frustration with the status quo understanding of smuggling and outmoded debates around the legalization of prostitution. Our research has shown us new dimensions of the issue that give us the opportunity to push the discourse into original, progressive analysis of rights, slavery, power, and emancipation. Our aim is to move the conversation from sex to slavery, from prostitution to power, and from rescue to rights.

Understanding the Problem

Many advocacy groups cite figures of more than 27 million people worldwide exploited in contemporary forms of slavery, with several million of those forced or tricked across borders (based on Bales [1999] 2004). The U.S. State Department estimates that up to 820,000 men, women, and children are trafficked internationally each year, while the International Organization for Migration cites a rough figure of 800,000 (U.S. Department of State 2009; International Organization for Migration 2011). The International Labor Organization (ILO) estimates that at least 1.39 million people are victims of commercial sexual servitude worldwide, though this figure includes both transnational and domestic trafficking. The U.S. data suggest that about two-thirds are women and girls. Much of this traffic is from east to west (Europe) or south to north (Latin America to the United States, Southeast Asia to Europe and the United States) (U.S. Attorney General 2007).

The good news is that UN standards, U.S. aid conditionality, and human rights network campaigns have inspired dozens of countries to prohibit trafficking in persons. There are educational, law enforcement, and victim assistance efforts in sending and receiving countries; via regional programs in North America, Europe, and Southeast Asia; and through global bodies such as the International Organization for Migration, the ILO, and UNICEF. The bad news is that almost a decade of anti-trafficking programs have done little to reduce the incidence or the harm of the phenomenon, and they may even have diverted attention from root causes of trafficking, as well as equally harmful practices of labor exploitation affecting even greater numbers. Burgeoning recognition of some of the structural determinants of slavery in migration and prostitution has not yet registered in appropriate policies or a deeper reorientation.

Inappropriate or disproportionate policies may result from ill-founded or incomplete understanding. The United States has the most comprehensive policy and has devoted the most bureaucratic and financial resources to the issue of any single receiving country—averaging around $80 million per year over the past decade. Yet its record under the Bush administration clearly shows the limitations of traditional concepts of trafficking in addressing the problem. In the U.S. Trafficking Victims Protection Act, perhaps the central single piece of legislation, trafficking is defined as when "a commercial sex act is induced by force, fraud, or coercion." Under the Bush administration, the United States ignored the broader UN definition, which encompasses sexual exploitation of voluntary migrants and other forms of nonsexual contemporary slavery. While the U.S. program is theoretically oriented around the "three Ps" of prevention, protection, and prosecution, prevention efforts are quite limited to a handful of education programs, and protection focuses more on training and subsidizing service providers than on direct victim assistance. The bulk of the funding and effort is in law enforcement, both in the United States and abroad. Under the terms of 2003 legislation, renewed in 2005, U.S. policy has even gone so far as to deny funding to health, migration, and sex worker assistance organizations for anti-trafficking empowerment and HIV-prevention programs if such NGOs tolerate or advocate decriminalization of commercial sex work. As recently as December 2010, congressional Republicans who claim to be concerned with trafficking blocked S.987—the International Protecting Girls by Preventing Child Marriage Act of 2010, a bill expressly designed to address one of the root causes and mechanisms of trafficking.

At the global level, some health workers and scholars believe that an overemphasis on trafficking hinders HIV prevention and empowerment of sex workers to protect themselves, as well as stigmatizing prostitutes on the basis of religion-based ideology (Pisani 2008). Worldwide, anti-trafficking programs devote far more attention and resources to prosecution than protection, and still less to prevention. For example, a best-case receiving country sensitive to social context—Australia—has committed almost $7 million per year to combating trafficking in Australia through improving detection and *prosecution*, while a counterpart sending-country program financed by the ILO in Thailand for *prevention* through education and job creation provides only around $1 million per year (Australian Government 2009; HumanTrafficking.org 2006). Similarly, the vast majority of policies seek source suppression rather than demand control.

Slavery is wrong, and trafficking is slavery—but so are other, often linked forms of migration and labor. As discussed by Choi-Fitzpatrick (this volume), it is important to recognize the multiple forms that power takes in the enslavement process—it is not always explicit and recognizable coercion. Sexual violence is wrong, but trafficking is not always violent—and some of the violence comes from its suppression and illegality. Women are not always safe at home, within their states, families, or workplaces—and empowering them is more effective than rescuing them.

Trafficking as Contemporary Slavery

Rethinking trafficking as one form of contemporary slavery will help us to see more clearly its roots, consequences, and connections to other forms of exploitive labor and smuggling. Choi-Fitzpatrick's chapter situates trafficking in the larger pattern of contemporary slavery, so we can benefit from the insights of existing scholarship and analyze the sources of the harm as disempowerment. He applies a multifaceted analysis of power to theorize the structural, cultural, and psychological sources of domination. This diagnosis leads to a better understanding of a prescription for emancipation based in the agency of all actors situated along the spectrum of enslavement.

Contemporary slavery may take new forms, but it must fundamentally be understood as an "extension and/or reconfiguration of enduring historical themes, rather than as distinctively modern developments" (Quirk, this volume). Quirk also points out that these "enduring historical themes" must be explored in greater depth, as they have critical and unexamined impacts on anti-slavery efforts, such as the historic connection between abolition and colonial conquest, which predisposes us to rescue rather than to restore rights.

Rethinking trafficking as slavery means rethinking our cultural constructions. Gulati's insightful study (this volume) of media depictions of trafficking in Britain, the United States, and Canada demonstrates empirically what has long been argued by advocates of a human rights approach to slavery. He shows that media reports: (1) tend to characterize the issue as mainly involving trafficking for sexual exploitation and (2) organized crime; (3) draw heavily on mainstream sources, ignoring alternative perspectives; and (4) tend mainly to consider more superficial and technical interventions. Gulati's sharpest critique is reserved for a media that tends to parrot dominant policy approaches, effectively limiting the public's exposure to competing perspectives on the issues at stake.

From Prostitution to Power

In Brysk's words, "The problem is powerlessness, not prostitution, and the solution to powerlessness is politics—not prohibition" (this volume). Human rights are increasingly understood to be claims against both governments and other sources of authority typically associated with trafficking and slavery (employers, military leaders, family members), while enforcement is the responsibility of all states (Brysk, this volume; 2005). Analysts of trafficking policy distinguish human rights versus law enforcement versus migration control versus moralistic approaches to trafficking, which prioritize different values of national security, cultural norms, and universal human dignity. But traffickers are not just criminals who can be suppressed by law and order; they are delegated agents of social control in exploitive systems of labor and corrupt regimes. Borders are not just demarcations of territory that can be better ordered, but violently contested market niches. Commercial sex is not just a transgression of socially approved channels for male sexual appetite, but an explicit commodification of female reproductive labor that turns some women into unwilling objects rather than self-determining persons. The common element is that individuals lack agency and control of exploitive social systems: human rights.

Wasilewski and Miller's contribution to this volume reminds us of the role that gender inequity plays in constructing trafficking as a form of violence against women. They show the differential state response to such violence depending on securitization of smuggling, not rights or protection for women who are victims. In a similar vein, Hebert (this volume) suggests the putative human rights approach undertaken by the United States in the form of the Trafficking Victims Protection Act of 2000 (TVPA) lacks a commitment to the indivisibility that underpins the human rights system, and it may in fact exacerbate vulnerability among the enslaved. In her chapter she makes the case that the United States' approach to trafficking is informed by concerns over security and insecurity and is based on prostitution rather than on powerlessness of the victims. Thus trafficked individuals are perpetual outsiders demonstrating the need for enhanced security. But not only is the trafficked individual a threat to the state's physical borders, she is also a threat to the state's moral authority. Trafficked individuals (and migrants in general) are the dreaded Other, a form of cultural contaminant (in this case in the form of a "helpless, disempowered female victim"). In this light, trafficked individuals are neither helpless victims (as in the moral crusader narrative) nor rights-bearing individuals (as in the human rights framework) but are instead seen as dangerous transnational actors. Hebert suggests that the TVPA, far from being a seminal human rights effort to end trafficking, may be better seen as a tool for the regulation of autonomy, especially an autonomy that threatens moral and national borders.

Moreover, *international* structures of power and political economy now help to constitute domination—even seemingly benign or neutral aspects of global governance. Both Charles Smith (focusing on Kosovo, Haiti, Sierra Leone, and Nepal) and Heather Smith (focusing specifically on Haiti) in this volume contribute to an empirically informed analysis of the ways international actors—in their cases, peacekeepers, themselves a product of earlier human rights victories—generate conditions ripe for human trafficking. These findings challenge assessments of international organizations that would see the influx of peacekeepers as a net-positive contribution to situations of radical instability. In a further move, Charles Smith suggests that when peacekeepers move on and demand diminishes, trafficked individuals are either moved to follow the demand or are repurposed for the very drug or arms trafficking that is often responsible for initiating destabilizing flows of weapons and narcotics—flows that are easily linked to the resurgence of conflict.

This cautionary assessment of international intervention is of a type with Quirk (this volume), who argues that a number of factors, including colonial imperatives and stylized notions of what it meant to be civilized, affected Britain's abolitionist policies and that global hierarchies undermine the export of empowerment. Gallagher (this volume) suggests that while the Trafficking in Persons (TIP) Reports mandated by the TVPA have prompted a stunning number of countries to comply with demands for new policies and approaches, it is not at all clear whether they have been effective in reducing levels of slavery (U.S. Government Accountability Office [GAO] 2006, 2007).

From Rescue to Rights

How can a human rights approach bring us from protecting our borders from prostitution toward empowerment and true global change? A human rights approach to trafficking and contemporary slavery reorients our analysis and response by showing that:

- people lacking human rights are the most vulnerable to trafficking and exploitation;
- trafficking and exploitation are violations of fundamental universal rights, not moral problems of perpetrators, victims, families, or cultures;
- sending states have a responsibility to protect the human rights of their citizens from all sources, including nonstate actors like employers, smugglers, and families;
- international responses to trafficking should focus on remedying and restoring rights, ideally through representation and not rescue;

- receiving states have a responsibility to protect the human rights of all residents on their territory, so crime and border control efforts relevant to trafficking must be rights-based and subject to monitoring and accountability as such.

This is echoed by van den Anker's call for a cosmopolitan model of global justice (this volume). Cosmopolitanism describes an approach in which individuals as well as states have duties across borders to make human rights accessible to all, whether they are in their home country or abroad. Such a model would ultimately serve to reduce human trafficking, especially, she points out, if this cosmopolitanism is recognized as also involving duties to those without citizenship. Clearly the process of recognizing and then obtaining such power and recognition is neither simple nor popular for enslaved individuals or their advocates.

And even in the United States, there are signs that new understandings may provide an opportunity for the further expansion of the human rights approach. The U.S. Trafficking in Persons office has recently highlighted the importance of several key human rights issues: ranking the United States alongside other countries; emphasizing that more people are trafficked for forced labor than for commercial sex; highlighting the significant number of men who are victims of trafficking; and challenging individuals to think about and reduce their slavery footprint (CdeBaca 2010). In her contribution to this volume, Gallagher points out that the Trafficking in Persons Reports generated by the TIP office have a capacity for both destruction and genuine innovation. The reports are modeled on U.S. legislation rather than the international legal standards of human rights law. This move effectively sidelines the core contributions of a rights-based response while generating the potential for violations of individual rights, whether through prosecution for a crime, detention, denial of migration, forced repatriation, required cooperation with authorities, gendered interventions, or blind raids. If the United States wants to improve the legitimacy of its anti-trafficking efforts and the TIP Reports, she argues, it must bring the standards for both into line with international legal norms. On a more positive note, she also argues:

The Reports have done more than perhaps any other single initiative to expose the breadth and extent of contemporary exploitation of individuals for private profit; they have shed light on practices and traditions that have too long remained hidden; they have exposed the complicity of public officials in trafficking-related exploitation; and they have compelled many governments who would not otherwise have done so to take action. (Gallagher, this volume)

Such a report from a longtime critic of the process should give some room for hope.

Civil society campaigns are a necessary complement to cosmopolitan justice and changes in state policy. Bales and Choi-Fitzpatrick conclude this volume with a call and orientation for civil society engagement in ending trafficking and empowering all victims of contemporary slavery. Solidarity with all migrants and all workers is the best human rights strategy for healing the harms of human trafficking.

Toward Rethinking

This volume is an effort to challenge governments, international organizations, corporations, nonprofits, and individuals to close the gap between our human rights ideals and bureaucratic, institutional, economic, and personal practice. Rethinking is the first step toward emancipation for all forms of contemporary slavery.

Rethinking trafficking as slavery and emancipation as human rights can guide us to improved scholarship and policy. From an academic perspective, more contextual analyses such as Gulati, Quirk, and Brysk show us that we cannot understand contemporary slavery without investigating its historical trajectory and cultural meanings. Our volume helps to build the emerging approach that shows how slavery and rights are historically constructed, in order to suggest how they can be deconstructed.

Our approach also aims to move the study of trafficking from protectionist polemic to political analysis. The contributions by Hebert, Wasileski and Miller, Gallagher, and Charles Smith each demonstrate that trafficking patterns and responses must be interpreted as outcomes of power and interests. As Brysk and others have pushed human rights debates to address the politics of "private wrongs"—human rights abuses committed by non-state actors—we must always ask what power structures drive trafficking and which domestic, international, and gendered elites benefit from it—even when they do not cause it directly.

Human rights scholarship struggles to locate the duties that correspond to rights. In our volume, Heather Smith, Christien van den Anker, Anne Gallagher, and Kevin Bales also move forward the call for responsibilities to protect and fulfill migrant, labor, and women's rights. Across the levels of global governance, state policy, and social movements, a humanitarian problem-solving approach must be expanded to systematically consider both rights and duties, and to hold all actors responsible for the rights implications of their interventions. Sending countries, host countries, international society, and domestic society are all the addressees of human rights claims.

Rethinking emancipation also generates and guides new approaches to policy. Our authors concur that trafficking policy must be a situated form of broader human rights policy, not an episodic campaign or intervention. If victims of trafficking are simply the weakest link in interdependent domestic and international systems of exploitation, chapters by Brysk and Choi-Fitzpatrick suggest that we cannot protect them without strengthening rights and empowerment for all women, all workers, and all migrants. Isolated anti-trafficking initiatives may easily push vulnerable populations into equally abusive forms of smuggling for other markets, nonsexual slavery at home or abroad, or domestic sexual exploitation replacing transnational prostitution. Rethinking trafficking as slavery also reminds us that for all forms of slavery, law enforcement and source suppression are not sustainable without structural demand control, usually located in host countries and markets. Some host countries' recent introduction of extraterritorial prosecution of their own citizens for sexual exploitation of children overseas is a first step, but greater control and stigmatization of host nationals' sexual exploitation of trafficked women at home is also needed. Choi-Fitzpatrick, Bales, and Brysk all emphasize that the move from protection to empowerment is a longer-term process of social change, not just a single intervention; true emancipation requires follow-up for liberated victims and longer-term economic and educational programs for at-risk populations.

More specifically, our authors recommend or imply the following policy changes. The chapters by Gulati and Bales and Choi-Fitzpatrick show that anti-trafficking policy must not be limited to government action, or even rescue-oriented campaigns, but must instead mobilize broader transnational social efforts for education, economic conditionality, and lobbying. Media, consumers, and educators must be shown the bigger picture, given incentives and resources, and directed to leverage points. In a different vein, the work by Wasileski and Miller, Hebert, and Gallagher critiques the insufficiencies and unintended consequences of U.S.-generated anti-trafficking legislation. The implication is twofold: enforcement-oriented legislation is necessary but not sufficient, and it must be coupled with supportive measures to reduce spillover effects on victims and diversion of the same abuses into other channels. Protection must not be tied to prosecution, and regulatory efforts must encompass the wider spectrum of violence against women—regardless of migration status. The essays by Charles Smith and Heather Smith deliver an important warning to international organizations to evaluate the impact of their intervention activities on trafficking and sexual exploitation, and to set up mechanisms of empowerment and accountability for the governed population vulnerable to abuse. Moreover, Heather Smith's comparison of the harms of intervention by different organizations suggests that democratization of international organizations is a necessary concomitant of global governance.

Finally, Van den Anker, Bales, and Choi-Fitzpatrick show the importance of establishing migrant and labor rights organizations and campaigns within broader human rights groups to complement any governmental or international intervention and to sustain longer-term emancipation. This is especially critical given the distortions of U.S. resistance to sex workers' organizations and most host countries' ambivalence regarding migrants' rights. Reframing labor, migrant, and sex-worker rights as human rights grants greater access to existing organizations and greater legitimacy and accountability vis-à-vis host governments.

Rethinking trafficking means rethinking how we see, understand, and embrace "the least among us," which is the true test of engaged human rights scholarship. Such rethinking involves overcoming several of the most difficult barriers to the development of human rights discourse: women's rights as human rights, labor rights as a confluence of structure and agency, the interdependence of migration and discrimination, the ideological and policy hegemony of the United States in setting the terms of debate, and the politics of global governance—and the international human rights regime itself. In this volume, by rethinking trafficking, we attempt to contribute to the larger project of rethinking and reclaiming human rights across borders.

PART I

From Sex to Slavery

Chapter 1

Rethinking Trafficking: Contemporary Slavery

Austin Choi-Fitzpatrick

Introduction

Over the last fifteen years, ever-increasing public, political, and scholarly attention has focused on human trafficking and modern slavery. This attention has been converted into action as pressure from international advocates has generated new international norms and policies. Advocacy within the United States has resulted in new domestic legislation. Subsequent pressure from the U.S. government has resulted in new legislation abroad, as well as extensive funding of projects intended to prevent trafficking, protect trafficked individuals, and prosecute perpetrators.

Action on the part of the United States has also generated a range of criticism, from both human rights advocates and scholars working on this issue. Since these critiques have come from many quarters, they have failed to generate a platform from which subsequent critiques (and efforts at amelioration) might be based. This volume can be seen as a clear argument for a human rights platform for ongoing critique, and subsequent reform.

This chapter contributes to this platform by introducing and briefly sketching a number of key issues, including: the existence of a growing body of work that I am calling a *field of contemporary slavery studies*; the importance of working within the rubric of *slavery*; the opportunity to better theorize the role of *power* in contemporary slavery; and the necessity of theorizing *contemporary abolition and emancipation* in addition to exploitation.

Contemporary Slavery Studies

Scholars contributing to our understanding of trafficking and slavery are engaged in a nascent and emerging interdisciplinary field of contemporary slavery studies. Indeed, one could argue that this field bridges research and movement fields as it increasingly involves the voices and contributions of grassroots activists and survivors of slavery as well as scholars and policy makers (Bales and Trodd 2008; Sage and Kasten 2006). This field of contemporary slavery studies has taken shape over the past decade with the emergence of special issues of journals and magazines, edited volumes and monographs in the popular and academic press, academic institutes on the topic, social movement organizations on college campuses, online and in major cities around the world, and with increased attention among members of the world policy community (governments, nongovernmental organizations, the United Nations and its affiliates, international nongovernmental organizations)—all eager to be seen tackling the issue with vigor. The momentum within national civil societies is clear, as is the salience of the issue within the world polity. Yet, despite this broad attention—or perhaps *because* of this attention—our understanding of *what* we are talking about, and what we hope to do about it, is sometimes hopelessly heterogeneous.

A steady stream of popular work has introduced this issue to the general public. For example, recent and popular works have sketched the issue in broad terms for a general public (Batstone 2007; Skinner 2009). The most popular theoretical overview, inarguably, is Kevin Bales's work emphasizing the historic dimension of modern slavery as well as its embedding in the global economy ([1999] 2004). Subsequent scholarly work has explored recent historic trends (Miers 2003), the crucial support this issue has received from evangelicals and second-wave feminists (Choi-Fitzpatrick n.d.; Hertzke 2004), the structural factors underpinning trafficking (Cameron and Newman 2008), the nature of demand (DiNicola et al. 2009), whether and how it intersects with issues of human rights (Obokata 2006), smuggling (Zhang 2007), security (Friman and Reich 2007), the global sex industry (Beeks and Amir 2006), gender (Aradau 2008; Lobasz 2009) and law (Gallagher 2010). Additional work has focused on the economic dimensions of the modern slave trade (Kara 2009; Shelley 2010), as well as specific regions, including the Balkans (Friman and Reich 2007), South America (Guinn and Steglich 2003), and Eurasia (Strecker and Shelley 2004).

Moreover, this recent literature has focused specific attention on the nature, scope, and quality of current data (Ali 2010; Feingold 2010; Laczko and Gozdziak 2005; Savona and Stefanizzi 2007; USGAO 2006), as well as contemporary policy trends (DeStefano 2008). Additional work has explored the predominant and preponderant emphasis on sex trafficking (Doezema 2010; Outshoorn 2004) and the overlooked role of labor organizing (Kempadoo 2005; Kempadoo and Doezema 1998). An emerging critical perspective on trafficking and slavery can be seen in a number of recent works, including volumes edited by Christien van den Anker (2004) and Kamala Kempadoo (2005). This volume continues this more critical conversation, broadening it to new arguments and targets.

In branding this efflorescence of work a *field of contemporary slavery studies*, I hope to delimit a body of academic and serious popular work on the issue, and to suggest opportunities to work comparatively and coherently in our efforts to better understand slavery and trafficking. Doing so recognizes a number of issues. First, this approach must recognize the diversity of the phenomena under consideration. Indeed it covers trafficking for sexual or labor exploitation, hereditary slavery, forced labor under military regimes and states, temple slavery, and the commercial sexual exploitation of children. Second, this approach recognizes the number and variety of perspectives on the issue, including migration, prostitution, child labor, and human rights, as well as cultural studies and history. Third, it is important to recognize the ways these different issues are connected to scholars' framing of the issue. By this I mean slavery is variously considered to be a matter for state-level intervention, a product of state-level intervention, a product of globalization, an issue connected to women's rights in particular or human rights in general, just to name a few. Finally, this approach recognizes the number and diversity of actors currently working to understand this issue. At any point in time, students, governmental officials and civil servants, nongovernmental organizations, social movement organizations, businesses, consumers, armed rebel groups, everyday people, and scholars are struggling to better conceptualize this form of exploitation. Not surprisingly, this complex issue has generated incredible enthusiasm as well as credible first steps within many of the sectors already listed.

The task that remains, I believe, is to integrate these resources, ideas, and opportunities under a common analytical umbrella. Such a rethinking, I argue, will allow us to move from thinking of trafficking as sex to considering the broader context of slavery, from understanding power as simple coercion to an analysis of domination, and from abolition to emancipation.

From Sex to Slavery

While the center of this field is focused on human trafficking and contemporary slavery, it overlaps significantly with many varied forms of abuse. It is crucial that efforts within contemporary slavery studies take slavery as the unit of analysis and the social phenomena of central concern. By slavery I mean a social and economic relationship in which *an individual is held against his or her will, through violence or threats of violence with little or no pay, for the purpose of economic exploitation* (Bales [1999] 2004). Thus, while contemporary forms of slavery differ in significant ways from more traditional forms of slavery, these core factors obtain (being held against one's will, threats/violence, and economic exploitation). My framing of slavery as occurring in multiple forms highlights slavery's position on a continuum of exploitation occurring around the world more than its historically fixed status as *the* "particular institution." In other words, slavery is no longer an institution, but instead a state of affairs that—whether short-term or life-long—best resembles a highly dysfunctional human relationship punctuated by violence and threats of violence. Thus, we can see being held against one's will, threats/violence, and economic exploitation as the key factors that connect contemporary slavery to its manifest prior forms.

With this central concept as a rubric or guide, we may then fruitfully work our way outward and determine whether other forms of abuse fit the definition. Many important forms of exploitation will not fit—such is the cost of conceptual and theoretical specificity. To date, the relationship between slavery and trafficking is poorly conceptualized and often abused. My call here is not to a new definition or theory, but to a more consistent use of an existing approach. For those who argue that slavery will not capture all phenomena currently debated by the "anti-trafficking community"—I agree. Understanding slavery's numerous forms and contexts wasn't easy in earlier movements against slavery, and we should not expect it to be any easier now, a point Quirk (this volume) makes to great effect.

Seen in comparative and historical perspective, slavery is one of humanity's most durable institutions. While its particular forms have changed—humans are more likely to be controlled than owned, for example—slavery has maintained a distinctive core. No matter what particular cultural or historic form it takes, slavery always involves the control of one person by another, through violence or threats of violence, for the purpose of economic exploitation. If we take the historical significance of slavery seriously, then we must account for its current manifestations in situations of forced labor, bonded labor, or trafficking for sexual or labor exploitation. Conceptualized in this way, human trafficking can be better understood as the modern slave trade—a critical but specific form of slavery. Perhaps those trading in humans are using new technologies, drawing on innovative organizational structures, and conducting their business with cutting-edge technology. Yet the core of our story—the ends—continues to be enslavement. We should not be surprised by new means.

But it is newly highlighted means that seem to generate the most consternation, and confusion. Not all prostitution is trafficking, not all smuggling is trafficking, and not all slavery is sexual. More heat than light has been generated in the explication of each of these relationships, and considerable confusion persists within the general public (as well as within sectors that should know better). Centralizing scholarly, policy, and advocacy energies around the rubric of contemporary slavery will allow for a welcome narrowing of these debates to focus on the critical social relation in question: when one person holds another against their will, through violence or threats of violence, with little or no pay, for the purpose of economic exploitation. A clear contribution to this end can be found in Quirk's chapter (this volume) in which he argues that contemporary slavery is not new. In fact, slavery never ended in some parts of the world. Examples abound: chattel slavery based on descent in Mauritania, Mali, and Niger, caste- and temple-based slavery in India based on debt or descent, and even the "white slavery" (1905) frame preceding the contemporary understanding of "sex trafficking" in the United States. Highlighting the continuity between seemingly historic manifestations and contemporary forms of slavery requires an identification of what Quirk (this volume) has called "enduring historical themes." As I argue below, current scholarship and advocacy have made more headway in conceptualizing slavery than analyzing emancipation. If the recent popularity of William Wilberforce has rightly emphasized the importance of social movement strategy and bold leadership, it has done so at the expense of the more complicated political and economic dynamics that ultimately determine the space in which social movement actors strategize (McAdam 1999). The goal of freedom will be best served by a round of issue consolidation that directs our attention to the issue at hand—slavery—and to the ways this issue has changed and evolved over time.

Power: From Coercion to Domination

Scholarship on contemporary slavery lacks a coherent treatment of the role of power. Theories of oppression, resistance, and the intersection of the two are under-theorized. Across the literature, a notion of *control* predominates, with few exceptions.[1] The most sophisticated development of a theory of power is found in Bales's (2004) direct adaptation of Gibbs's work on control, which Gibbs defines as: "*overt* behavior by a human in the belief that 1) the behavior increases or decreases the probability of some subsequent condition and 2) the increase or decrease is desirable" (1996, 27). As Brysk argues in this volume, however, anti-trafficking efforts are often hampered by "concentration on coercion rather than more complex structural violence." Both Gibbs and Bales draw on power as control—what has been called power's first dimension. Additional purchase can be obtained through the incorporation of power's two additional dimensions, as identified by sociologist Stephen Lukes.

Lukes's fundamental contribution is the argument that power has three dimensions: the first entailing overt decisions, the second entailing non-decisions, and the third comprised of structural power (the "sheer weight and shape of institutional frameworks") (Barrett 2002). In this way Lukes focused scholars' attention on: (1) explicit decision-making and control over specific political and cultural contexts; (2) hidden strategies for keeping *potential issues* out of these contexts; and (3) the prevalence of false consciousness in eliminating concern over one's real interest. While it has faced subsequent criticism, this approach provides an opening to explore slavery in light of cultural forms of power as well as the more explicit interpersonal use of force.

The prevailing conceptualization of power in the literature appears to have rested at Lukes's first dimension of power: overt control. Yet a rapid review of contemporary slavery's manifestations readily demonstrates that enslavement is a complex process and the forms of control, coercion, and power exercised by slaveholders are not only physical (power's first dimension) but also psychological and cultural (power's second and third dimensions).

This approach is exactly that described by Lukes' structural power—the process of precluding the thought of resistance. This more nuanced approach to power can be applied with great effect to contemporary studies of slavery. Part of the utility in this approach lies in the way it foregrounds the role of culturally embedded power structures such as caste, class, citizenship, and gender. Historians of the American experience of slavery have done significant work on this issue, and Quirk's chapter in this volume begins to apply these theories to contemporary cases.

Seen from this perspective, therefore, power operating in Lukes's third dimension—through culture, assumptions, and pretexts—must be identified and named if there is any chance for emancipation, eradication, and abolition. Within the literature on social movements and social change, the dominant assumption has been that social-movement activity targets the state, as it has often been considered the actor of greatest significance. Recent scholarship has challenged this approach, observing that social movements for human rights target a number of institutions, both state and non-state (Armstrong and Bernstein 2008). Moreover, private authority within and across borders can be challenged by transnational campaigns (Brysk 2002; Keck and Sikkink 1998).

Such multi-institutional and transnational approaches allow for a more comprehensive mapping of the power systems involved in the patterning and enforcing of quiescence. These approaches also suggest novel and complex targets for movement challengers and human rights activists. For this reason the authority targeted by the anti-slavery efforts may range broadly, from the authority of a local landowner to dominant cultural conceptions of rightful personhood (Macwan et al. 2010). In the caste system— illegal but widespread—individuals live at the intersection of economic power systems, cultural power systems, and gendered power systems and within often corrupt political systems. In rural India, for example, the state often represents a distant and abstract force, while power dynamics related to caste, class, and gender occupy far more of the life-world. Efforts to end slavery must challenge the articulation of power at these points— caste, class, gender—as well as in more traditionally recognized seats of power (the slaveholder's coercive force; the judge's gavel; the legislator's pen). Additional attention to the complex nature of power will add to our understanding of individual power *over* the enslaved as well as structural power *through* culture and institutions. This shift—from power *over* to power *through*—also provides an opportunity to more usefully conceptualize agency and emancipation. Emancipation is more than abolition; it is a transformation in consciousness, social structure, and political empowerment.

Beyond Abolition: Toward Emancipation

The literature on contemporary slavery suggests there are a number of paths out of slavery: (1) escape, death and disappearance, about which very little is known and almost no data exists; (2) externally initiated raids, from sympathetic nongovernmental organizations (NGOs) or police; and (3) internally or externally initiated collective action, from within the community itself or facilitated by sympathetic NGOs. While collective action interventions occasionally occur, most contemporary anti-slavery efforts are focused on the second of these three paths: externally initiated raids. Indeed, raids lie at the center of the themed approach advanced by the U.S. State Department: *Rescue, Rehabilitation, and Reintegration*. This clever alliteration belies the complexity of the task it describes while relying on a number of crucial misconceptions. Alternative approaches relying on community or labor organizing have been pursued by sex workers around the world and have met with some success. To date, however, wider adoption of this strategy has been an exception (for example, the Coalition of Immokalee Workers' efforts in Florida). Here I argue that the experience of such groups points to the importance of a shift from rescue, rehabilitation, and reintegration to an approach that is based in *Resistance, Representation, and Rights*.

The first stage in this process—rescue—is a nearly universal, relatively well understood, and generally recognizable and stable stage. This stability, however, should not be confused with support, a fact attested to by most of the contributors to this volume. The process of rescuing individuals through raids is actively contested on the grounds that it is rooted in a denial of agency (Agustin 2007; Jones 2003). Much of the debate around the use of raids and rescues pivots around what happens next: the less well conceptualized, and more unevenly instituted, Restoration and Rehabilitation phases of the intervention process.

Rehabilitation is often taken to mean some sort of psychosocial stabilization combined with a return to one's (presumably normal economic and social) life. What this approach acknowledges in theory, it ignores in practice. Enslaved individuals come instead from contexts of grinding poverty or social dependency—as seen in the broader picture of gender inequity and intrafamily violence across borders depicted by Wasilewski and Miller (this volume). Little practical attention is given to the complexity of the life that a "restored" survivor should "reintegrate" into. A simple assessment of the term "reintegrate" suggests several underlying assumptions. Most notably, "reintegrate" implies that the person went anywhere. The vast majority of the people impacted by slavery live in India, where bonded labor confines people in their own communities, which they have never intended to leave. Most people living in slavery do not actually go anywhere. The second assumption is that if an individual *has* gone anywhere, he or she would like to return. In Immokalee, Florida, or Southern California, survivors of forced labor rarely want to return to Mexico or Guatemala or wherever they are from. They often want to simply return to work and be paid a fair wage without suffering from abuse.[2] The third, and final, assumption is that an effort should be made to return the (ideally psychosocially rehabilitated) individual to their community. This approach is considered to be complex, but preferred, despite the fact that the literature is clear that poverty and violence (within the home or from the state) are significant precipitating "push" factors in the trafficking or enslavement process.[3] As Brysk points out (this volume), current policies are rooted in a neoliberal assumption that coerced victims can simply be returned to the market where they will be able to pursue other viable choices and to supportive families and societies. These assumptions are both simplistic and false.

The shortcomings of these approaches become clear when one attempts to apply the Rescue, Restore, and Rehabilitation model's assumptions to actual anti-trafficking efforts, whether they are initiated by outside actors or through grassroots struggles for emancipation. For these reasons, I suggest a new rubric. First, I argue that the way people come out of slavery should be thought of as involving either rescue or *resistance*. By resistance I mean to emphasize public struggle drawing on existing oppositional consciousness and everyday forms of resistance. My sense is that former slaves are better able to avoid reexploitation when they emerge from slavery as the result of collective action. This action has the potential to generate a critical collective identity that ideally roots the newly emancipated in an awareness of their dignity and rights.[4] Second, I argue that an individual (or collective) assessment of dignity and rights is more valuable when it can be harnessed though *representation*. Successful and enduring emancipation should result in new political, economic, social, and legal roles and claims for the newly emancipated. Such an approach recognizes that "the problem is powerlessness, not prostitution, and the solution to powerlessness is politics—not prohibition" (Brysk, this volume). In fact, this challenge may explain why in the United States little federal funding has been available to groups working to identify victims of labor exploitation or to those who have adopted community-organizing models. While this situation has slowly changed over the past decade (CdeBaca 2010), it is also being challenged by contemporary debates over immigration and rights-worthiness of immigrants and migrants (see van den Anker, this volume).

Resistance and representation within a community generate new relationships between slaveholders and those held in slavery. The complexity of these new social relations is critical to activists and scholars willing to consider human rights violations more sociologically—that is, as a complicated relationship between two or more people within a particular sociocultural context. Most existing anti-slavery models only consider legal remedies for perpetrators (that is, *prosecution*). Yet recent advocacy and scholarship on restorative justice and experiences in the aftermath of mass atrocities suggest more stable solutions must be found, as perpetrators and victims may live the rest of their lives together within the same community. As Bales has suggested ([1999] 2004; Bales and Choi-Fitzpatrick, this volume), emancipation's victories in the United States were hollowed out through the reemergence of status-quo social relationships enforced through sharecropping and segregation. To avoid this fate, we encourage policies and interventions that empower oppressed individuals while making every effort to address the attitudes and behaviors of the enslaving class or caste. This clearly requires more than stronger legislation, larger awareness campaigns, and better-trained law enforcement.

I argue that such challenges to the status quo represent a shift from a rescue model of victim maintenance to a *rights* approach to sustainable emancipation. Sketching the contours of a human rights–based approach to anti-slavery work is a project central to this volume. At the most fundamental level, a rights-based approach recognizes the critical importance of both protection and empowerment (Brysk, this volume). The importance of protection is reinforced by several of the volume's contributors. Brysk points out the increased number of violations perpetrated by private actors, van den Anker calls for a cosmopolitan model of global justice that would see individual rights that transcend borders, Hebert critiques the TVPA's lack of commitment to the indivisibility of human rights (Whelan 2010), and Gallagher questions whether existing efforts at protection have borne fruit.

A human rights approach places individual actors—whether prior to, in the midst of, or after enslavement—at the center of any effort to address conditions of exploitation. The critical value here is agency, a human capacity present in even the most dire straits (Scott 1987, 1990). While much has been said with regard to agency and resistance among those working in commercial sex, this issue has not been theorized more broadly, for example among bonded agricultural workers.

A human rights approach would additionally clarify the challenging relationship between an individual's rights as a "victim" versus as a "worker" versus one's rights as a "woman," were one individual to inhabit each category. The role of victim is complicated if an individual has chosen the work but not the conditions. If a person has chosen employment in the commercial sex industry (or as a stonebreaker), only to find themselves held against their will, without pay, for economic exploitation, they inhabit two statuses: as a worker and as a victim. Their subsequent status as a victim is clear, while their status as a worker should remain intact. The reality of this condition has gained traction in the TIP office at the USG: "there is less duping and kidnapping of naïve victims than there is coercion of people who initially agreed to do the work" (CdeBaca 2010). It is good that this is being recognized. Unfortunately, this is the easy part. The empowerment of enslaved individuals has often meant letting migrant men return to the informal economies that produced abuse in the first place. This option is less frequently available to women, perhaps because they are perceived to have fewer real options. Put bluntly, men are frequently allowed to choose between statuses (worker or victim), while status is more frequently selected for women (that of a victim). Whatever the case, a human rights approach would empower survivors of trafficking to self-identify as worker, victim, both, neither, or some other category.

Conclusion

This chapter has argued that broadly dispersed and oft disjointed efforts to understand trafficking and slavery should first be named ("contemporary slavery studies") and that this newly branded field of scholarship should take the concept of slavery as a first principle of sorts. Such a solution is of little interest to most advocacy-oriented efforts, as they are understandably keyed to specific issues (migration, child rights, etc.), but is necessary to advance scholarly understanding. I then propose that additional attention should be paid (by both scholars and advocates) to the nature of power and the importance of contemporary abolition and emancipation. Understanding abolition and emancipation will require shifting our attention from rescue to resistance, from restoration to representation, and from reintegration to rights. Such a human rights approach must also better consider the roles, rights, and responsibilities of perpetrators in post-intervention social relations.

The gap between the human rights approach advocated in this volume and that currently pursued by governments, corporations, and the voting, consuming public is significant (Chuang 2006). In our concluding chapter, Kevin Bales and I advance a number of recommendations for each of these communities. We argue that earlier experiences with slavery and abolition hold critical lessons. Both slavery and abolition are part of much broader trends within cultural and religious change, the global political economy, and nationally oriented civil society. For this reason, the successful eradication of slavery will require the engagement of governments, intergovernmental organizations, businesses, religious and cultural groups, social movement organizations, and individual communities. Rooting these efforts in a human rights approach will better serve individuals held in slavery, slaveholders perpetrating injustice, and the broader human community working to abolish slavery.

Chapter 2

Uncomfortable Silences: Contemporary Slavery and the "Lessons" of History

Joel Quirk

Introduction

Over the last decade, the various practices that fall under the rubric of contemporary slavery have generated a level of public interest that has not been matched since early twentieth-century campaigns against both "white slavery" and forced labor in the Congo Free State. Numerous governments have recently drafted new anti-slavery (mostly anti-trafficking) laws. Some legislatures have even established specialized anti-slavery agencies and taskforces. Various reports have been drafted, additional protocols and procedures have been established, and a range of rehabilitation schemes and training programs have been introduced. These official activities have followed in the wake of a remarkable change in public consciousness from the late 1990s onward. From a situation in the 1980s where few nonexperts were aware that forms of slavery remained a problem, things have recently reached a stage where there are relatively few people who are not aware that slavery remains a global problem. As part of this latest phase in the evolution of organized anti-slavery, a number of anti-slavery activists and other commentators have recently looked to earlier historical periods for instruction and inspiration in the continuing fight against contemporary slavery. In keeping with larger trends, most of these recent historical incursions have focused upon various aspects of the history of transatlantic slavery, while remaining largely silent regarding the related history of slavery and abolition in other parts of the globe.

In this chapter, I explore a number of linkages between historical practices and contemporary problems, paying particular attention to various complications arising out of this selective approach to history.[1] The main point of departure for this particular project revolves around the contemporary ramifications of an uncomfortable historical relationship between the legal abolition of slavery and European imperialism. To help make sense of this relationship, I have divided this chapter into two main sections. In the first section, I examine some of the key features of the history of slavery and abolition in West Africa between 1807 and 1960. By providing a snapshot of some major developments during this period, I aim to develop an alternative framework from which to evaluate some of the historical "lessons" that have recently been drawn by anti-slavery activists and other commentators. This is the task of the second section, which begins by considering some of the ways in which the history of slavery has been represented in recent works, and then goes on to consider how additional issues and associations come to light once this larger history becomes part of the conversation.

Slavery and Abolition in West Africa, 1807–1960

Slavery and enslavement have been practiced by most peoples at most times for the course of thousands of years. While European slave systems in the Americas have consistently attracted the lion's share of both popular and scholarly attention, the last two decades have also seen the consolidation of a now extensive literature concerned with slavery and abolition in other parts of the globe.[2] Until relatively recently, slavery was an integral feature of both social and economic life in most parts of the Americas; North Africa and the Middle East; southern Europe; Russia; the Indian subcontinent; East, South-East, and Central Asia; and sub-Saharan Africa. Both pre- and postabolition practices in these regions raise a number of uncomfortable questions regarding the causes and consequences of the legal abolition of slavery, and therefore pose a number of problems for orthodox assumptions and representations derived from "New World" experiences. In order to develop this line of argument, I have chosen to focus upon the history of slavery and abolition in West Africa, which offers a valuable case study from which to reflect upon the broader causes and consequences of the abolition of slavery outside the Americas.[3] The time period to be discussed begins with the passage of legislation abolishing the British transatlantic slave trade in 1807, and it concludes at the peak of decolonization in Africa in 1960.

For political elites in West Africa,[4] the passage of the 1807 legislation had both immediate and long-term consequences. Over the course of the eighteenth century, the British had consolidated their position as the premier slave trader in the Atlantic. Their unilateral withdrawal not only meant that local elites in places such as the Gold Coast (Ghana) lost a key trading partner, it was also symptomatic of a larger transformation in sensibilities that eventually called into question the legitimacy and long-term viability of slavery within Africa as a whole (Quirk and Richardson 2008). In the first half of the nineteenth century, British anti-slavery efforts were chiefly geared toward European slave traders, resulting in the expenditure of considerable diplomatic and naval resources on anti-slavery suppression efforts. This far-reaching campaign also impinged upon elites in West Africa. British agents secured (largely ineffectual) agreements with various local rulers to help prevent trading, and also periodically deployed their navy against coastal sites supplying other European slavers (Eltis 1987, 164–84; Miers 1975, 43–55).

The transatlantic slave trade eventually came to an end in the 1860s, after three and a half centuries that saw approximately 12.5 million slaves embarked on ships bound for the Americas via the "Middle Passage" (Eltis and Richardson 2008). The staggered closure of the various branches of this Atlantic trade had important consequences for venerable slave systems in both West and West Central Africa. A number of key themes can be briefly highlighted here, starting with the growth of "legitimate" (that is, nonslave) commerce. In the decades that followed 1807, the export trade in palm oil and other agricultural products substantially increased in parts of West Africa. This trade was presented as a way of developing commercial alternatives that would offer a viable alternative to African involvement in transatlantic slave trading (Curtin 1964, 125, 270–72, 428–31). This strategy proved to be completely misguided. In the Bight of Biafra, to take one key example, British merchants moved from trading in slaves to trading in palm oil, while their African counterparts "engaged in both trades simultaneously" (Northrup 1976, 359).

The rise of "legitimate" trade was not simply ineffectual. By stimulating demand for various trade goods, it actually ended up contributing to a further expansion in the long-standing use of slave labor across West Africa. This outcome is captured by Paul Lovejoy and David Richardson, who observe that:

> expanding production of commercial crops, whether for export overseas, as in the case of gum arabic and palm oil, or consumption within West Africa, as in the case of kola nuts, grain and cotton, provided a major impetus to slavery within Africa. (1995, 46)

Historians continue to debate the levels of dislocation and adaptation occasioned by the end of Atlantic slave trading. There is one area, however, where there is substantial agreement: the marked growth of slavery and enslavement in West Africa during this period (Lovejoy 2000, 140–252; Manning 1990, 126–49). This development is usually attributed to a combination of long-term and immediate factors, with centuries of involvement in regional and transcontinental slave systems intersecting with new developments such as the closure of the Atlantic trade and the growth of new political centers.

From a political standpoint, warfare, commerce, and slavery regularly proved to be a potent combination. Especially prominent here is the Sokoto Caliphate, which was founded in 1804–8 in what is now northern Nigeria. Building upon a successful call for *jihad* from Shehu Uthman dan Fodio, the caliphate embarked upon a "continuous military campaign lasting the rest of the century with enslavement as a basic aim" (Lovejoy 2005, 20). With religious identity serving as a key source of differentiation, the caliphate waged war against many of its neighbors in both West Africa and elsewhere, building the largest empire in sub-Saharan Africa with a slave population estimated to be "in excess of 1 million and perhaps more than 2.5 million" (Lovejoy and Hogendorn 1993, 1).[5] This total may have represented as much as half of the overall population, and it needs to be placed alongside the 800,000 slaves emancipated by the British in 1834, the 500,000 slaves in Haiti during the 1780s, and the nearly 4 million slaves who inhabited the southern United States in 1860 (Davis 2006, 298; Drescher 2002, 4; Geggus 1982, 23).

Slaves in the Sokoto Caliphate were forced into service in a variety of capacities, with agricultural production (both small-scale and plantation), concubinage, domestic work, and military service being especially prominent. Recent captives were also sold in large numbers, and thus ended up in the Trans-Saharan slave trade into North Africa and the Middle East. Over the course of the eighteenth and nineteenth centuries, the standard of *jihad* was raised on numerous occasions in West Africa, offering ideological justification for protracted wars of conquest and enslavement (Klein 1998, 37–58; Searing 1993, 173–75, 190–99). While the life of a slave meant different things to different people, even slaves who were fortunate enough to eventually secure relatively favorable terms of service, such as some slave soldiers and concubines, still experienced the profound dangers and dislocations associated with the experience of violent enslavement, and the familial separation, forced migration, cultural reconfiguration, loss of status, and prospect/reality of public sale that their captivity invariably entailed.[6]

European agents usually had little or no direct involvement in developments within the interior of West Africa. Prior to the colonial "Scramble" in the final third of the nineteenth century, European rule was limited to small coastal enclaves, with French authority going little beyond island bases in Saint Louis and Goree in Senegal, and British rule being confined to a small colony in Sierra Leone, fortifications on the Gold Coast, and coastal sites such as Lagos (annexed in 1861) in the Bight of Biafra.[7] During the mid-nineteenth century, the delegitimation of slavery presented two major challenges. First, there was the status of slavery under colonial jurisdiction, as governors came under metropolitan pressure to take action against local slavery and slave trading. This marked a departure from centuries of historical precedent, as European agents in Africa, the Middle East, and other locations had long favored a policy of either noninterference or active exploitation of non-European slave systems. With limited resources at their disposal, administrators were reluctant to interfere with the valued property of their African subjects. Second, there was the role of anti-slavery in complicating relations with neighboring rulers. The two main issues at stake here were the status of runaway slaves seeking sanctuary and the effect of anti-slavery ordinances on trading relationships.

One early example of these dynamics comes from the Gold Coast. When the British Parliament passed the much celebrated emancipation act of 1833, there was initially some confusion over whether the Gold Coast was included, but a subsequent order in council determined that it—along with chartered companies in India and East Asia—was not affected, allowing the continuation of support for slavery. While limited restrictions on slavery were introduced in 1843 and 1851, they were not effectively enforced. The 1843 measures also contained a provision against the return of runaways, which was also set aside until 1863, when a reversal of policy provoked an armed response from the neighboring Asante. In keeping with larger trends, administrators resisted more proactive measures by disingenuously claiming that slavery was "benign" and should be allowed to continue (interventions to address ill treatment notwithstanding) (Dumett and Johnson 1989, 71–78; Getz 2004, 54–68; Opare-Akurang 1999, 148–56).

Similar patterns are also in evidence in French Senegal. When the French Parliament legally abolished slavery in the Caribbean in 1848, this legislation also extended to colonies in Africa. Having unsuccessfully resisted the introduction of this legislation, administrators in Senegal also found themselves in a difficult predicament. When the 1848 legislation came into force, there was rejoicing among about 6,000 freed slaves (their masters were eventually paid a modest indemnity for the loss of their property), but its long-term impact would be muted by strategic and economic calculations. While former slaves in the tiny colonies experienced qualified gains, French officials succumbed to pressure from their neighbors by fabricating dubious justifications for ignoring a requirement not to return runaway slaves (unless they were fleeing from French enemies) and also making an artificial distinction between subject and citizen, which protected the rights of the former to keep their slaves. As French military forces conquered more territories, officials also made a further distinction between colonies and protectorates, enabling them to minimize the scope of their anti-slavery obligations (Getz 2004, 69–159; Klein 1998, 19–36, 66–67; Mbodji 1993, 200–2002; Searing 1993, 175–87). A similar strategy would also be used in Sierra Leone and the Gold Coast (Opare-Akurang 1999, 148; Rashid 1999, 216). Numerous justifications for diluting, ignoring, or otherwise subverting official anti-slavery commitments were offered by colonial officials (among others) well into the twentieth century. It is also important to emphasize, however, that the cautious/complicit character of these strategies often owed at least as much to "native" opposition as to European hypocrisy. With even the best will (and ample resources) in the world, ending slavery and the slave trade would have remained a very challenging proposition, owing to slavery's integral socioeconomic role in much of the region.

In order to further evaluate historical developments during this period, it can be useful to think in terms of three main themes: (1) the extent to which anti-slavery policies and pronouncements provided sustenance to other political and economic interests; (2) the extent to which anti-slavery conflicted with or otherwise compromised other strategic interests; and (3) the extent to which other related practices and procedures, such as forced labor, fatally compromised whatever qualified progress was made combating slavery. When it comes to the first theme, the key point at issue is the Scramble for

Africa, which saw European powers rapidly extending their authority over continental Africa between the 1870s and 1914. Ending slavery was regularly invoked as a justification for unprovoked wars of conquest during this period. This is most notoriously associated with the Congo Free State and the later Italian invasion of Ethiopia, but it also applies to less familiar cases, such as the British conquest of the Sokoto Caliphate in 1897–1903 (Lovejoy and Hogendorn 1993, 10–19). Most historians do not list anti-slavery among the primary *causes* of colonial expansion, but it clearly helped to legitimate decisions that were primarily made for other reasons. It remains an open question, however, whether this contribution proved decisive. Since European colonialism predates anti-slavery by many centuries, it is likely that other justifications would have sufficed if anti-slavery had not been a factor.

If we look more broadly, however, it becomes evident that anti-slavery not only helped to justify specific policies, it also featured prominently in larger ideologies of European superiority and paternalism. During the nineteenth century, both slavery and anti-slavery acquired particular prominence within Europe as key markers of collective identification and differentiation. As an emblem of more general "savagery" or "backwardness," the presence of slave raiding and slave trading in Africa offered both further confirmation of the superiority of European "civilization" and further impetus to a widespread approval of the desirability and legitimacy of colonial "tutelage." Framed in these terms, anti-slavery can be best understood as a core component of a larger ideological mindset that imbued the Scramble for Africa— and colonialism more generally—with a level of coherence and conviction that both muted critics and inspired supporters.[8]

The second theme to be considered is the extent to which anti-slavery compromised other strategic interests. On this front, the available evidence suggests that anti-slavery obligations frequently entailed economic costs, political complications, and/or foregone opportunities.[9] By taking measures against slavery, however qualified and tentative, colonial agents risked antagonizing key political constituencies (sometimes to the point of armed rebellion), undermining trade links and commercial networks, and generally creating complications that would not have otherwise existed. In most colonies, administrators faced a fundamental dilemma: "To please audiences at home, slavery had to be abolished. But to keep colonies safe and profitable, slave owners could not be alienated" (Getz 2004, 183). With limited resources available for compensation or robust intervention, most colonial agents favored a long-term, incremental approach to ending/ameliorating slavery,

but they were sometimes compelled to endorse stronger measures by periodic scandals, external pressures, and slave resistance. In the vast majority
of cases, both strategic calculations and economic interests chiefly found
expression in various efforts to *minimize* costs, rather than maximize gains.

One notable area where anti-slavery obligations and colonial interests
were closely aligned was the suppression of slave raiding and trading, which
were viewed as a threat to colonial authority and commercial expansion. With
the consolidation of colonial rule, large-scale raiding and trading were steadily
suppressed across West Africa (Getz 2004, 161–63; Klein 1998, 122–28;
Miers and Roberts 1988, 21). Although residual practices persisted well into the
twentieth century, the decline of large-scale slaving nonetheless represented
a blow to the viability of slavery more generally, making it harder to acquire
"fresh" supplies. When it came to the millions of Africans already enslaved,
the picture was very different. While the content of anti-slavery policies
varied among jurisdictions, several common elements can be identified,
starting with concerted attempts to minimize as much as possible the scope
and severity of slavery. In order to rationalize their cautious/complicit approach, administrators sought to distinguish "domestic" slavery in Africa
from the horrors of slavery in the Americas. While a minority of slaves served
on relatively favorable terms, references to the "mild" character of "domestic" slavery usually had more to do with political expediency than descriptive accuracy. If slavery could be passed off as "benign," then a long-term,
minimalist approach to abolition could be justified as responsible and desirable (Dumett 1981, 193; Getz 2004, 71, 122; Klein 1998, 62, 97–99, 136; Quirk
2006, 590–91).

These conceptual gymnastics were both reflected in and further reinforced
by a variety of legal strategies that were designed to bring about gradual reforms rather than radical transformation (Miers 2003, 32–38). This legislative
pattern can be found in places such the Gold Coast (1874), Nigeria (1901),
French West Africa (1905), and Sierra Leone (1928). The most common approach
involved formal moves to end and/or restrict slavery as a legal category,
rather than a lived reality (Getz 2004, 101; Klein 1998, 134–40). This meant
that slave masters—at least in theory—could no longer appeal to colonial
institutions to uphold their former prerogatives, but if slaves remained within
their masters' orbit, there was no guarantee that colonial agents would directly intervene. This typically placed the onus on slaves to initiate change,
and when many remained tied to their masters (through socialization, surveillance, and/or lack of viable alternatives), it was disingenuously presented

as a conscious "choice." In this environment, slavery in West Africa was subject to a "slow death" measured in decades rather than years. One snapshot of this larger trajectory comes from Martin Klein, who has calculated that there were 3–3.5 million slaves in French West Africa (spanning from Senegal and Mauritania to Niger) during the 1900s. At the time of decolonization in 1960, perhaps 200,000 people continued to be subject to some form of slavery (Klein 1998, 194, 252–59). Another perspective comes from Paul Lovejoy and Jan Hogendorn, who have calculated that there were around 390,000 to 400,000 slaves in northern Nigeria—the heart of Sokoto—during the 1930s (Lovejoy and Hogendorn 1993, 277–84). While these rough snapshots indicate a substantial decline from the late nineteenth-century peak, they do not reflect well on decades of colonial rule. While colonial agents in the field were aware of this situation, more senior figures offered repeated assurances that slavery had "effectively" ended, and that those who remained in bondage were no worse than "serfs" or "retainers."

The final theme to be considered here is the complex relationship between anti-slavery and other colonial policies. While European efforts to abolish slavery in West Africa left a great deal to be desired, the main point should not be whether or not more could have been done to end slavery, but instead whether other related aspects of colonial rule fatally undermined whatever progress was made in this area. On this key point, it is important to (re)emphasize that colonialism in Africa was systematically defined by violence, destruction, deprivation, and exploitation on a cataclysmic scale.[10] While many grievous abuses could be highlighted here, the one issue of particular importance in this context is the systemic use of forced labor. The most egregious example of forced labor comes from the Congo Free State (Grant 2005, 39–78; Hochschild 1998), which saw perhaps 10 million deaths—perhaps half of the local population—but forced labor was also applied more broadly throughout Africa.

Colonial officials justified forced labor practices as an unfortunate necessity, which arose from acute labor shortages, urgent public requirements, and the innate failings of "native" peoples. The logic of "necessity" proved to be highly malleable. In the early twentieth century, it was invoked to justify the extensive use of forced labor on public works and (more contentiously) private projects (Derrick 1975, 159–66; Grant 2005, 22–24; Johnson 2003, 91–106). It was also invoked in times of war. This included both localized wars of colonial conquest and the global struggle of two world wars (Killingray 1989, 483–501; Killingray and Mathews 1979, 6–32). During the First

World War, millions of Africans were forced into service using highly coercive techniques. As porters, they transported great burdens long distances for meager rewards. Tens of thousands of Africans died of disease, starvation, and exhaustion. As conscripted soldiers, they fought on fronts in Africa, Western Europe, and the Middle East (with thousands of slave soldiers serving in northern France) (Conklin 1997, 143–73; Klein 1998, 216–19, 233–35; Killingray 1989, 490). As a general rule, these burdens fell hardest upon slaves or ex-slaves. This usually involved either (1) fugitive slaves being forced into service, or (2) slaves being dispatched by their masters to satisfy quotas, or call-ups. During the colonial period, labor practices in West Africa involved an unstable combination of slave labor and related practices, forced labor for the colonial state, and an expanding market for wage labor, most notably in urban areas, which became increasingly prominent following the First World War.

If the abolition of slavery represents an achievement that is worthy of contemporary emulation, what should we make of the fact that it frequently occurred as a consequence of colonial conquest and imperial imposition? Instead of clear-cut historical "lessons," we must instead confront a cautionary tale that does not reflect well upon either Europeans or Africans. As we have seen, some of the main issues at stake here are (1) the rhetorical use of anti-slavery to justify colonial conquest, (2) widespread complicity in the continuation of slavery for extended periods under colonial rule, and (3) the introduction and/or expansion of other coercive labor practices and human rights abuses. It is also clear, moreover, that the tentative pace of reform can also be traced to extended resistance by African elites, who continued to regard slavery as a legitimate and valuable institution. In this often ambiguous environment, slaves and ex-slaves frequently found it necessary to take matters into their own hands. By the 1930s and 1940s, slave populations in West Africa were no longer measured in millions, but there also continued to be a sizable minority of slaves who had experienced little or no change. In a number of countries in West Africa, the continuing legacies of these historical slave systems remain with us to this day.

Contemporary Slavery and the "Lessons" of History

The history of slavery and abolition has served a number of contextual, intellectual, and political functions within recent treatments of contemporary forms of slavery. Here, as elsewhere, the primary frame of reference has been the history of transatlantic slavery in general and events in the British Empire and the United States of America in particular. It is also clear, moreover, that the selection and representation of specific issues and events have been heavily influenced by current political agendas, resulting in a tendency to concentrate upon the successful campaigns that culminated in legal abolition, rather than the hundreds of years when slavery was practiced without major political opposition (long-standing slave resistance notwithstanding). By surveying the activities and achievements of the pioneers of organized anti-slavery, modern activists and other commentators have sought to identify compelling lessons and orientations that can be called upon to shed new light upon more recent challenges.

Within the recent literature on contemporary slavery, the history of legal abolition has been primarily conceptualized in terms of (1) a strategic framework and (2) a historical inspiration. As a strategic framework, anti-slavery has been chiefly approached from an organizational perspective, with pride of place going to the tactics and techniques used by anti-slavery activists in Britain and the United States, such as petitions, publications, organizational networks, boycotts, legal proceedings, public meetings, artistic icons, and parliamentary maneuvers. Framed in these terms, organized anti-slavery can be best understood as a historical prototype that not only occupies a foundational position as the first in a long line of related humanitarian projects, but also continues to offer important insights for modern political activism. As a historical inspiration, organized anti-slavery has been chiefly viewed as an enduring source of ethical and political inspiration. This starts with the personal virtues demonstrated by leading abolitionist figures such as William Wilberforce and Harriet Tubman, whose commitment to their cause has been identified as a compelling personal example for modern individuals, but it also extends to the achievements of organized anti-slavery as a whole. By successfully agitating for the abolition of slavery in the face of tremendous political and economic obstacles, anti-slavery pioneers are said to have illustrated that fundamental changes are both possible and desirable.

One prominent example of these various themes comes from *Creating the Better Hour: Lessons from William Wilberforce* (2007), edited by Chuck Stetson. This collection is designed as a companion piece to a prominent documentary on William Wilberforce, which was promoted among evangelical audiences in both Britain and the United States during 2007 and

2008. In his chapter on "The Birth of Issue Campaigning," Stetson argues that "William Wilberforce and Thomas Clarkson pioneered what we would recognize today as issue campaigning and lobbying methods in the fight for the abolition of slavery" (Stetson 2007, 87). As part of a stylized survey of the personal virtues and organizational strategies of British abolitionists, he observes that "it took forty-six years for Wilberforce and his colleagues to achieve the unachievable: the total eradication of slavery from the British Empire" (Stetson 2007, 89). No mention is made of the continuation of legal slavery under British authority in territories in the Gold Coast or India post-1834, or to the subsequent relationship between the British Empire and the legal abolition of slavery in Africa. In its broad contours, *Creating the Better Hour* is divided into three main sections: (1) the personal virtues of William Wilberforce and the Clapham Circle; (2) efforts to complete the legacy of William Wilberforce; and (3) Wilberforce as a model for effecting change.[11] Despite an explicit remit that is designed to explore underlying connections between historical practices and contemporary problems, I can identify only one brief reference in the book to the history of slavery outside the Americas, which comes from Caroline Cox in a chapter on slavery in Sudan (Cox 2007, 241–42).

A similar attempt to integrate historical and contemporary issues can be found in *Slavery: Now and Then*, edited by Danny Smith (2007). This collection is advertised as "an investigation into modern slavery by the leading human rights authorities of our time in the context of the transatlantic slave trade." The first half of the book comprises ten chapters devoted to various forms of contemporary slavery. None of these chapters offers much in the way of historical context. This comes in the second half, which provides a potted history of slavery that starts in the Ancient world and ends with the abolition of transatlantic slavery. Smith echoes many others in his description of British anti-slavery as the "the first human rights campaign," which was based upon a unique combination of organization, leadership, narrative, and public engagement (Smith 2007, 184). Building upon their "resolute commitment," these pioneers "contributed to an extraordinary action: the end of the slave trade and, eventually, slavery as a whole." In his historical survey of the end of transatlantic slavery, Smith provides a brief list of dates on which slavery was legally abolished in the Americas (Smith 2007, 203),[12] together with a more sustained treatment of developments in Britain and the United States. The history of the legal abolition in territories elsewhere is not mentioned at all.[13]

The two collections discussed above are somewhat unusual, because they give equivalent billing to historical practices and contemporary problems. Most recent works on contemporary slavery have not engaged with the history of slavery to this degree. Some have included brief allusions. Others have bypassed the history of slavery entirely.[14] This informal separation between past and present can be partially attributed to a popular belief that "new" and "old" slavery display quite different characteristics, and are primarily driven by different dynamics.[15] One key result of this lack of interest in history is a widespread belief that "old" slavery effectively ended in the nineteenth century, and thus has little bearing upon ongoing problems that are now over a century removed from legal abolition (van den Anker 2004, 1; International Labor Organization 2001, 10). This belief is not confined to modern anti-slavery circles; it also applies more broadly. One high-profile example of this approach comes from former U.S. president George W. Bush. In a major address to the United Nations General Assembly on September 23, 2003, Bush described the importance of the fight against contemporary slavery in the following terms:

> We must show new energy in fighting back an old evil. Nearly two centuries after the abolition of the trans-Atlantic slave trade, and *more than a century after slavery was officially ended in its last strongholds*, the trade in human beings for any purpose must not be allowed to thrive in our time. (Bush 2003b, my italics)

The presence of such a basic historical error in a heavily vetted presidential address is emblematic of a widespread lack of recognition of the global dimensions of slavery and abolition. Historical slave systems outside the Americas have also tended to be overlooked in recent works on social movements,[16] more general histories of human rights,[17] and discussion of reparations for the history and legacies of slavery.[18]

The various sources identified above reveal a selective and ethnocentric approach to the history of slavery and abolition. While the early history of organized anti-slavery undoubtedly offers many important insights into both historical practices and contemporary problems, serious problems can arise when one component—however important—in a larger historical trajectory is consistently allowed to stand in for the entire story. By selectively engaging with the early history of anti-slavery, much of the recent literature on contemporary slavery has overlooked the full spectrum of issues and complications associated with the history of slavery. In order to develop this overall line of argument, the following remarks focus on three main issues: (1) the relation- ship between mobilization and abolition, (2) the underlying motivations behind legal abolition, and (3) the path-dependent relationship between historical practices and contemporary problems.

I begin with popular mobilization. While the pioneers of organized anti-slavery clearly faced daunting political obstacles and are undoubtedly deserving of significant respect, it is important not to limit our historical horizons to political activism in Britain and the United States. If we look more broadly, it is possible to identify three main paths to the legal abolition of slavery. The first path revolved around popular mobilization. In this fa- miliar model, which is epitomized by Britain but also imperfectly applies to the northern United States, France, and Brazil, a strong popular commit- ment to anti-slavery crystallized prior to the passage of key anti-slavery legislation. This proved to be the historical exception, not the rule. The second path revolved around armed conflict. In this model, which is chiefly appli- cable to Haiti (San Domingue), the United States, and many parts of Latin America, the legal abolition of slavery primarily occurred as a consequence of revolution and war, with associated losses of blood and treasure (Blanchard 2008; Geggus 2006, 209–52; Hahn 2009, 55–114). In the century after 1787, more enslaved people of African descent living in the Americas were liber- ated through violent conflict than through popular mobilization. Here, as elsewhere, the collective actions of both slaves and ex-slaves made a vital contribution, as slaves took advantage of the narrowest of opportunities to challenge their enslavement through flight, force of arms, and other forms of contestation and negotiation (Quirk 2009, 66–70, 90–91).

The third and final path revolved around "top-down" external pressures. In this model, which applies to most parts of continental Europe, Africa, the Middle East, and South, Central, and East Asia, the legal abolition of slavery was not driven by popular mobilization, but was instead set into motion by cumulative external pressures. While there is no doubt that anti- slavery activists forged powerful coalitions in Britain and the United States, it can be difficult to point to even remotely comparable movements in most other parts of the globe. In the vast majority of cases, there were no large-scale petitions, anti-slavery tracts, popular mobilizations, meetings, or boycotts (Drescher 1987, 50–66). Outside of periodic outrage at external intrusions, public opinion was rarely aroused, leaving vested interests and political elites to grapple with external anti-slavery pressures. The main sticking point here is the nexus between anti-slavery and colonialism. While the abolition of slavery may well have been a positive development (at least in the long term), it frequently came about through processes that at best left a great deal to be desired, and at worst heralded the acceleration of other systemic human rights abuses. While popular mobilization played a crucial role in placing anti-slavery on the agenda, it was European imperialism that translated this agenda into a global phenomenon. If we only focus on the first half of the equation, we will be left with an incomplete picture. Once European imperialism is included, anti-slavery may no longer serve as a historical inspiration.

This brings us to the second theme identified above: the underlying motivations behind legal abolition. On this front, it is necessary to analytically distinguish between two main impulses, or orientations, that paved the road to legal abolition. One impulse is connected with the familiar idea of racial and/or human equality. While this impulse was undoubtedly present within some parts of the early anti-slavery movement, its influence can be easily overstated. Here, as elsewhere, it is important not to unduly accentuate themes that are held to "anticipate" contemporary values. The second, less familiar, impulse revolves around what (anti-)slavery was held to signify, or otherwise symbolize, about the distinctive virtues (or vices) of specific communities. If we limit discussion to the first of these impulses, it becomes very difficult to come to terms with the fact that Europeans continued to officially support anti-slavery policies during the late nineteenth century, at a time when powerful essentialist models, such as social Darwinism and "scientific" racism, had ostensibly confirmed that the physiological gulf between European and non-European peoples was deep, pervasive, and all but insurmountable (Adas 1989; Hawkins 1997; Keene 2002). While there were undoubtedly enlightened individuals among anti-slavery activists who were committed to human equality (especially in the United States), they represented the exception, not the rule. In keeping with larger historical precedents, societies in the nineteenth and early twentieth centuries were deeply hierarchical, reflecting entrenched social and institutional cleavages based upon sex, class, race, and "civilization." Organized anti-slavery was chiefly based upon a well-constructed claim for better treatment for a depressed category of persons, but this did not necessarily require human equality, only a much more qualified commitment to sufficient commonality.

At this juncture, it is necessary to emphasize the contribution of prevailing ideologies of collective honor and paternalism. From this standpoint, the key issue was not slavery *per se*, but instead what slavery gradually came to signify about the "backward" or "uncivilized" character of various communities. This dynamic played a key role in organized anti-slavery from the very beginning. In Britain, to take one key example, anti-slavery activists were able to transform the treatment of slaves into a symbolic referendum on prevailing conceptions of religious virtue, political exceptionalism, and national identity (Colley 1992; Quirk and Richardson 2010). Within this frame of reference, taking action against slavery offered a vehicle for redeeming and further reinforcing unique British and/or Christian virtues. With the legislative changes of 1807 and 1833, the demarcation between British anti-slavery (often embodied by the "noble work" of the Royal Navy) led to various displays of self-congratulation, as Britons contrasted their anti-slavery zeal with others who continued to sanction slavery.

With the passage of time, the status of slavery emerged as an international test of "civilized" standing and collective honor. In intra-European settings, rulers would seek to advance and/or defend their standing as "civilized" powers by taking action against slavery. In extra-European settings, these divisions were partially subsumed by a common European identity and common "civilizing" mission, resulting in an ideology of "benevolent" paternalism where peoples who considered themselves blessed with "superior" virtues were held to be duty bound to assist "lesser" peoples. Rulers across Africa, Asia, and the Middle East would also end up officially endorsing anti-slavery in an (often ineffectual) effort to escape colonization and demonstrate their own "civilized" credentials (Allain 2006, 214–16; Gong 1984). In all of these settings, it was not required to be a committed abolitionist to take up the cause (or, more commonly, signal the appearance of commitment to the cause). Challenges to collective honor and cumulative external pressures instead served as the principal catalyst. This is important on several levels. It not only provides both a key insight into why many rulers took steps against slavery in the absence of strong domestic anti-slavery sentiment, it also helps to explain why so many anti-slavery laws proved ineffective: the officials who were responsible for enforcement were not convinced they were necessary. While nongovernmental anti-slavery activism was by no means absent from the equation in the late nineteenth and early twentieth century, it tended to take the form of specialized groups working in conjunction with governments. Popular support for anti-slavery in Britain and the United States rapidly fell away following key legislative victories in the 1830s

(Britain) and the 1860s (the United States) (Temperley 1972; Welch 2009, 70–128).

This brings us to the third and final theme identified above: the path-dependent relationship between historical practices and contemporary problems. On this front, a narrow focus upon transatlantic slavery once again offers an insufficient foundation from which to evaluate the sources of—and solutions to—a variety of contemporary problems. The main point at issue here is an informal separation between past and present, or "old" and "new," in which the history of slavery and abolition is at least tacitly assumed to have little or no *direct* causal connection to ongoing problems.[19] Most recent works have tended to attribute the "rise" of contemporary slavery to new innovations, such as economic globalization, technological change, Cold War collapse, and demographic trends. While there is no doubt that recent developments—both macro and micro—have affected the character and composition of various practices, most forms of contemporary forms of slavery can best be understood as an extension and/or reconfiguration of enduring historical themes rather than as distinctively modern developments.

The historical roots of contemporary problems are especially evident in many parts of West Africa, where the persistence of residual cases of "classical" slavery and descent-based discrimination in countries such as Mauritania, Mali, and Niger can be primarily traced to previous failures to end slavery under colonial rule (Klein 2009, 26–44; Seddon 2000). A similar pattern also applies to other enduring forms of human bondage such as Trokosi "cult" slavery in places such as Ghana (Edwards 2000, 69–73; Krasniewski 2005, 141–150). When modern campaigners object to "slave chocolate" sourced from plantations in West Africa, they are also following in the footsteps of earlier campaigns against the use of forced labor in cocoa production under colonial rule (Grant 2004). If we consider Africa as a whole, we also encounter recent cases of wartime enslavement in countries such as Liberia, Sierra Leone, the Democratic Republic of Congo, Sudan, and Uganda, which once again represent a resurgence/reconfiguration of historical patterns of slave raiding (Fegley 2010, 203–28; Jok 2007, 143–57; Quirk 2010). Other major concentrations of contemporary slavery, such as bonded labor in the Indian subcontinent, can also be traced to earlier failures to take effective action against historical slave systems (Chatterjee 1999; Prakesh 1990). While a slightly different story applies when it comes to human trafficking, this is mainly because the primary antecedent on this occasion is not "classical" slavery but instead late nineteenth- and early twentieth-century campaigns against "white slavery" (Quirk 2007, 181–207).

Concluding Remarks

This chapter brings together a number of different literatures, placing the history of slavery and abolition in West Africa in conversation with a series of recent works dealing with contemporary forms of slavery. By focusing upon selected aspects of transatlantic slavery, many recent efforts to generate "lessons" from the past have largely overlooked an uncomfortable historical relationship between the legal abolition of slavery and European imperialism. Once this relationship becomes part of the conversation, the history of anti-slavery becomes a story of caution and complication, as well as instruction and inspiration. While anti-slavery pioneers undoubtedly played a decisive role in the fight against slavery in places such as Britain and the United States, events in other parts of the world reveal a much less salutary picture. Over the course of the nineteenth and early twentieth century, anti-slavery was caught up in larger patterns of European imperialism and colonialism. For many peoples outside Europe, this regularly meant conquest, violent death, dispossession, discrimination, and exploitation. It is possible to argue that these global conquests would have been even more brutal if anti-slavery had not been part of the equation, but this is an argument that rests upon the role of anti-slavery in mitigating harm rather than promoting human welfare. Once this broader historical trajectory is taken into account, we can also begin to rethink the underlying causes behind the various practices that fall under the rubric of contemporary slavery. Instead of being driven by distinctively modern developments, most forms of contemporary slavery have complex historical roots, but these connections and associations have tended to be obscured by a widespread assumption that the history of slavery concluded in the nineteenth century, and therefore has no direct bearing upon more recent problems. When most recent aspects of the history of slavery and abolition are downplayed or disregarded, we may not be fully equipped to tackle current problems.

In this context, the relationship between pre- and post-abolition practices in West Africa potentially offers an innovative starting point from which to further refine efforts to combat slavery today. When it comes to many examples of contemporary slavery, such as the worst forms of child labor or bonded labor, it has been demonstrated time and again that legal injunctions are necessary but not sufficient, and that a range of additional strategies, both direct and indirect, are required in order to gradually reduce the overall scope and severity of what are often deeply rooted problems. From a diagnostic standpoint, the history of West Africa offers both negative and positive examples. The ambiguous achievements of the past make it necessary to resist the temptation to prematurely conclude (or allow others to conclude) that the problems involved can be easily resolved. On the other hand, the remarkable historical resilience that has been consistently demonstrated by enslaved Africans—in both Africa and the Americas—can also offer an additional dimension to contemporary advocacy by focusing attention on various ways of encouraging individual agency and resistance. On these and many other fronts, the history of slavery and abolition in Africa offers further insights, ideas, and cautionary tales that go well beyond more familiar stories of Western political activists.

Chapter 3

Representing Trafficking: Media in the United States, Great Britain, and Canada

Girish J. "Jeff" Gulati

Introduction

The trafficking of persons across borders for sexual, labor, and other forms of exploitation is a subject that has captured the attention of international organizations, activists, and policy makers that range the ideological spectrum. A 2000 United Nations Protocol established guidelines on how nations should combat trafficking and assist victims. In the same year, the Trafficking Victims Protection Act became law in the United States with near unanimous support, establishing the first and most aggressive effort to date in the punishment of traffickers, protection for victims, and prevention programs (Stolz 2007; Wyler, Siskin, and Seelke 2009). Since then, new anti-trafficking initiatives have been adopted in several countries, most notably in Great Britain and in Canada. There also has been increased bilateral and regional cooperation, with major agreements adopted by the Council of Europe and the European Union.

The recent flurry of government activity indicates that there is a growing awareness of the horrors of human trafficking and the exploitation of people around the globe and in their own countries. It also would seem that a consensus has emerged on the extent of the problem, the reasons the problem exists, and the actions that need to be taken to put an end to this modern-day form of slavery. Yet, a significant number of academics, news commentators, and activists have called into question the numbers that are used to describe the problem, the reasons trafficking occurs, and how it should be addressed. Given these contrasting perspectives, have a broad range of ideas been represented in the news-media coverage of human trafficking?

The news media serve an essential purpose in a democratic society by giving voice to established groups and organizations in society and serving as a forum where ideas about public policy can be debated and selected on the strength of their arguments. The representation of different viewpoints should reflect the true diversity of groups in society, however, by giving voice to the unorganized, presenting the ideas of outsiders and nonelites, and exposing the public to alternative ideas and arguments (Curran 2005). This role allows the media to influence the nature of the debate by deciding what information is included and excluded from the public sphere and how many points of view are represented. Without media coverage, solutions that might be effective are left off the table and current policy may not get a full critique. Studies of foreign policy issues where there is consensus within the policy community (Mermin 1999) have shown that the media's role has been to reflect the government agenda and frame news stories in a way that echoes the arguments of the major participants in the policy-making process (Jacobs and Shapiro 2000; Jones and Baumgartner 2005; Kingdon 2003).

Most of the scholarship on human trafficking to this point has focused on documenting the horrors of trafficking (for example, Farr 2004; Kangaspunta 2003; Kligman and Limoncelli 2005), measuring the extent of the problem (for example, Raymond and Hughes 2001; Weitzer 2007; Zhang 2007), and analyzing the causes of trafficking and the actions taken to combat it in various countries (for example, Friman and Reich 2007; Gallagher 2006; Nieuwenhuys and Pécoud 2007; Outshoorn 2004). There have yet to be studies, however, of how the media have covered human trafficking. In this study I examine how well news media in the United States, Great Britain, and Canada have performed with respect to representing the various viewpoints on trafficking. I begin by summarizing briefly public policy toward trafficking and then review in some detail the critiques of recent policy initiatives in order to establish a reference point by which we can assess the representativeness of the coverage. From a content analysis of the coverage of human trafficking in six quality newspapers between 2000 and 2005, I show that only a limited range of viewpoints have been represented, which has served to legitimize the views and decisions of established policy makers while marginalizing alternative viewpoints and criticism.

The Evolution of a Social Problem

Public Policy Responses to Trafficking: 1910–2005

Human trafficking and, more specifically, the trafficking in women for sexual exploitation are not new phenomena and have received intermittent attention from governments and international organizations during the past 150 years (Langum 2007; Outshoorn 2004). The economic dislocations caused by the collapse of communism in the Soviet Union and Eastern Europe, a continued globalization of the world economy, and a flourishing international sex industry and sex tourism trade helped anti-trafficking NGOs and activists bring the issue of trafficking to the attention of policy makers and international organizations in the early 1990s.

In the United States, an unlikely coalition of feminists, progressive Democrats, and Republicans who closely identified with the evangelical Christian community worked closely with the Clinton administration to pass the Trafficking Victims Protection Act (TVPA). The Act expanded the tools available to law enforcement for apprehending and prosecuting traffickers, increased the penalties for those convicted of trafficking offenses, authorized assistance programs for victims overseas, and directed the president to establish a public awareness campaign and programs designed to enhance economic opportunities for women who are at a high risk for becoming victims of trafficking. The Act also required the government to issue an annual assessment of other nations' efforts to combat trafficking (the State Department's annual Trafficking in Persons Report) and authorized the president to sanction nations that allowed trafficking to continue unabated. The bill received near unanimous support in Congress and was signed by President Clinton on October 28, 2000 (Miko 2004; Stolz 2005, 2007).

Further reauthorizations of the Act have substantially increased federal spending for the Department of Justice (DOJ), Department of State, and the Immigration and Naturalization Service to combat trafficking and assist victims. A number of task forces, assistance centers, and training programs have been established, and victims who cooperate with law enforcement are granted nonimmigrant "T" visas to allow them to remain in the United

States. U.S. action abroad included requiring the U.S. Agency for International Development to work with international organizations to fund programs and organizations; DOJ and State to train foreign law enforcement and immigration officers to better identify traffickers and victims at the border; and U.S. embassies and consulates to work with other countries in heightening public awareness, and targeting messages to potential victims (Stolz 2007; Wyler, Siskin, and Seelke 2009).

In the same year that the TVPA was moving through Congress, the Clinton administration actively worked to draft the language of a 2000 United Nations Protocol to Prevent, Suppress, and Punish Trafficking in Persons, Especially Women and Children, and advocated its passage. One significant outcome of the protocol was an agreement on language defining trafficking, which was somewhat narrower than what was outlined in the TVPA. Making the distinction between voluntary and involuntary prostitution, the UN defined trafficking as "the recruitment, transportation, transfer, harboring or receipt of persons, by means of threat or the use of force or other forms of coercion, of abduction, of fraud, of deception, of the abuse of power or of a position of vulnerability or of the giving or receiving of payments or benefits to achieve the consent of a person having control over another person, for the purposes of exploitation" (UNODC 2004). This language would serve to guide future policy initiatives for combating trafficking in many countries (Masci 2004; Miko 2004; Outshoorn 2004).

New initiatives to combat human trafficking in the United Kingdom began in 2003 with passage of the Sexual Offenses Act and in the following year with the Asylum and Immigration Act, both of which expanded the definition of trafficking and increased the maximum penalty for sex trafficking. As a result, there has been a substantial increase in raids, arrests, and prosecutions, which in some cases have been carried out under the authority of anti-trafficking statutes. In addition, the UK government established new agencies to dismantle trafficking rings, share trafficking intelligence with law enforcement, and develop training modules for attorneys prosecuting trafficking crimes. More resources were allocated for programs designed to encourage victims to assist in trafficking prosecutions, and to provide care for trafficking victims. And there have been strong efforts in educating the British public about trafficking.[1]

Canada's Parliament also moved to expand the definition of trafficking and increase penalties by revising its criminal code (Law C-49) and passing the Immigration and Refugee Protection Act in 2005. These two acts also prohibited a defendant from profiting from a trafficking act and prohibited Canadians from engaging in child sex tourism abroad. The Canadian government has adopted a much more accommodating posture toward trafficking victims by granting renewable temporary residency permits and providing them with health care and counseling services without requiring their testimony against their traffickers. Other government efforts include the organizing of anti-trafficking training for law enforcement, victim service providers, and NGOs in Canada; an increase in funding for awareness and anti-trafficking programs around the world; and the imposition of alternative sentences on men convicted of soliciting prostitution.[2]

Canada, the United Kingdom, and the United States also have joined several multilateral efforts to combat trafficking. In 2004, NATO adopted a Policy on Combating Trafficking in Human Beings that committed member countries to provide training to NATO personnel participating in peacekeeping missions and to support law enforcement efforts in host countries. The United Kingdom joined similar agreements adopted by the Organization for Security and Cooperation in Europe, the Council of Europe, and the European Union.

The sudden burst of activity and general approval among anti-trafficking activists with U.S. leadership in combating trafficking would suggest that there is an overwhelming consensus on how serious the problem of trafficking is and how it should be addressed. For the most part, this is an accurate picture. There is a high degree of agreement on the objectives among those in the anti-trafficking policy community. Yet, it should not be surprising that there are criticisms of the UN and Western nations' response to dealing with trafficking. The most common complaints voiced among those in the anti-trafficking community at congressional hearings and appearing in mainstream foreign policy publications about U.S. government policy are that enforcement should be more vigorous, that law enforcement agencies should be empowered further by providing additional money and training to combat trafficking, and that greater resources should be directed to border security. The U.S. government is urged to be more honest about reporting which countries have been doing a poor job in combating trafficking and putting economic and greater diplomatic pressure on nations that refuse to improve their record. There also have been calls for increased aid to international assistance programs and more services for trafficking victims in the United States. Critics have urged reforms of the T-VISA process and eligibility criteria, which require most victims to testify against their abusers even though many fear that their families will face retribution or they are too ashamed to discuss their experience (Gallagher 2006; Kapstein 2006).

The Human Rights Perspective

Most scholars and activists who have been assisting trafficking victims have praised the United States for its international leadership and sincere efforts in combating human trafficking. Yet they are critical of the narrow lens with which U.S. policy makers have conceptualized the problem. Almost all of the attention has been placed on the trafficking of women and children for the purpose of sexual exploitation, while other forms of labor slavery and trafficking involving men have been largely ignored, which in turn has led to a gross underestimate of the problem (Feingold 2005; Zimmerman 2005). Furthermore, these scholars and activists provide a broader view of the reasons that human trafficking continues to be an international problem. While they agree that organized criminal networks contribute greatly to the problem, they also attribute responsibility to poverty, social inequality, and lack of economic opportunities in the developing world. In many new democracies, economic liberalization has contributed to new inequalities and dislocation. In addition to the economic turmoil, military conflicts and political upheaval, persecution, and violence across the globe also encourage people to seek refuge and opportunities abroad, making them particularly vulnerable to trafficking networks (Gill 2007; King 2004; Kligman and Limoncelli 2005; Salt 2000).

Globalization (and regionalization) exacerbates the problem by contributing to the economic and political instability in many of these countries, while creating a demand in western nations for cheap labor (Kligman and Limoncelli 2005; Skeldon 2000). Technological innovation in transportation and communication further facilitate organized crime's ability to prey on these vulnerable populations (Friman and Reich 2007). In addition, advances in gender equality in the West and more women working outside the home have created a demand for domestic servants and child care providers (Ehrenreich and Hochschild 2004). This, in turn, has created a demand among Western men for Eastern European, Asian, and Latin American women, who fit the stereotype of a docile, passive, and obedient wife (King 2004). Western demand not only encourages trafficking into Western countries, but also creates a market for "sex tours" of origin countries where prostitution is either legal or tolerated (King 2004; Singh and Hart 2007). This problem is particularly acute near U.S. military bases and where international peacekeepers are stationed (Kligman and Limoncelli 2005).

For women, the impact of globalization, economic and political transformation, and increasing social inequality has been even more harmful. In many of the origin countries, there already is severe gender inequality and limited educational and economic opportunities for women, long-standing societal oppression of women, and women face abusive conditions in their own homes (Gill 2007; Kangaspunta 2003; Kligman and Limoncelli 2005; Salt 2000; Skeldon 2000). Government officials, the police, border security agents, and even international peacekeepers have cooperated with criminal networks to lure women into prostitution by deceit, coercion, or force (Mendelson 2005). There also is a high incidence of family members selling their children or relatives to traffickers (Friman and Reich 2007). While many women initiate contact with traffickers with referrals from neighbors, friends, and family, none of these women are fully aware of the life that awaits them and the terms of their transport (Platt 2001; Zimmerman 2005). But many do have hopes of obtaining better opportunities elsewhere in the sex industry (Agustin 2005; Skeldon 2000) or are simply searching for adventure and a more exciting life (Salt 2000).

This more comprehensive view of the problem requires solutions that go beyond empowering law enforcement with more resources and authority. While there is support for assisting foreign governments with their enforcement and services (Shauer and Wheaten 2006), there is concern about the value of this approach in countries where government officials and law enforcement personnel have been involved in trafficking enterprises or place a very low priority on addressing problems experienced by marginalized people. More emphasis is placed on empowering women (Agustin 2005; Friman and Reich 2007) and assistance for economic development more generally (Skeldon 2000) and penalizing corporations that hire trafficking victims (Gill 2007; Salt and Stein 1997). Scholars from the human rights perspective also echo the concern of the policy community that more should be done to assist victims (Gallagher 2006; Haynes 2004), to inform the public (Kligman and Limoncelli 2005), and to place pressure on governments that fail to address trafficking, regardless of their strategic position or value in the war against international terrorism (Friman and Reich 2007; Kapstein 2006). There also are suggestions to extend protections to sex workers and allow U.S. assistance to go to organizations that do not take a firm prohibitionist stand on prostitution (Nieuwenhuys and Pécoud 2007; Platt 2001; Shauer and Wheaten 2006; Singh and Hart 2007).

An "Alternative" Critique

Another group of scholars and activists criticizes U.S. policy from a "sex-positive" feminist (for example, see Agustin 2007; Andrijasevic 2007; Chapkis 2003; Doezema 2000; Kinney 2006; Kuo 2002) or neocolonialism perspective (for example, see Kempadoo 2005; Outshoorn 2005). These views are echoed frequently in the leading progressive news magazines (for example, see Cockburn 2006; Critchell 2003; Jones 2007; Katayama 2005; Lustig 2007; Nathan 2005; Schafer 2005). These critics question the estimates made by the United States and the United Nations of the extent of the trafficking problem, which they argue are based on faulty methodology and extrapolations. They point to the widely varying estimates in government reports and the negligible increase in prosecutions and victim rescues observed in the United States since the 2000 Act (Weitzer 2007). They also challenge the conventional definition of human trafficking, which designates as victims all "sex workers" who have traveled across borders in hopes of seeking a better standard of living. In addition, they do not view as victims undocumented immigrants who enter another country seeking work simply because they received assistance entering their destination from another person (Agustin 2007; Chapkis 2003; Doezema 2000).

These scholars and activists also claim that these high and erroneous estimates are advanced mostly by conservative Christians who are on a moral crusade against all forms of female sexual liberation, which they see as threatening to the traditional family structure. Religious conservatives are joined by "radical" feminists who view prostitution as exploitation of women and male dominance and a justification for continuing violence against women and gender inequality. Reminiscent of the move against "white slavery," this coalition's strategy has been to generate outrage among the American public in order to build support for more draconian solutions to combat prostitution and criminalize other elements of the sex industry (Abbot 2007; Agustin 2007; Chapkis 2003; Doezema 2000; Weitzer 2007).

Others see the anti-trafficking efforts as a form of cultural imperialism, a defense of neoliberal economic interests, and an excuse to restrict the movement and economic opportunities of women and other marginalized people.

They point to information campaigns funded by the United States to warn potential victims about traffickers' methods and motives as really being subtle attempts to discourage migration to western countries. In terms of solutions, these alternative voices propose legalizing prostitution, treating prostitutes as workers rather than victims, and helping them obtain safer working conditions and health care. They also call for more liberalized immigration laws in the United States and Western Europe (Andrijasevic 2007; Chapkis 2003; Kempadoo 2005; Kinney 2006).

Media Framing of Public Policy

The news media contribute to the democratic process by giving voice to a diverse set of groups and exposing the public to a range of ideas and arguments. In practice, which groups and viewpoints get represented is a result of news organizations' decisions about what they should try to cover from the seemingly endless number of problems, activities, and events. Journalists can know and develop an understanding about a limited number of stories that rise to the agenda, and only a small fraction of these stories appear in print or on television newscasts (Gans 2005; Schudson 1980; Tuchman 1978).

In addition to choosing what to cover, journalists are routinely making decisions about how to logically structure their stories to make them accessible and intelligible for their audiences. Choices are made about how much background to include in a story, which facts and interpretations to include and exclude, and which sources to use and quote. Further choices are made about how much prominence and significance to give within the narrative to the specific ideas and information that are selected for inclusion and to the format of the presentation. Decisions about what is selected and given more salience can have a profound influence on how a social problem is discussed in the public sphere and the actions taken by policy makers. How a story is framed influences how a problem is defined, what are determined to be causes of the problem and its consequences, and what solutions are seen as effective in alleviating the problem (Entman 1993).

The literature on the news-gathering process suggests that rather than influencing the nature of the debate, the news media mostly echo the narratives presented by the major participants in the policy process and thus help support the dominant views. Organizational routines (such as beat reporting and a reliance on official sources) limit the ideas and information that can get included in a story (Gans 2005; Klinenberg 2003; Schudson 1980; Tuchman 1978). Alternative perspectives and policy prescriptions adhered to by groups that do not intersect with established beats are omitted, as are individuals and groups whose ideas might seem to undermine the legitimacy of established institutions or run counter to the dominant ideology and middle-class values (Larson 2006).

The need to strive for balance and the preference for presenting stories around a conflict frame would suggest that conventional news organizations will try to include multiple viewpoints even when there is clear consensus or a dominant view, and the minority views seem illogical or are shared by only a few people or groups on the fringe (Gans 2005; Schudson 1980; Tuchman 1978). But studies of media framing of foreign policy issues and controversies among U.S. news organizations suggest that alternative viewpoints are covered in only limited circumstances, and rarely do the media provide critical analysis in foreign policy debates (Entman 2004). Alternative views will be reported only when there are disagreements among elites, particularly if they are voiced by members of Congress or individuals within the foreign policy establishment (Althaus 2003; Bennett 1991; Bennett, Lawrence, and Livingston 2007; Mermin 1999; Robinson 2002). Leaders of foreign governments and prominent international figures often provide criticisms of U.S. policy and alternative views, but the U.S. media has been reluctant to feature these alternative views, which would not seem objective or credible to American readers. Yet even domestic sources that are viewed as objective or at least credible, such as academics and policy analysts, are rarely given a voice when there is consensus among lawmakers (Mermin 1999).

The literature on media framing of public policy suggests that the media coverage of human trafficking has been presented in a way that has marginalized alternative views on trafficking and criticisms of current policy and, as a result, legitimized the dominant view on trafficking and the approach to combating trafficking. When examining specific aspects of the coverage of human trafficking in recent years, we should expect to see:

(H_1) human trafficking characterized mostly as sex trafficking and prostitution;

(H_2) viewpoints mostly voiced by official and other establishment sources, that is, foreign policy elites and activists in the anti-trafficking policy network;

(H_3) the view that organized crime and other criminal activity have
been the primary cause for trafficking; and

(H_4) that the main way to combat trafficking is to build on current
policy, that is, more law enforcement, protection programs for
victims, and prevention campaigns.

Since only the U.S. media system has been the subject of extensive research
regarding media framing and coverage of foreign policy making, it is unclear if these hypotheses will hold for other media systems. It is possible that
these same patterns occur in other countries that have been making strong
efforts at combating human trafficking and that have a media system structurally similar to the one in the United States. For example, journalistic
professionalism is a central feature of the media systems of Canada and the
Great Britain, suggesting that there is a heavy reliance on official sources as
in the United States. There are some notable differences among these three
media systems, however, that may produce some variation in the coverage of
human trafficking. In the United States and Canada, news reporting tends
to be presented in an informational and narrative style and generally re-
frains from commentary. In addition, rather than catering to a particular
political party, Canadian and American media tend to have a centrist orientation and emphasize stories that appeal to white, middle-class consumers.
In Great Britain, news reporting includes more commentary and tends to be
more interpretive (Hallin and Mancini 2004), creating a framework with
which to be critical of government policy.[3] Thus, we may see that the British
media use a more diverse set of sources, reflect a more comprehensive view
of the causes of trafficking and solutions to combat it, or are more critical of
government policy.

Data and Methods

To examine the sources and arguments used in recent media coverage of
human trafficking in the United States, Britain, and Canada, I identified all
articles on the subject that were printed in a sample of authoritative and
widely read (by both the policy makers and the public) newspapers from the
three countries between January 1, 2000, and December 31, 2005. The newspapers chosen for analysis were the *New York Times* and the *Washington
Post* for the United States, the *Times of London* and the *Guardian* for Great

Britain, and the *Toronto Star* and the *Globe and Mail* for Canada. The *New York Times* was selected for this study because it is considered the most influential media source in the agenda-setting process, among both policy makers and other media organizations (Dearing and Rogers 1996). While less of an authority on foreign policy issues, the *Washington Post* also is widely read by national policy makers and political elites in the United States. Although the other four papers do not have the same influence as their American counterparts, each is considered an authoritative news source and has a large mass audience (Teitz 1999).

The relevant articles were obtained from Lexis-Nexis, which maintains a full-text archive of all articles appearing in the print edition of these newspapers during the study period.[4] After removing duplicate and irrelevant articles, I identified 837 articles that were printed over the six-year period: 181 articles in the *New York Times*, 174 articles in the *Washington Post*, 140 in the *Times*, 120 in the *Guardian*, 97 in the *Toronto Star*, and 125 in the *Globe and Mail*.

Figure 3.1 displays a summary of the number of articles published by year. Although the American papers published the most articles on human trafficking during the study period, more articles were printed in the Canadian papers in 2000 and in the British papers in 2001. The coverage in all three countries dropped significantly in 2001, most likely because much of the media's attention was on the aftermath of the terrorist attacks in the

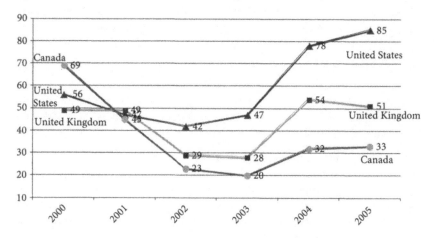

Figure 3.1. Media coverage of human trafficking in the United States, Great Britain, and Canada, 2000–2005

United States on September 11. Beginning in 2002, the U.S. media provided the most coverage of human trafficking, while the Canadian media provided the least coverage. This is somewhat surprising given that the most recent policy initiatives have originated out of Canada and Great Britain. On average, 59 articles appeared in the two American papers between 2000 and 2006, 43 articles appeared in the two British papers, and 37 articles in the two Canadian papers.

Of the 837 articles on human trafficking appearing in six newspapers during the study period, 79 percent appeared as news stories, 9 percent as editorials and commentary, 4 percent as letters to the editor, and 8 percent in the form of news summaries, lists, or transcripts. The average word count for the news stories was 660, while the average count for all the articles was 720 words. Only about one-fifth of the articles were placed in a highly visible location and in a position to capture the public's attention: 6 percent of the articles appeared on the front page of the main section, and 2 percent appeared on the first page of another major section. In addition, 12 percent appeared on the op-ed pages, the section of the newspaper that tends to be read by policy makers and the paper's most politically aware readers. The vast majority of articles, however, 65 percent, appeared elsewhere in the main section, and the remaining 16 percent appeared inside other sections.

But as can be seen in Table 3.1, there was a clear difference in the types of articles printed and the placement of articles by country. In the American papers, there was a greater tendency for a discussion of trafficking on the op-ed pages, with 13 percent of the stories appearing as editorials and 7 percent appearing as letters to the editor. In the two Canadian papers, only 8 percent of the articles appeared as editorials and letters, and only 5 percent appeared in this form in the two British papers. The articles in the two American newspapers also were more prominently placed than the articles printed in the other papers. As Table 3.1 also shows, 11 percent of the articles in the *New York Times* or *Washington Post* appeared on the front page of the main section or the first page on another major section, and 19 percent of the articles appeared on the op-ed pages. Thus, nearly one-third of all articles were placed in a location that could potentially have an impact on the public agenda. For the two Canadian papers, 15 percent of the articles were placed in one of these prominent locations. For the two British papers, however, only 7 percent, or two articles were prominently placed. It is pos-

Table 3.1. Article Type and Placement by Country

	Country			
Type of article	*US* %	*Great Britain* %	*Canada* %	*All* %
News story	67.9	87.7	87.4	79.2
Editorial/signed commentary	13.2	4.2	6.8	8.7
Letter to the editor	7.3	1.2	1.4	3.8
News summary or list	11.5	6.9	4.5	8.2
Placement of article	%	%	%	%
% Front page, A section	7.0	3.5	5.4	5.5
% Op-ed pages	19.4	3.8	8.1	11.6
% Front page, non–A section	3.7	0.0	1.8	2.0
% Elsewhere, A section	54.4	73.5	73.0	65.2
% All other sections/pages	15.5	19.2	11.7	15.7
# of articles	355	260	222	837

sible that the infrequent discussion of human trafficking on the op-ed pages in the British and Canadian papers was the result of not having the reputation as the agenda setters for policy makers in the same way that the *New York Times* or *Washington Post* have on U.S. federal policy makers even while enjoying large circulation numbers.

To examine the sources and arguments used in recent news media coverage of human trafficking, I performed a detailed content analysis of the 837 identified articles. The format of the questions and coding protocol for the content analysis were adapted from prominent published studies of media framing (Gilens 1999; Iyengar 1991; Klinenberg 2003; Project for Excellence in Journalism 1998) and from more recent reports published by the Project for the Excellence in Journalism. These themes included issue focus, sources used, and the representation of specific ideas and details about causes and solutions. The lists of possible sources included groups and individuals having a role in the policy process. Lists of causes and solutions cited by the media were created by identifying the full range of views expressed in the writings and statements of official policy makers, scholars, and activists that were outlined above. For each of the three lists, open-ended answers were available as options so that ideas not expressed in the academic and policy discourse could be included as well.[5]

Media Coverage of Human Trafficking, 2000–2005

Issue Focus

As discussed above, human trafficking refers to trafficking of persons for sexual exploitation, labor slavery, and the smuggling of migrants across borders. A common criticism of U.S. policy is that the focus has been almost entirely on sex trafficking and prostitution and has largely ignored labor trafficking unless it falls within the context of combating illegal immigration (Ehrenreich and Hochschild 2004; Kempadoo 2005; McGill 2003). The American, British, and Canadian print media coverage seems to have corresponded closely to governmental efforts in each of the three countries. Over half of the articles that addressed human trafficking referred to the issue in terms of sex trafficking, prostitution, or pornography (54 percent), while only one-fifth referred to the issue in terms of labor exploitation (20 percent). The public's concern about illegal immigration in many Western nations (see, for example, Pew Research Center 2009; Transatlantic Trends 2009) has also been reflected in the coverage, with 29 percent of the articles framed as an immigration issue. This greater focus on sex trafficking supports the hypothesis that (H_1) human trafficking has been characterized mostly as sex trafficking and prostitution and has helped legitimize the dominant conceptualization of trafficking.

There were some significant differences in the issue emphasis in the coverage across newspapers (see Table 3.2). Whereas 60 percent of the articles in the U.S. papers and 54 percent of the articles in the British newspapers focused on sex trafficking and prostitution, only 43 percent of the articles in the *Toronto Star* and *Globe and Mail* papers did so. Rather, the Canadian papers framed almost half of their coverage of trafficking in terms of immigration and human smuggling. Immigration was the focus of 29 percent of the articles in the two British newspapers and only 17 percent of the articles in the two American papers. One explanation for the greater emphasis on immigration in Canada was that there happened to be a number of reported cases of human smuggling, many of which had ended tragically during the study period. Moreover, Canada serves as a transit country for

Table 3.2. Issue Focus by Country

	Country			
Issue Focus	US %	Great Britain %	Canada %	All %
Sex trafficking/prostitution	60.0	54.2	43.2	53.8
Labor trafficking	21.7	18.1	18.0	19.6
Immigration/human smuggling	17.7	29.2	48.2	29.4
National security	2.2	2.7	0.0	1.8
Adoptions, illegal	2.0	3.8	2.7	2.7

trafficking of persons into the United States (U.S. Department of State 2009), and many articles described the problems faced by rescued victims seeking refugee status.

Sourcing

About three-fourths of the articles analyzed cited one or more sources that referred to trafficking: 39 percent cited at least one source, and 38 percent cited more than one source. Information obtained from government officials and policy makers in the form of official press materials, personal interviews, or second-hand accounts was the most common source, used in 43 percent of the articles (see Table 3.3). It is not surprising that so many stories used information derived from government officials, given that they are the quintessential official source and that they are readily accessible on the most common beats.

Another common source used in the coverage was law enforcement personnel, including prosecutors, defense attorneys, border agents, and police (23 percent). Law enforcement personnel also are considered official sources and are accessible to reporters on the "crime" beat or those covering immigration. The third and fourth most common sources cited were individuals associated with a nongovernmental organization (19 percent) and representatives of the United Nations or one of its agencies (13 percent). NGO representatives are likely considered experts in issues related to trafficking and can provide valuable knowledge and perspectives. They are not located in areas that neatly intersect with news beats, however, and thus have to be aggressive in making themselves known and available to the media in order to have their voices

Table 3.3. Sources Cited

Source	Official Source?	% of Articles Cited
Government officials, policy makers, or agencies (not police)	Yes	43.1
Law enforcement officials	Yes	22.6
NGOs, activists, etc.	Mix	19.4
UN or UN agencies (UNESCO, ILO, IOM, etc.)	Yes	13.0
Traffickers, employers, customers, etc.	No	12.1
Victims	No	9.3
Professors, analysts, or other researchers	Mix	7.2
Witnesses/family/victims' advocates	No	5.4
Other journalists	Mix	3.7
Religious groups/leaders	Mix	1.9

heard. What also helps them attract media attention is their relationship with official sources. Although this group of sources comprises a great diversity of activists, every representative cited was affiliated with a group associated with the anti-trafficking policy community (for example, Human Rights Watch, International Justice Mission, International Labor Organization, Poppy Project, etc.). None of the groups that are considered to represent the positions of sex-positive feminists and other alternative views are included in the newspaper coverage during the study period. Rather, most of these groups cited have a good working relationship with Western governments and the UN and support an abolitionist position on prostitution.

The victims of trafficking are sourced in only 12 percent of the stories. Not only is it hard to find trafficking victims to interview for a story, but it is also challenging to get victims to discuss their experience with others. Many fear that their traffickers will harm them or their families if they discuss their ordeal or their traffickers, while others are ashamed of their experience (Gallagher 2006; Haynes 2004). Prosecutors also have had difficulty interviewing victims and getting them to talk on the record for the same reasons, which explains why so few victims in the United States have obtained T-Visas (DeStefano 2008).

Only 9 percent of the stories used a trafficker, employer, customer, or other person involved in the trafficking as a source. The ones used as sources tended to be accused employers or traffickers who were waiting to be prosecuted. While it is understandable that most traffickers would avoid the media in order to not attract police attention, the ability of journalists to obtain confidential and frank interviews with people responsible for so much of the criminal activity could provide valuable and useful information to policy makers for crafting solutions to the problem.

One group of sources that has the potential to provide alternative viewpoints is academics. Only 7 percent of the articles cited an academic or policy analyst as a source, however. Again, those cited tended to be associated with the main policy-making community and activists or were even part of recent policy-making activity. Alternative voices tended to be associated with descriptive information and details. On a few occasions, these voices provided an alternative, albeit tempered perspective. For example, in a May 12, 2005, article in the *New York Times*, an International Labor Organization researcher urged the World Bank to focus more on poverty-reduction programs in addition to stepping up law enforcement activities. In a May 19, 2006, *Washington Post* article, a law professor and attorney representing three health organizations challenged the U.S. government's policy of requiring groups receiving funds for AIDS work, as a condition for receiving those funds, to denounce prostitution, and criticized policies that made it difficult to teach prostitutes about AIDS-prevention methods.

The sources cited in the newspapers varied by country, but not in a way that was expected. The newspapers in each country relied mostly on official sources and infrequently upon the people who were the most acutely involved in or affected by the trafficking, that is, the victims and their families, traffickers, buyers and customers, and other witnesses. The major difference was that there was a more even balance between official and other sources in

Table 3.4. Sources Cited by Country

Country	Type of Source Cited		
	Official %	*Mixed* %	*Unofficial* %
United States (N = 355)	55.5	32.1	23.4
Great Britain (N = 260)	72.3	22.7	23.1
Canada (N = 222)	65.3	25.2	19.4
All (N = 837)	63.3	27.4	22.2
Chi square	18.787	7.394	1.431
P	0.000	0.025	0.489

the two American newspapers than in the British and Canadian newspapers (see Table 3.4). While Hallin and Mancini's (2004) analysis of the British print media suggests that the *Times* and the *Guardian* should have been less likely to rely on official sources because of their tradition of being more interpretive and analytical, this analysis shows that this is not the case, at least for the coverage of human trafficking.

Causes

At least one cause was mentioned in 61 percent of the articles, and two or more were mentioned in 31 percent of the articles. There was no cause cited in 39 percent of the articles. Thus, over one-third of the coverage failed to discuss any causes at all and was not in a position to educate the public or policy makers about the reasons for human trafficking. The most commonly mentioned set of causes, cited in 40 percent of the articles, was criminal activity, including forms of fraud, deception, and coercion (see Table 3.5). Trafficking activity perpetrated by organized crime networks was mentioned specifically in 26 percent of the articles. The next most cited causes were poverty and lack of economic opportunities (13 percent), war and political violence (9 percent), corruption by government officials (8.5 percent), and the selling of victims by family members (7.5 percent).

The ranking of causes provides support for the hypothesis that the dominant narrative when discussing the causes of trafficking has been the "crime frame" (H_3). Grouping the various specific causes into general frames shows even more clearly that the crime frame has been the dominant narrative most often used. Whereas 47 percent of the articles mentioned at least one cause as being crime or poor law enforcement, 28 percent mentioned a political, socioeconomic, or cultural cause for trafficking. Causes cited by alternative scholars and activists were even less mentioned, that is, that the problem of trafficking has been exaggerated or is the result of Western demand. A Western demand for cheap labor was cited in only 3 percent of the articles. In addition, women attracted to the sex industry were cited in only 4 percent of the articles. Together, the sex-positive feminist and neo-imperialist frames were prominent narratives in only 13 percent of the articles.

To be even more confident that the alternative views were being marginalized and that the official view was further legitimized by the coverage, I coded for the presence or absence of any questioning about the definition of

Table 3.5. Causes Cited

Cause	Perspective	% of Articles Cited
Criminal activity/deception	Crime/Legal	39.5
Organized crime networks	Crime/Legal	25.7
Poverty, lack of economic development	Societal	13.4
Political violence/upheaval	Societal	9.4
Government/police corruption	Crime/Legal	8.5
Family selling girls/children	Crime/Legal	7.5
Sex tourism from Western and other countries	Alternative	6.5
Poorly enforced laws that already exist	Crime/Legal	5.1
Women and girls voluntarily drawn to prostitution, sex industry, excitement of urban life	Alternative	4.1
Gender discrimination/low status of women	Societal	3.3
Demand from Western and other countries for cheap labor	Societal	3.0
Cultural tolerance and/or indifference	Societal	2.6
Lack of educational opportunities for women	Societal	1.8
Local demand for cheap labor	Societal	1.8
Lack of international cooperation/collaboration	Crime/Legal	1.8
Local demand for sex	Societal	1.6
Abductions after Indian Ocean tsunami, 2004	Crime/Legal	1.1
Too strict an immigration policy in West	Alternative	0.4
Globalization	Societal	0.2
Criminalization of sex work	Alternative	0.0

trafficking or the extent of the problem. Only two articles raised any questions about the meaning of trafficking, but neither in a way that was critical of government policy. In an October 24, 2005, *Washington Post* review of the Lifetime Network's mini-series *Human Trafficking*, the reviewer criticized the filmmaker's incoherence in documenting the problem. And an article in the *Globe and Mail* on April 14, 2005, quoted a policy analyst who also served as an attorney for the accused trafficker, asserting that the foreign migrants his client hired for his massage parlor were not prostitutes and, thus, had not been trafficked. As far as the extent of the problem was concerned, any questioning of numbers was about how the problem was being underestimated. In one case, an official of the Russian government maintained that the number of illegal adoptions was nonexistent or, at worst, greatly exaggerated.

In Table 3.6, the causes are collapsed into three broad categories and presented for the three countries. The two British papers stand out not only for using the crime frame the most often, but also for citing more often the

Table 3.6. Causes Cited by Country

	Type of Cause Cited			
Country	Crime %	Societal %	Alternative %	No cause cited %
United States (N=355)	39.2	26.2	7.9	46.8
Great Britain (N=260)	54.2	31.9	18.8	30.0
Canada (N=222)	49.5	27.0	14.0	36.5
All (N=837)	46.6	28.2	12.9	38.8
Chi square	14.768	2.634	16.341	18.448
P	0.001	0.268	0.000	0.000

sex-positive feminist and neo-imperialist frames. The higher tendency to cite the crime frame may be partly the result of the heavier reliance by the British papers on official sources. The two American papers also stand out, but by using both the crime frame and the alternative frames the least often. This difference may be the result of 47 percent of all the articles in the *New York Times* and *Washington Post* not citing any cause at all. For the *Times* and the *Guardian*, only 30 percent of the articles failed to cite any cause.

One way to account for the difference between the American and British papers in the frequency of citing causes is to examine the ratios of criminal-to-societal and criminal-to-alternative citations. The ratio of criminal-to-societal citations is highest in the Canadian papers (1.8) and lowest in the American papers (1.5). For the British papers, the ratio is 1.7. But at the same time, the American papers had the highest ratio of criminal-to-alternative citations (5), followed by the Canadian papers (3.6), and then the British papers (2.9). Examining the data in this way indicates that the major difference among the three countries is that the British and Canadian media have been better at representing the alternative perspective than the American media, although all have given prominence and helped to reinforce the dominant perspective on the causes of human trafficking.

Solutions

Most of the recent coverage on human trafficking by the major print media in the United States, Great Britain, and Canada did not discuss any solutions at all. Approximately 54 percent of the stories did not include reference to a proposed solution or policy currently in place; 20 percent cited only one solution, while 25 percent cited two or more. As expected, the most commonly cited solution in the coverage was stricter law enforcement, cited in 15 percent of the articles (see Table 3.7). The second most commonly cited solution was political change and reform (14 percent), one of the major themes appearing in the advocates of the human rights perspective. The next three most common solutions all echoed calls for building on current policy: implementing new laws (10.6 percent), promoting greater international cooperation (10.5 percent), and tightening or more strictly enforcing immigration policy (7 percent). Increasing assistance for victims was cited as a solution in 7 percent of the articles. An investment in human development needs such as education, income generation, and social services in origin countries was cited in 6.5 percent of the articles. Very few articles raised the possibility of

Table 3.7. Solutions Cited

Solution	Perspective	% of Articles Cited
More effort/resources aimed at enforcement or prosecuting traffickers and/or customers of prostitutes	Current policy	14.5
Political change/reform	Human rights	13.5
Legal measures	Current policy	10.6
International collaboration	Current policy	10.5
Stricter immigration controls	Current policy	7.0
More assistance for victims	Human rights	6.5
Invest in human development	Human rights	6.2
Raise public awareness	Current policy	5.7
Sanctions imposed by United States	Current policy	4.3
Treat victims as witnesses or refugees rather than criminals/reform visa process	Human rights	3.3
Legalize prostitution	Alternative	2.4
Raise status of women	Human rights	2.3
Diplomacy	Current policy	2.0
Liberalize immigration laws	Alternative	1.7
Information campaigns warning potential victims	Current policy	1.6
Stricter anti-prostitution laws	Current policy	1.4
Labor rights	Human rights	0.7

Table 3.8. Solutions Cited by Country

	Type of Solution Cited			
Country	Current Policy %	Human Rights %	Alternative %	No solution cited %
United States (N = 355)	38.0	21.1	1.4	53.8
Great Britain (N = 260)	35.4	28.1	5.0	53.1
Canada (N = 222)	33.3	25.7	6.8	56.8
All (N = 837)	36.0	24.5	3.9	54.4
Chi square	1.362	4.149	11.430	0.731
P	0.506	0.126	0.003	0.694

liberalizing immigration laws or legalizing prostitution. There was little discussion or mention of improving the condition of women, and almost nothing about improving labor standards in either origin or destination countries. Together, 36 percent of the articles cited a source advocating a solution that would build on current policy, while 24 percent cited a solution that addressed the root cause of trafficking. Only 4 percent of the articles included calls for liberalizing immigration laws or legalizing prostitution.

I also coded for the presence or absence of specific criticism of government policy with respect to their own government's actions and to government action in other countries. In almost all the cases where a criticism of government policy was cited, either at home or abroad, it was to present an argument for doing more to enforce existing laws or help victims rather than to advocate going in a new direction. The only article that was critical of government policy was in the *Globe and Mail* on June 21, 2005. An article headlined "DNA Tests Add a Risky Delay, Refugees Say" presented criticism of a Canadian government policy that required DNA tests of family members of trafficking victims living abroad before they could enter the country to be reunited with their parents or children. While the purpose of the policy was to prevent fraud, the result was a disheartening delay for a number of vulnerable and traumatized people.

In Table 3.8, the solutions are collapsed into three broad categories and presented for the three countries. There were no differences in the frequency with which current solutions or the criticisms voiced by human rights advocates were represented. While the Canadian papers did cite solutions such as liberalizing anti-prostitution and immigration laws significantly more often than British or American newspapers, these solutions still represented only 7 percent of the coverage. On the whole, the analysis of the solutions cited in the major print sources in the United States, Great Britain, and Canada supports the hypothesis that the media coverage of human trafficking has emphasized the view that (H_4) *the main way to combat trafficking is to build on current policy.*

Conclusions and Implications

This is one of the first studies to examine how the media have covered the issue of human trafficking. The study has revealed that the coverage of human trafficking has increased significantly since 2002, particularly in the American media. The American media also were more likely to publish editorials, commentary, and letters to the editor on human trafficking and to place the issue in prominent locations. The American, British, and Canadian media all conceptualized the trafficking problem more in terms of sex trafficking rather than of labor trafficking, although the Canadian newspapers also conceptualized the problem as one of immigration and human smuggling. The news coverage relied almost exclusively on government officials and law enforcement personnel as sources, and conveyed the view that the problem is the result of organized criminal networks and that the appropriate remedies are increased resources for law enforcement, enhanced legal measures, and assistance for victims. While the print media in the United States, United Kingdom, and Canada have helped to bring the horrors of human trafficking to the attention of their readers, they have done a poor job of representing the various viewpoints on the issue. Most of the coverage tended to reflect the view of the dominant actors, and there was almost no questioning of positions and statements of official sources.

The reasons for the inadequate and unrepresentative coverage likely are the routines of conventional news organizations that make it difficult for journalists to be exposed to views that do not neatly intersect with their established beats (Gans 2005; Schudson 1980). The need to be objective creates even more reliance on official sources, which also happen to be available at common beats such as the U.S. State Department and the United Nations. Reporters who have the crime beat or immigration beat also are prone to frame their stories in ways that mirror current government policy. Additionally, journalists covering foreign affairs and human rights issues such as human trafficking are stationed in the capital city of foreign countries or their own embassies and consulates, where much of their information comes from government press releases and statements (Graber 2010). Since there does not seem to be much disagreement on the policy goals and methods, it is difficult for journalists to write about the alternative perspectives or critiques (Entman 2004). It is also likely, moreover, that journalists have ignored sources and views that challenge the values and legitimacy of core institutions or do not report on solutions that have a high cost in order to avoiding troubling their audience. It may be that establishment groups are more aggressive in promoting themselves to the media, while many academics are less knowledgeable about media relations. And the more radical voices may be unwilling to play the "media game," especially with members of the mainstream media (Larson 2006).

The difficulty of reporting on a phenomenon that exists largely underground and is highly complex cannot be discounted as an explanation for the inadequate and unrepresentative coverage. A journalist's job is to streamline and simplify information for the public. This can lead journalists to refrain from framing a story in a way that is contrary to the dominant narrative or including additional information that contradicts the prevailing structure of the story. At the same time, many journalists might lack the expertise to understand this complex issue themselves (Casselman 2004). And the ever declining resources for investigative reporting and international coverage may be partly to blame for the misleading coverage as well (Flournoy 2004; Ricchiardi 2008).

The way that human trafficking has been covered has consequences for the policy process and the individual trafficking victims. Good, effective solutions are not even considered, and ineffective policies are not terminated or improved. For example, more money could be directed toward exposing corrupt government officials and law enforcement personnel who are complicit in trafficking or look the other way.

While there was some evidence to suggest that the British newspapers were even more reliant on official sources and more likely to represent the dominant viewpoint, while the Canadians were less reliant on official sources and more likely to print alternative views, for the most part, the media coverage in the United States, United Kingdom, and Canada produced a similar product. By studying the media's coverage of human trafficking with a comparative approach, it has been possible to uncover the influence that professional norms can have on news gathering and reporting across varying cultural and institutional contexts.

Rather than serving as a watch dog on government and as a vehicle for a critical assessment of policy debates and outcomes, the findings from this study suggest that, indirectly, the media has had an important role in anti-trafficking policy by limiting how many competing views of the causes of the problem are discussed and the range of recommended policy alternatives considered. More disconcerting is that the media seem to have been following the lead of those whom they should be watching.

PART II

From Prostitution to Power

Chapter 4

Rethinking Trafficking: Human Rights and Private Wrongs

Alison Brysk

Over the last decade, international humanitarian campaigns and policy have begun to address the horrific and increasing transnational sexual exploitation of women and children. While this is a welcome development, it is too often based on a distorted understanding of trafficking, violence, and globalization. Sexualized, individualistic myths regarding trafficking limit appropriate attention and response to victims of a wide range of globalized exploitation and coercion—including the intended beneficiaries of anti-trafficking efforts.

The fight against slavery is seen as the first international human rights movement, but the persistence and revival of this ancient evil shows that in an era of globalization, a prohibited public crime has morphed into a massive private wrong. "Private wrongs" are contemporary patterns of human rights abuse committed by nongovernmental forms of authority: from firms to families (Brysk 2005). While the enslavement of tens of millions of Africans in the Americas was state-sanctioned and sometimes state-sponsored, modern slavery operates in the gaps of governance: in rural backwaters, failed states, and the freefall of illicit migration. Its victims, like most current forms of exploitation, are second-class citizens and "disposable people"— women, children, outcasts, and the marginalized poor (Bales 2004).

The key to understanding and combating private wrongs is to recognize these affronts to human dignity as abuses of power as much as any act of government, unmasking their justification as states of nature, cultural traditions, or personal choice. Slavery is not an accident or an atavism; it is a predatory strategy of commodification of fellow human beings in a privatizing world. In this "race to the bottom," traditional inequities and stigmas are brands signaling who can be exploited and how. Women are especially vulnerable to the sex trade—but women are equally vulnerable to exploitation in the "maid trade," and any other traditional role where domestic disempowerment meets globalized displacement.

Prevailing constructions of international commercial sex have brought attention to a tragic underside of globalization, but they generate incomplete responses to abuse and obscure linked forms of exploitation. Anti-trafficking policies depart from an assumption of free individual women, or parents on behalf of children, who are coerced or egregiously misled to be smuggled across borders and then continuously pressured and abused to engage in sex work. It is assumed that such women were not and would not engage voluntarily in sex work, that other employment options exist or are not exploitive, and that trafficking is uniquely harmful due to its nature. Recognizing transnational forms of slavery and sexual violence is a necessary but not sufficient response to trafficking and the wider spectrum of sexual abuse and transnational labor exploitation; this initial response corresponds more to our own cultural norms than the moral equality and self-determination of the victims. More specifically, the coercive model of trafficking dodges a deeper analysis of globalization's structural pressures on decision making in households, and the social delegation of authority over women to households rather than state authorities in a kind of embedded second-class citizenship (Brysk 2005).

Policies based on these neoliberal assumptions of coerced victims who can be freed for other viable choices do not serve even the preponderance of their intended beneficiaries: victims of transnational sexual exploitation. First, anti-trafficking policies framed to protect "innocent" women from sexual slavery ignore or slight prior sex workers, or other women who migrate voluntarily to engage in sex work but are subsequently exploited—often the most vulnerable populations. Second, international policy and especially American policy focuses disproportionately on culturally recognizable European victims of east-west traffic, when the vast majority of victims are intraregional in the global south. Third, policies often aim to stop commercial sex rather than the violence, exploitation, and other harms associated with it—and with other forms of labor and migration.

The disproportionate emphasis on trafficking within migration policy also slights the wider set of persons exploited and abused across borders. The individualistic emphasis and sexual focus of anti-trafficking efforts fails to address the wider issue of structural violence and economic determinants of all forms of trafficking, labor abuse, and exploitive smuggling. Such policies also fail to recognize the much broader sexual abuse of women integral to many forms of exploitive globalized labor, such as sexual harassment and rape in sweatshops and the "maid trade." Finally, by putting sexual exploitation first and assuming that women are uniquely degraded by sex, anti-trafficking policy diverts attention from equally harmful and widespread forms of labor exploitation that affect equally "innocent" men and children, as well as women toiling in dangerous and debilitating nonsexual jobs.

What would a human rights approach look like? The struggle for human rights rests in a dual mandate of protection and empowerment. Internationally recognized human rights provide a universal range of rights to freedom of movement, labor rights, and physical integrity—freedom from torture, abuse, and rape. While human rights originated as a claim against governments, they are now widely understood to hold against all agents of authority: from guerrillas to employers to families. And human rights go beyond a humanitarian appeal for succor to assign a responsibility for remedy. In the first instance, an individual's state must protect his or her rights, but where citizenship is absent or unavailing, all states are responsible for providing protection if not empowerment to all residents of their territory—especially refugees (Brysk 2002).

The problem is powerlessness, not prostitution, and the solution to powerlessness is politics—not prohibition. Private wrongs like trafficking are ameliorated when new groups are recognized as human, new leverage points of global connection are discovered, and new claims for governance are recognized as determinants of human dignity (Brysk 2005). This is more than just "prevention" in the narrow sense—it implies using the international human rights regime to move toward governance for the most marginal. Elements of this system must include UN monitoring and coordination, pressure by strong powers, legal and development assistance to willing but weak governments, and sanctions on regimes that tolerate this abuse (discussed by van den Anker, Gallagher, and Bales and Choi-Fitzpatrick later in this volume). But above all, it means providing political channels and leverage to victim populations and at-risk groups.

Rights at Risk: Sex, Lies, and Globalization

Women now comprise almost half of international migrants. Women are trafficked within and across borders for various forms of female-typed labor: from "nimble-fingered" sweatshops to the "maid trade," from mail-order brides to prostitution. Women are highly vulnerable to sexual harassment and exploitation in *all* of these forms of labor, but the level of coercion is usually highest in transnational prostitution. While regional patterns of female factory and domestic labor mirror those of males, the export of female sexual services follows distinct geographic patterns: East–West and South–North.

The numerical preponderance of people trafficked *domestically* are men indentured for debt slavery in rural areas of developing countries, or forced labor in dictatorial regimes and war zones. Significant numbers of male and female children are also enslaved on plantations, in informal factories, as domestic servants, as beggars, and as child soldiers. The largest flows of domestic labor trafficking are within the poorest countries and regions: Africa, South Asia, and the Middle East.

Although international sex trafficking is an especially egregious violation of almost every fundamental freedom, enacted on especially vulnerable populations, other forms of labor exploitation and abuse are even more widespread and affect greater numbers of people. For example, the International Labor Organization (ILO) estimates there are nearly 700,000 child domestic workers in Indonesia alone, and Human Rights Watch has identified that country as one in which a large number of such workers face "slave-like conditions," including frequent physical and sexual abuse (Human Rights Watch 2006). This is a far larger and more vulnerable affected population *in one country* than the maximal estimates of Eastern European women trafficked to the West for sexual exploitation. Similarly, the International Organization for Migration estimates that in 2007 alone, there were 26 million internally displaced persons as a result of political conflict or natural disaster (along with 11 million refugees)—and these vulnerable groups face very similar threats to their rights and well-being as trafficking victims do (International Organization for Migration 2011). Although women trafficked for sexual exploitation are especially at risk of abuse due to displacement, the number of women co-

erced or pressured into prostitution *within* their countries far exceeds trafficking victims, with little international attention or pressure. For example,
some sources estimate that Iran, a relatively closed society where trafficking is
not a major factor, hosts 200,000 to a million women working as prostitutes
under degrading, repressive, and exploitive conditions—and increasingly
threatened by HIV infection (Saba 2003).

The website www.bayswan.org/traffick/, run jointly by the Global Alliance Against Traffic in Women, the Network of Sexwork Projects, the International Human Rights Law Group, and Human Rights Watch, monitors
the effects and shortfalls of anti-trafficking initiatives. Part of the problem is
an overestimation and concentration on coercion rather than more complex
"structural violence" as a determinant of sexual exploitation. A single but
suggestive 2009 London Metropolitan University survey of migrants in sex
work in the UK concludes that

> interviews with 100 migrant women, men and transgender people
> working in all of the main jobs available within the sex industry, and
> from the most relevant areas of origin (South America, Eastern Eu-
> rope, EU, and South East Asia), suggest that although some migrants
> are subject to coercion and exploitation, a majority are not.... ap-
> proximately 13 per cent of female interviewees felt that they had
> been subject to different perceptions and experiences of exploitation,
> ranging from extreme cases of trafficking to relatively more consen-
> sual arrangements. Only a minority, amounting approximately to 6
> per cent of female interviewees, felt that they had been deceived and
> forced into selling sex in circumstances within which they had no
> share of control or consent. (Mai n.d.)

Moreover, a report by the Global Alliance Against Trafficking shows that
anti-trafficking programs too often impinge on the rights of the people they
are supposed to help. Based on research in a range of sending and receiving
countries—Australia, Bosnia and Herzegovina, Brazil, India, Nigeria, Thailand, the United Kingdom, and the United States—the report shows that
women who are "rescued" from trafficking may be indefinitely detained
against their will in police facilities or shelters, involuntarily deported,
forced to provide evidence that puts them and their families at risk, or even
abused or harassed by law enforcement officials. In other cases, young
female migrants and potential border-crossers are profiled and subjected to

preemptive scrutiny and interdiction that restricts their freedom of movement in the name of protecting them from trafficking (Global Alliance Against Traffic in Women [GAATW] 2007, 2009). Thus, some argue more broadly that a "rescue industry" undercuts the rights of migrant sex workers when it types them as "innocent victims" in need of humanitarian protection rather than displaced agents in need of migration rights (Agustin 2007).

Worldwide, programs concentrate disproportionately on women trafficked from Eastern Europe and Southeast Asia to Western Europe and the United States, when the vast majority of exploitation occurs in South Asia, Africa, and the Middle East—either intraregionally or domestically. Moreover, trafficking in Africa and the Middle East is more likely to involve children, and to mix sexual exploitation with other forms of forced labor and even institutionalized slavery (United Nations Office on Drugs and Crime [UNODC] 2006). But both positive aid and legal assistance and negative U.S. sanctions have been focused by cultural construction and geopolitics, not need. For example, almost half of U.S. anti-trafficking funding went to East Asia or the Western Hemisphere, and only 14 percent to Africa (Ribando 2007). U.S.-sponsored Tier 3 sanctions have only been imposed on a handful of countries that overlap with pariah regimes sanctioned by the United States for other reasons—such as North Korea, where severe strictures on migration suggest that high levels of trafficking are unlikely.

The United States should be a best case for anti-trafficking efforts, since it has a willing and relatively effective state, legislation in place since 2001, and an attentive civil society coalition of religious, feminist, and human rights advocates for trafficking victims. Yet with an estimated incidence of "as many as 17,500 people" per year, the United States limits special protective visas for trafficking victims to 5,000 per year—and actually grants only several hundred (Ribando 2007). According to the State Department's mandated annual Trafficking in Persons report for 2008, the Department of Justice's Civil Rights Division and U.S. Attorneys' Offices in 2008 initiated 183 investigations, charged 82 individuals, and obtained 77 convictions in 40 human trafficking cases (13 labor trafficking, 27 sex trafficking). On the victim assistance side, the Department of Health and Human Services (HHS) certified 286 foreign adult victims in FY 2008, and issued eligibility letters to 31 foreign minors—which enabled them to receive special protective visas and social services. At the same time, one of the few genuine preventive measures that indicates both responsiveness and unmet need, the National Human Trafficking Resource Hotline, received a total of 4,147 calls, including more than 550 tips on possible human trafficking cases and nearly 400 requests for victim care referrals (U.S. Department of State 2009). Completing the picture, U.S. sources report that in 2007 only 3,427 traffickers were convicted worldwide (Ribando 2007)—keeping in mind the rough estimates of 800,000 victims annually.

In a parallel distortion, the large number of women trafficked South to North to sexually service migrant co-ethnics, a significant proportion of the Mexico–United States flow, receives much less attention and assistance than East–West or Southeast Asian prostitution and sex tourism. The harms of this form of trafficking are reported to be especially high, with extremely harsh living and working conditions and frequent physical abuse. While there are problems of receiving country law enforcement and social service access to this population of at-risk or trafficked women within diasporas, a conceptual barrier to greater enforcement is the implicit assumption that these women are in some sense governed (or even literally owned) by their communities rather than the authorities of the receiving country. At the U.S.-Mexico border, the problem is exacerbated by a failure on both sides to distinguish smuggling from trafficking, resulting in U.S. smuggling-suppression policies that drive migrants further underground into the arms of traffickers. Conversely, Mexico's practical toleration and legislative confusion regarding smuggling fails to protect its own most vulnerable citizens from exploitation (Cicero-Dominguez 2005). The Bilateral Safety Corridor Coalition (BSCC), an inter-American coalition of sixty NGOs and government agencies, has begun to raise awareness and deliver services to this population, and has received funding and provided training to U.S. border enforcement, justice, and social service agencies (BSCC 2011).

Sex work is not always slavery; sometimes it is "freely" chosen as the best of a terrible range of options available to poorly educated young women in patriarchal developing countries. Some of the distorted typing of trafficking as uniquely coercive and harmful obscures the pressures and violations of both alternative forms of migration and alternative domestic employment, as well as the sexual exploitation of "normal" practices in many sending countries. The "maid trade" is the main migration alternative beyond sex work for many young women from sending regions. For example, Saudi Arabian households employ an estimated 1.5 million domestic workers, mainly from Indonesia, Sri Lanka, the Philippines, and Nepal. Many of these migrants suffer egregious exploitation, "slavery-like conditions," and even sexual abuse (Human Rights Watch 2008). In parts of Latin America and Asia, young women who gain employment at home are likely to be employed in informal or low-wage export-oriented production, that is, sweatshops, with extremely high rates of sexual harassment and abuse. As fieldwork in the Dominican Republic shows, for example, it is perfectly rational for a woman in this situation to conclude that if she is going to be coerced into providing sexual services, she might as well get paid for it—and possibly escape some draining physical toil (Cabezas in Brysk 2002) In sending regions of South Asia and Africa, some young women naively but knowingly enter the sex trade fleeing "normal" customary domestic practices such as forced marriage, bonded domestic labor, and routine domestic violence.

Finally, the narrowed emphasis on transnational sexual exploitation sometimes deflects attention from equally harmful forms of nonsexual exploitation, transnational and domestic, enacted upon equally vulnerable populations. While there has been ample attention to child labor in export-oriented industrial sweatshops, for example, there has been much less coverage of routine domestic and intra-regional child labor on plantations and in mines. As the recent State Department report on trafficking notes, without offering a policy response parallel to anti-trafficking efforts:

> Some 20 to 30 percent of the world's gold comes from artisanal mines throughout Africa, South America, and Asia. . . . of the two million children who work in goldmines worldwide, many are forced, often through debt bondage, to do back-breaking work in hazardous conditions. Child laborers in gold mines face a number of dangers: In West Africa, children rub mercury into their hands before sifting soil through their fingers. In South America, children reportedly wash gold while standing in waist-deep water contaminated by mercury. Prolonged mercury exposure causes retardation, blindness, kidney damage, and tremors. . . . In Bolivia, trafficked boys as young as eight help detonate dynamite in the interior of gold mines. Traffickers in the Democratic Republic of the Congo subject children to debt bondage in gold mines, forcing them to work nine to ten hours daily digging tunnels and open-pit mines. In gold mines in Ethiopia, children are forced to work an average of 14 hours a day, six days a week. Children trafficked from Burkina Faso, Guinea, and Mali to gold mines in Côte d'Ivoire are held in slavery-like conditions and forced to work 10 hours a day, seven days a week. They receive little food and meager pay. In 2008, a Guinean child told the Associated Press he was promised $2 a day for his work in a gold

mine but received only $40 after six months of backbreaking, co-erced, and hazardous labor. (U.S. Department of State 2009)

Private Wrongs—The Problem Is Power, Not Prostitution

A deeper analysis of the differential response to trafficking may permit a more complete understanding and commensurate response to exploitation and abuse. Opposition to trafficking springs from a set of incomplete and even contradictory moral intuitions that can be addressed by a more systematic human rights approach. Yet even a conventional human rights approach must be broadened to encompass violations by nonstate actors and empowerment in the social vs. civic realm: private wrongs.

Why has policy seized so narrowly on trafficking, and adopted such a partial perspective on the nature and sources of the phenomenon? The narrative of trafficking has particularly salient features for contemporary Western publics, vis-à-vis other types of human rights abuse. The frame of transnational sexual labor exploitation was initially established as "white slavery" (Kempadoo and Doezema 1998). It thus taps into the moral capital of the anti-slavery campaign, often deemed the first modern human rights movement. In a morally regrettable yet politically powerful semantic move, *white* slavery emphasizes the "unnatural" threat of enslavement to a portion of a population generally exempted from this peril. Differential attention to Eastern European women promotes ready identification by Western publics with the subset of victims who are culturally and racially similar. Talk of slavery taps into Judeo-Christian religious imagery that appears to transcend ideology, avoiding more challenging sociological frames of labor exploitation or the highly contested issue of immigration rights.

And the slavery frame garners a special historical resonance from the dominant society most resistant to universal human rights—the United States—as one of the most mainstream American organizations ties trafficking to "American values":

We tell our children about the slave trade of Africans to the Americas. We speak of the atrocities that were committed. We speak of noble ideals and shun the thought that these things ever occurred in our history. And we pledge that no living thing shall ever be enslaved again to another. And while we recite these words, thousands of women and children across the world are being trafficked as slaves across U.S. borders and abroad. ("Ending Human Trafficking," National Association of the American People, posted at City Limits Radio, www.citylimits radio.com/?p=192, originally available at www.thenaap.org)

Moreover, the United States has a particular history of Protestant condemnation of prostitution and a quest for social purity through the abolition rather than prevention or regulation of socially harmful activities.

The trafficking frame also draws on the most palatable form of feminism: the struggle to end violence against women. Internationally, the humanitarian protection rubric and transnational networks combating violence against women have succeeded in gaining much greater response than equally costly but chronic or contested economic, cultural, or social rights struggles (Keck and Sikkink 1999). Trafficked women, as "people out of place" (Brysk and Shafir 2004), bridge the universal individual claims of displaced persons and the claims of traditional family values—as they are uprooted from the ascribed protection of home and family. Moreover, even within the violence-against-women frame, *sexual* violence receives greater recognition and priority. This is partly a reflection of decades of feminist education regarding the differential vulnerability of women and girls to these forms of abuse, but it also articulates with cultural scripts of female sexuality as fascinating yet also dangerous and inherently degrading.

International sex trafficking is properly defined as the subjugated and exploitive sale of sex across borders. Like other forms of labor migration, sex trafficking follows dual market and organizational logics: supply and demand plus availability of smuggling and receiving networks. A supply of desperate and vulnerable women (and families, in the case of children) is generated by the collapse of local economies, due to endemic poverty, political conflict, and/or pressures of globalization. Conversely, demand is highest in areas that have benefitted from globalization, with high flows of tourism and migration. Smuggling and receiving networks often developed around other illicit flows, such as drugs or weapons, but flourish in weak states and articulate with local institutions of gender inequity. International abuse of women grows from preexisting domestic practices of commodification of female reproductive labor, such as prostitution, forced marriage, and domestic service, as well as patriarchal control of women's movement, education, and employment—enforced by gendered violence. In the broader context of contemporary slavery, Bales's overall predictors of trafficking levels in a given country are corruption, infant mortality, youth population, food production, population density, and conflict (Bales 2005, 139).

Trafficking = supply (globalization + gender inequity) x demand (globalization + gender inequity) x networks (weak states + smuggling social capital + control of violence)

This type of analysis is supported by evidence such as a study by La Strada International, a coalition of nine NGOs in Eastern Europe, that shows systematically how trafficking is both a cause and a consequence of violations of women's human rights in that region. Patriarchal stereotypes, domestic violence, domestic employment inequity, informalization of female-typed labor in both sending and receiving countries, feminization of poverty in transitional economies, and shortfalls in social support services that differentially affect women are all linked to higher rates and harms of trafficking (La Strada International 2008). The problem is power, not prostitution. If we want to stop subjugated commodification, we must empower its victims. Specifically, we must disable the mechanisms of subjugation by gender— multiplied by race, class, and caste—that enable exploitation. And if we want to diminish the harms of trafficking, we must reduce the violence, stigma, and second-class citizenship of subjugated women and sex workers— not seek to eradicate commercial sex. What kinds of policies would support this deeper approach to trafficking and its associated forms of exploitation?

Rights and Responsibilities: From Exploitation to Empowerment

More broadly, how could an enhanced analysis of the roots and nature of trafficking help to design better policies worldwide? First, a human rights approach to trafficking as a private wrong would begin by strengthening protection from receiving states and international entities, and reorienting prosecution to serve protection rather than vice-versa. A better distinction between forced and free sex work means that protection for victims must be delinked from prosecution of traffickers, and protective services and status must be offered without conditionality. Complementing this, victims of non-coercive sexual exploitation must be offered access to expanded mechanisms of legal and financial accountability for labor abuse.

On the other hand, protection for victims of coercion may be more effective under a broader rubric of refugee status rather than the narrower trafficking niche, with expanded status for "well-founded fear of persecution" by non-state and transnational actors. There is some emerging precedent for this in leading states such as Canada's extension of gender-based asylum, and even recent U.S. rulings on protected status for victims of female genital mutilation and domestic violence that point in a similar direction.

Attention to prevention means empowerment, in sending states and migrant communities. Since *all* forms of migration are potentially exploitive, strengthening labor rights and labor organizations of *all* migrants—including sex workers' organizations—is an antitrafficking and a human rights strategy. The challenge is to ensure that trafficking is not marginalized from such forms of empowerment and relegated to a humanitarian ghetto, and that undocumented migrants are not legally or socially isolated from state protection and self-defense. Advocacy groups may be needed to bridge the gap on an interim basis, but their goal should be to establish a legal framework and social capital for self-representation by migrant workers in sending and receiving states.

Since *all* forms of labor are linked to sexual abuse in conditions of gender inequity, the best remedy and prevention from the harms of trafficking and other forms of sexual exploitation are programs and policies to increase women's incomes, educations, and reproductive freedoms. This power gap is greatest in sending countries, but the private sphere—and especially the commercial sex industry—is the most unequal workplace in developed countries, warranting particular policy focus. The linkages between privatization of developing countries' economies and the potential for unaccountable labor exploitation by transnational actors and migration push warrant special scrutiny in debates on the legal status of sex work and migrants in receiving nations.

Finally, anti-trafficking policy should triage prosecution and protection more by level of harm than type of abuse. While this does happen to some extent with the priority granted to prosecuting sexual exploitation of children, a triage by harms mandates a broader shift in the regional and demographic focus of receiving country and international institution programs. While anti-trafficking funds and programs focus on the most visible and Western-linked populations, more harmful forms of sexual exploitation are usually linked to poorer sending regions, greater gender inequity, servicing of other migrants or domestic indentured labor, and weak states. Developed receiving states can and should increase monitoring and "access to justice" programs for their less visible populations, as well as greater outreach to zones of intensified exploitation. This also means that all forms of exploitive labor in a country or region must be considered and prioritized by harm, rather than automatically focusing first on the sex trade. Even religious and some feminist advocates predisposed to attribute inherent harm to sex work should realize that greater attention to mitigating the harms of nonsexual labor should indirectly decrease sex trafficking by improving the alternatives for a vulnerable population.

Conclusion

The era of globalization has increased awareness of private wrongs and accelerated some forms of cross-border labor exploitation. But it has also distorted attention and response to a variety of abuses, through historical, cultural, and sociological stereotypes. A better understanding of freedom, sex, and development will allow us to expand a human rights approach to these private wrongs.

Under the direction of Secretary of State Hillary Clinton, the 2009 U.S. State Department Report shows signs of a modest conceptual breakthrough in the understanding of trafficking along the lines suggested in this essay. The report now begins with a broader discussion of forced labor that frames transnational prostitution as one facet of trafficking, and the 2008 legislation encompasses fraud and exploitation following voluntary migration. The U.S. report explicitly states that prior employment in sex work for adults or parental consent to exploitation of children should not diminish accountability for forced labor. The new report also highlights the emerging U.S. practice of forcing traffickers to pay restitution to victims, which has the potential to increase the effectiveness of enforcement by diminishing the profit motive of traffickers. It is too soon to tell how, or how fast, these new understandings will improve U.S. policy.

What is clear is that the best anti-trafficking policy is universal, indivisible human rights. Human rights mean voice and choice. Victims of sexual exploitation need the same things as all migrants, and all workers: recognition, monitoring, resources, access to justice, and organization. Rethinking trafficking can help us to rethink rights, responsibility, and the solidarity it will take to end all forms of contemporary slavery.

Chapter 5

The Sexual Politics of U.S.
Inter/National Security

Laura Hebert

Introduction

Once an invisible issue, the problem of human trafficking has captured public and political attention over the past decade, as evidenced by the many books, films, and college courses that today speak to the subject, as well as the myriad anti-trafficking laws and policies that are now in place at the national and international levels. This is a development welcomed by activists around the world who have struggled to bring international visibility to exploitative labor conditions associated with globalization. But, as Alison Brysk observes, the implementation of anti-trafficking efforts has also become a "relatively easy way [for states] to enact modern norms and burnish humanitarian credentials, without undertaking structural political or economic reform" (Brysk 2009, 14).

Political leaders today commonly articulate trafficking as a human rights violation that requires the adoption of a victim-centered approach. The U.S. government, in particular, has characterized its enactment of the 2000 Trafficking Victims Protection Act (TVPA) and its institutionalized monitoring of trafficking initiatives internationally as indicative of its leadership role in promoting international human rights standards. The TVPA explicitly identifies trafficking as a form of modern-day slavery, the continuation of which is deemed contrary to the country's founding principles that uphold the "inherent dignity and worth of all people" (U.S. Senate 2000, 1468). But a review of core provisions of the TVPA raises questions of the extent to which the Act represents a progressive departure from the more typical security-oriented response to trafficking, and thus whether it is capable of targeting the broader social structures of gender, ethnicity, class, and global North/South relations that have made possible the enslavement and involuntary servitude of humans in both the past and the present. Moreover, with the support of antiprostitution abolitionists, the U.S. government has used its platform in the trafficking arena to export its moral opposition to prostitution through prohibiting the appropriation of anti-trafficking funds for organizations that do not explicitly condemn the practice (U.S. Senate 2003, 12), serving to perpetuate a "trafficked victim" archetype that acknowledges only those totally deceived or subject to extreme forms of violence as "innocent" and worthy of assistance. The U.S. case illustrates that although the framing of trafficking as a human rights issue may positively signal the legitimization of human rights norms in domestic and international political relations, the concept of human rights is also vulnerable to cooptation for purposes that may be contrary to international human rights principles.

In the United States, the language of "human rights" and "human rights violations" is usually reserved for discussions of *other* states. In this essay, I turn the critical lens inward. I begin by engaging the question of what it means to adopt a human rights approach to trafficking, before turning to an examination of whether U.S. policies and practices fulfill international human rights standards. Building on an analysis of the consequences of restrictive immigration policies for trafficking survivors in this country, I argue that the government's construction of trafficking as externally driven and experienced ignores how the physical and psychological integrity of international "Others" has too often been sacrificed in the name of U.S. security. Probing the constitutive relationship between gender and U.S. inter/national security reveals the self-interested impulses behind the TVPA, while also exposing the lack of self-reflexivity among U.S. leaders regarding the human rights implications of their domestic and foreign policy decisions. I conclude the essay by arguing that it is precisely through revealing how the privileging of state security over the welfare of trafficked persons has proven counterproductive to the goal of eradication that spaces are opened for reenvisioning anti-trafficking policies as instruments for the advancement of human rights norms and practices.

The Conceptual Framing of Human Trafficking

Although "trafficking" has entered mainstream political conversation over the past decade, the term remains highly contested. It is not uncommon for policy makers, academics, and activists to be working with different definitions of trafficking even when studying the same cases, which invariably influences who is considered to be a "victim," how cases of trafficking are handled by state and nonstate actors, and what recommendations are made with prevention in mind. The closest to a consensus definition that exists is offered by the United Nations (UN) Protocol to Prevent, Suppress, and Punish Trafficking in Persons, Especially Women and Children, attached to the UN Convention Against Transnational Organized Crime (UN CTOC):

> "Trafficking in persons" shall mean the recruitment, transportation, transfer, harboring or receipt of persons, by means of the threat or use of force or other forms of coercion, of abduction, of fraud, of deception, of the abuse of power or of a position of vulnerability or of the giving or receiving of payments or benefits to achieve the consent of a person having control over another person, for the purpose of exploitation. Exploitation shall include, at a minimum, the exploitation of the prostitution of others or other forms of sexual exploitation, forced labor or services, slavery or practices similar to slavery, servitude or the removal of organs. (UN Protocol 2000, Article 3a)

Although one can scarcely imagine more inelegant phraseology, what is important about this definition is that it leaves room for acknowledging internal trafficking, it recognizes the multiple forms that trafficking may take, and it distinguishes trafficking from other forms of criminal activity by reference to the use of force, coercion, fraud, or deception for the purposes of exploitation.

The debate over how to define trafficking has been accompanied by the proliferation of conceptual frameworks intended to highlight the factors that drive trafficking, to shed insight into the power relations informing trafficking responses, and to contribute to the development of preventive strategies

(Piper 2005, 209–13; Samarasinghe 2007, 25). Of the various framing schemes that have emerged, three analytical approaches are most relevant to a study of the U.S. government's anti-trafficking activities. The *migration* and *organized crime* approaches have dominated U.S. anti-trafficking policies to date, together representing a national security orientation that looks to the immigration and criminal justice systems as "frontline" agents responsible for protecting U.S. citizens from dangerous outsiders. In contrast, the *human rights* approach represents a normative, still-in-process effort to establish minimum standards for the treatment of trafficked persons, guided by the principle that all humans are endowed with inherent dignity and worth, regardless of national origin or any other status.

The Migration Approach

The migration approach begins with the assumption that the supply and demand of trafficked persons is driven by socioeconomic conditions in both the source and destination countries, conditions heightened by the stratifying effects of globalization along gender, ethnic, and geographic lines. In the source countries, low education levels, high unemployment, and poverty push individuals to migrate with the expectation of improving their economic status, leaving them vulnerable to the predation of traffickers. The proximity of countries of destination, their lax immigration or border control policies, and/or the relative strength of their economies in turn creates openings both for the employment of illegal migrants and the generation of higher profit margins for traffickers. Although the migration approach doesn't ignore the role of criminal networks in facilitating and profiting from trafficking, its emphasis is on migrant laborers themselves, particularly the factors that motivate them to leave their home communities and draw them to particular destinations, as well as the illegal status of their movement and labor (Uçarer 1999, 231–32).

International trafficking as an irregular form of migration is by definition distinguished from smuggling by the use of force, coercion, fraud, or deception for purposes of exploitation. Underscoring the distinction between smuggling and trafficking is not to deny that smuggling is hazardous or may lead to exploitation. But smuggling implies that the person smuggled has given consent to a border crossing, usually for purposes of economic migration. If at the point of destination the transported individual is subject to force, coercion, fraud, or deception, we are no longer talking about smuggling, but rather trafficking. But for the governments that have historically approached trafficking through a migration lens, the problems of trafficking and smuggling share similar solutions: reinforce border security, tighten visa policies, and increase the penalties imposed against foreign nationals who are caught engaging in criminal behavior. Trafficked persons are thus effectively conflated with undocumented migrants, with the individual's illegal status superseding any abuses that may have been perpetrated against her.[1]

The migration approach heavily influenced the U.S. government's response to trafficking up to the turn of the twenty-first century. Prior to the adoption of the TVPA, an individual who was discovered to have been trafficked to the United States was almost certain to be detained by immigration authorities and ultimately deported to her home country, significantly reducing the willingness of trafficked persons to come forward and seek out assistance for the harms they had suffered. The enactment of the TVPA arguably marked the U.S. government's shift away from the migration approach and its tendency to conceal the injurious nature of trafficking. Under the TVPA, trafficking is recognized as a "contemporary manifestation of slavery" and a "grave violation of human rights" (U.S. Senate 2000, 1466, 1468). The Act increases penalties for trafficking offenses, while affirming that victims of "severe forms of trafficking" should not be held criminally liable for illegal acts they committed as a consequence of being trafficked, including entering the country unlawfully or being employed without legitimate documentation (U.S. Senate 2000, 1468). It calls for protective and social assistance measures to be made available to victims and presents opportunities for temporary and permanent residence in the United States, albeit under specific conditions to be discussed below (U.S. Senate 2000, 1474–80). And it recognizes the need for preventive efforts to reduce the vulnerability of specific populations to trafficking, including education and income-generating programs and the launching of public awareness campaigns (U.S. Senate 2000, 1474). All of these stipulations are highlighted by U.S. officials to confirm the TVPA's status as a "victim-centered" law that assigns priority to the rescue of trafficked persons and their reintegration into society. But although the TVPA may represent an advance over the government's previous trafficking policies, its victim-friendly provisions remain in tension with its criminal justice–oriented provisions, particularly those relating to the role of organized crime networks as agents of trafficking.

The Organized Crime Approach

The link between human trafficking and organized crime has been established internationally under the United Nations Convention Against Transnational Organized Crime (UNCTOC), which defines an organized criminal group as "a structured group of three or more persons, existing for a period of time and acting in concert with the aim of committing one or more serious crimes . . . in order to obtain, directly or indirectly, a financial or other material benefit" (UNCTOC 2000, Article 2a). Although human trafficking has been widely framed by governments, international organizations, and activists as an egregious *human rights* violation, the decision of the UN to attach the Trafficking Protocol to the UNCTOC has served to privilege trafficking as a subset of organized criminal activity under international law, rather than as a violation that imposes human rights obligations on states.

Interpreted alongside the CTOC, the scope of the UN Protocol covers those cases of trafficking offenses that "are transnational in nature and involve an organized criminal group" (UN Protocol 2000, Article 4). Under the Protocol, state parties are obligated to adopt a number of measures in order to prevent, detect, and punish trafficking in persons, including: (1) criminalizing trafficking under domestic law; (2) strengthening border controls and improving cooperation with other national border control agencies; (3) providing training to law enforcement and immigration authorities to better intercept organized criminal activities; and (4) ensuring that travel or identity documents issued by the state are secure and not easily altered or replicated (UN Protocol 2000, Articles 5–12). The mandatory nature of the law enforcement-related provisions for parties to the Protocol is unequivocal. In stark contrast, the language employed in the Protocol to address the status of victims is far less prescriptive.

In calling for the adoption of remedies to protect and assist victims of trafficking, the Protocol states that "*in appropriate cases and to the extent possible under its domestic law,* each State Party shall protect the privacy and identity of victims of trafficking in persons" (UN Protocol 2000, Article 6, Section 1, my emphasis). "Each party *shall consider* implementing measures to provide for the physical, psychological and social recovery of victims of trafficking," such as housing, counseling, medical assistance, and employment and training opportunities (Article 6, section 3, my emphasis). "Each State Party *shall endeavor* to provide for the physical safety of victims of trafficking in persons while they are within its territory" (Article 6, section 5, my emphasis). States Parties *"shall consider"* adopting laws or other measures to allow trafficked persons to temporarily or permanently remain in their states, *in appropriate cases* (Article 7, my emphasis). And States Parties shall facilitate the process of repatriating trafficked persons, *preferably* voluntarily (Article 8, Section 2, my emphasis). Even though these suggested measures may mark an improvement over the historical treatment of trafficked persons as criminals, they are just that—*suggestions.* As a consequence of its attachment to the UNCTOC and the significant discretion it affords governments in the adoption of victim-related measures, the Protocol effectively sanctions the prioritizing of state security over the individual well-being of trafficked persons.

This same privileging of state security is evident in the United States' trafficking law. The TVPA explicitly constructs trafficking in persons as "a *transnational* crime with national implications," underplaying the problem of internal trafficking (U.S. Senate 2000, 1469, my emphasis). The Act recognizes that trafficking is "increasingly perpetrated by organized, sophisticated criminal enterprises," with the profits from trafficking contributing to the further expansion of criminal networks in the United States and internationally. Affirming trafficking as a serious offence in the interest of deterring future trafficking, according to the TVPA, requires "proscribing appropriate punishment, *giving priority to the prosecution of trafficking offenses,* and protecting rather than punishing the victims of such offenses" (U.S. Senate 2000, 1469, my emphasis). As a consequence of the primacy granted to legal action against traffickers, the purported "rights" accorded to foreign victims in the form of protection and benefits are made contingent on being certified by government officials as a victim of a severe form of trafficking, with the exception of individuals under the age of eighteen. To be eligible for certification requires that the individual be "willing to assist in every reasonable way in the investigation and prosecution of severe forms of trafficking in persons" (U.S. Senate 2000, 1476). Individuals who are unwilling to cooperate with authorities in proceedings against their traffickers thus face the same prospects that existed for those when the migration approach to trafficking prevailed: detention and deportation as an undocumented migrant or as a foreign national whose forced labor violated U.S. criminal law.

The Human Rights Approach

Under both the migration and organized crime approaches to trafficking, the impetus behind national and international interventions is to disrupt the illicit movement or behavior of those who traffic in humans and/or are trafficked in order to undercut perceived security threats. In contrast, the human rights approach foregrounds the physical, psychological, and/or sexual injury perpetrated against the trafficked person, regardless of any criminal behavior she may have engaged in during transit or in the performing of forced labor.

The human rights approach draws its inspiration from the Universal Declaration of Human Rights (UDHR), the foundational document of the UN human rights system that identifies the minimum conditions necessary for humans to live lives of dignity, to fulfill our potential as humans, and to realize global freedom, justice, and peace (United Nations General Assembly 1948). The UDHR is implicitly grounded in the notion of indivisibility, the idea that the civil, political, economic, social, and cultural rights that humans possess by virtue of our very humanness are interrelated and mutually dependent, with the realization of each right being conditional on the enjoyment of all other rights. Moreover, each of these rights is understood to be an *entitlement* that is inherent to all humans regardless of status, rather than privileges that must be earned or that may be lost or taken away (Donnelly 2003, 7–8).

The drafters of the UDHR recognized that even though human rights are inalienable entitlements, the ability of individuals to enjoy these rights requires an authority capable of ensuring their promotion and realization, a duty that falls first upon the government of the country of which an individual is a citizen (Donnelly 2003, 8–10). Nonetheless, in its preamble the UDHR also anticipates that fulfilling its promise as a "common standard of achievement for all peoples and all nations" requires action at the national *and* international levels to secure universal adherence to human rights norms, an especially vital provision in light of the frequency with which government action or inaction poses the most immediate threat to the ability of individuals to fully enjoy their human rights. Thus, although the state-citizen relationship has traditionally formed the core of the international human rights system, this system has proven adaptive to recognized changes in the nature of threats to human dignity, as is illustrated by the "obligation-to-protect" imposed on governments that host refugees fearful of persecution in their home countries in the 1951 United Nations Convention on the Status of Refugees.

Trafficking in persons is widely identified by national and international actors as among the most urgent human rights issues of the twenty-first century, a practice that violates the commitment of the international community to eradicate all forms of slavery and servitude. In framing trafficking as an egregious human rights violation, policy makers, academics, and activists alike tend to characterize the anti-trafficking mechanisms that have been adopted by states and international organizations as *human rights* instruments. Building on the principles contained in the UDHR and elaborated in later human rights documents, however, a human rights approach to trafficking must meet certain criteria to qualify as truly human rights–oriented. At a minimum, trafficked persons must be recognized as individuals empowered to claim human rights that are not contingent on fulfilling duties or meeting particular status requirements, including the rights to security of person, to freedom from enslavement or forced labor, to freedom from torture, to equality before the law, to privacy, and to fair and just remuneration for one's labor. Interventions must explicitly acknowledge the harm suffered by trafficked persons, rather than penalize them for criminal offenses they committed as a result of being trafficked. And the protection and assistance offered to trafficked persons must be extended on an equal basis, rather than implicitly or explicitly perpetuating a standard they must meet in order to be deemed blameless for their victimization and thus worthy of support.

Ideally, a human rights approach to trafficking will also engage the principle of indivisibility that underlies the human rights system. Emek Uçarer has argued that a weakness of the human rights approach is that, "unlike the migration framework, it seeks to rectify primarily the consequences of trafficking and tends not to address its root causes" (1999, 236). I argue instead that taking seriously the mutual interdependence of human rights signals the need to go beyond treating the symptoms of social problems to work toward eliminating structural constraints to transformative change. The integrative human rights framework established by the UDHR gives us the conceptual tools for devising strategies that better attend to the ethical implications of anti-trafficking interventions (e.g., affirming the equality of all individuals and their right to equal protection, regardless of nationality and other status) and offers us a language for articulating the specific harms suffered by trafficked persons. Even more important, it points the way to the fundamental conditions that must exist for hierarchies of gender, race/ethnicity, and class to be dissolved and for human beings to flourish—developments vital for reducing the likelihood of individuals' becoming victims or victimizers.

A human rights approach therefore places the survivor of trafficking in the forefront, emphasizing the need to protect trafficked persons from further harm, respond to their immediate and transitional needs, and work to alleviate the conditions that give rise to the vulnerability to victimization in the first place. This is precisely what the United States purports to do through the TVPA, with Senator Brownback of Kansas describing the Act as "the most significant human rights legislation" of the 2000 Congress (Chaddock 2000, 2). Rather than taking the human rights credentials of the TVPA—or its author—for granted, it is imperative that this claim be subject to close scrutiny, especially given the United States' self-designated role as the leading authority on trafficking.

The United States as the Global Authority on Trafficking

> *Our commitment to human rights is much more than a practical*
> *necessity, although it is certainly that. It's an expression of the*
> *values we share with people of every culture and every faith. It is a*
> *responsibility that comes with our leadership in the world, and a*
> *quality that strengthens our ability to lead.*
>
>   Secretary of State Warren Christopher
>   (Christopher 1996)

U.S. economic, political and military dominance at the turn of the twenty-first century has afforded the U.S. government the power and political space to establish itself as the world's human rights "watchdog." As a recent illustration of the United States' surveillance authority, the TVPA not only closes identified gaps in the United States' internal response to trafficking, but it additionally calls for the creation of an office under the authority of the State Department responsible for evaluating whether states identified as source, transit, or destination countries for "a significant number of victims of severe forms of trafficking" have met the minimum standards for eradicating trafficking *established by the United States* (U.S. Senate 2000, 1474). Each year since 2001, the Office to Monitor and Combat Trafficking (TIP Office) has released a Trafficking in Persons Report (TIP Report) that documents U.S. efforts to combat trafficking, offers examples of anti-trafficking "best practices" around the world, and, most importantly, places countries identified as having a significant problem with trafficking into "tiers" that correspond to the degree to which they have fulfilled U.S. standards.

The tier system has been revised since the Act's initial implementation. At present, countries that have received 100 or more reports from victims of trafficking over the course of the previous year[2] are placed into one of four categories: (1) *Tier 1* countries are those identified by the State Department as being in full compliance with the minimum standards established by the TVPA; (2) *Tier 2* countries are not yet in full compliance with these minimum standards, but are making substantial efforts to achieve compliance; (3) *Tier 3* countries are not in compliance with the minimum standards and are not making the necessary efforts to bring their policies and practices in line with the TVPA; and (4) *Tier 2 Watch List* countries are those considered to merit close attention because their placement in the tier structure changed since the last TIP Report or they are Tier 2 countries that require additional evidence of significant progress in meeting the TVPA's standards (U.S. Department of State 2007a).

Where a country falls in this tier system matters, given that countries classified as Tier 3 may be subject to U.S. sanctions. Under Section 110 of the TVPA, those Tier 3 countries that are recipients of U.S. economic and/or security assistance may have this assistance withheld, with the exception of humanitarian or trade-related foreign assistance. Tier 3 countries that are not currently recipients of U.S. assistance may be penalized through the withholding of funds for official educational and cultural exchanges. In addition, the U.S. president reserves the authority to direct the heads of international financial institutions such as the World Bank to deny nonhumanitarian, non–trade-related, and non–human rights–related assistance to Tier 3 countries. While the sanctions policy represents an attempt to strengthen the enforcement powers of the TVPA, its potential impact is diminished by the right of the president to refrain from imposing punitive measures of any kind if doing so is in the national interest of the United States.

A review of the tier system reveals the lack of uniformity in the imposition of sanctions and the frequency with which national interests have trumped the TVPA's objectives. Forty-five countries were categorized as Tier 3 in the

TIP Reports from 2003 to 2009,[3] twelve of which were subject to partial or total (nonhumanitarian, non–trade related) sanctions. Of these countries, eight were already subject to U.S. sanctions, with the TIP sanctions having minimal or no effect, including Burma, Cuba, Eritrea, Iran, North Korea, Sudan, Syria, and Zimbabwe.[4] Among the remaining thirty-three countries, nineteen were considered to have taken sufficient steps in the four months following their designation as Tier 3 to avoid the imposition of sanctions. The government granted waivers to the other fourteen countries on the basis of U.S. national interests, with the exemptions for Algeria, Bahrain, Kuwait, Malaysia, Oman, Qatar, and Saudi Arabia explicitly justified by the government as necessary to "effectively prosecute the Global War on Terror" (U.S. White House 2008; U.S. Department of State 2009).

Beyond concern for the political motivations informing classification and sanctions decisions lies the question of the legitimacy of the United States' positioning itself as the global authority on trafficking in persons. As the quote by Warren Christopher illustrates, the United States has long envisioned itself as the world's leader in promoting international human rights norms. But although the U.S. government's rhetoric in the area of human rights is strong, its record speaks to weak support for international human rights mechanisms in practice. As of June 2010, the United States has failed to ratify the 1966 International Covenant on Economic, Social, and Cultural Rights, the 1979 Convention on the Elimination of All Forms of Discrimination Against Women, and the 1989 Convention on the Rights of the Child. The U.S. Senate took forty years to ratify the widely supported 1948 Convention on the Prevention and Punishment of the Crime of Genocide, taking this step in 1988 only after imposing a number of reservations to the Convention (Power 2002, 163–69). The United States also took twenty-six years to ratify the 1966 International Covenant on Civil and Political Rights, the convention that is most in line with the principles underlying the American Declaration of Independence. And, although U.S. resistance to the International Criminal Court has eased under the Obama administration, the U.S. government has not yet ratified the Rome Statute, ostensibly out of concern that U.S. troops will be subjected to frivolous prosecutions.

The U.S. government's decision to withhold support for core international human rights mechanisms is disappointing. One could reasonably claim, however, that the United States is already meeting its obligations under international human rights law. If we limit human rights responsibilities to the traditional relationship between states and their citizens, U.S. support for international human rights mechanisms may be construed as largely symbolic, since U.S. law generally reflects respect for human rights standards and American citizens are afforded a high degree of political and social freedoms. For the U.S. government to position itself as the global promoter and protector of human rights, however, arguably places an additional burden on the United States to defend not only its domestic human rights record, but also the human rights consequences of its domestic and international policies for non-U.S. citizens.

Trafficking and the Gendered Effects of U.S. Inter/National Security Policies

In its TIP Reports, the State Department recognizes that no country, including the United States, is immune from the problem of trafficking in persons. Nonetheless, the TIP reports generally demonstrate limited self-reflexivity or willingness to acknowledge the shortcomings of U.S. responses to trafficking. Furthermore, although each year since 2003, reports by trafficking victims in the United States exceeded the 100-case threshold set by the State Department for inclusion in the TIP report, it was not until 2010 that the Obama administration finally subjected the United States to tier ranking. Not surprisingly, the United States was classified as a Tier 1 country that is in full compliance with the minimum standards established by the TVPA (U.S. Department of State 2010).

Evaluation of U.S. anti-trafficking efforts has largely been reserved for the "Assessment of U.S. Government Activities to Combat Trafficking in Persons" reports, released annually by the Department of Justice's Office of Legal Policy since 2003. But, even these assessments have primarily reiterated the strong commitment of the United States to combat trafficking and catalogued the benefits and services provided to victims, the number of investigations and prosecutions of traffickers that have occurred over the given fiscal year, the international grants the United States has provided to governments and nongovernmental actors, and the training and outreach programs that have been conducted across U.S. agencies and departments. In its 2003 and 2004 assessments, the Department of Justice offered relatively comprehensive recommendations for improving U.S. activities (U.S. Attorney General 2003, 2004). By the assessment for fiscal year 2005, the recommendations section of the report had dwindled to half a page, and by 2006 it was dropped altogether (U.S. Attorney General 2005, 2006). Over the past couple of years, the Department of Justice has identified several core recommendations in each assessment that it follows up on in the subsequent assessment (U.S. Attorney General 2009). But, read together, the Department of Justice's assessments and the TIP reports leave the impression that the United States has reached the stage where it is more or less "getting it right" in dealing with a problem that originates outside of the country, with the onus on Tier 2 and 3 states to clean up their act if trafficking is to be abolished. The self-construction of the United States as a "destination" country for a problem that is externally driven has allowed the United States to avoid confronting the implications of its foreign policy decisions for fostering conditions conducive to trafficking abroad—obscuring, for example, how the history of U.S. government support for military prostitution entrenched the sex industry in Asia over a period of decades, helping to fuel the problem of trafficking in the region today (Enloe 1993; Moon 1997; Truong 1990). It has also obscured the gendered and gendering nature of contemporary U.S. inter/national security policies and their human rights effects.

U.S. Immigration Policies and Trafficking

The language of human rights pervades American foreign policy discourse but is nearly absent in domestic political discourse, even among civil society actors. Reflecting the taken-for-granted assumption that U.S. values and policies embody universal human rights principles, rarely do Americans refer to human rights in the context of discussions about the problem of poverty, or violence, or inequities in education in the United States. Instead, references to "civil rights" and "political rights" are ubiquitous, while the language of "*human* rights" is most often invoked by U.S. political leaders when calling attention to the failure of *other* states—usually in the global South—to comply with international obligations in the treatment of their citizens. Given that the U.S. government itself has articulated trafficking in persons as a grave violation of human rights, to broach the topic of trafficking in persons *within* and *to* the United States significantly complicates the representation of human rights violations as a *foreign* problem.

Government statistics on the scale of trafficking in the United States have fluctuated considerably over the past decade. In its TIP report released in June 2002, the government estimated that 50,000 women and children were being trafficked into the country for purposes of sexual exploitation each year. The government has since dramatically scaled back this figure, and now estimates that approximately 14,500–17,500 people are trafficked into the United States each year for multiple purposes of exploitation (U.S. Attorney General 2006).[5] The 2010 TIP report identifies the United States as a source, transit, and destination country for trafficked persons (U.S. Department of State 2010), but U.S. law enforcement agencies do not track internal cases, impeding an assessment of the magnitude of the problem domestically and further reinforcing perceptions of trafficking as driven by forces outside of U.S. borders.

Policy debates in the United States over how to curtail the problem of trafficking interconnect with the highly emotive issue of illegal immigration. Policy makers and the public alike have long identified illegal immigration as a threat to U.S. economic security, public safety, and even American identity, with state and national elections often coinciding with heightened demands for the reform of the country's immigration laws. In theory, those foreign nationals trafficked to or within the United States and subject to forced labor are to be granted a status distinct from undocumented migrants or aliens who breach U.S. criminal laws. But the fate of trafficked persons continues to be inseparable from U.S. immigration laws and policies. In the wake of the September 11 terrorist attacks, analysts of U.S. immigration policies have uniformly detected a marked tightening of restrictions, with one observer commenting that immigration and terrorism have become "inextricably linked in the U.S. public debate on security" (Kerwin 2005, 749). The Illegal Immigration Reform and Immigrant Responsibility Act of 1996 had previously instituted strict measures intended to crack down on illegal immigration, including doubling the number of border agents, establishing new documentation requirements for immigrants, enhancing penalties for nonimmigrants who overstay their visas, and increasing the grounds for excluding or removing noncitizens (Fragomen 1997, 438–42). Following the 2001 terrorist attacks, the administration of immigration policies and services was reorganized and placed under the responsibility of the Department of Homeland Security (DHS), with the fusing of immigration and security serving to further bolster the surveillance and coercive powers of immigration authorities (Kerwin 2005, 749). Although particular sectors of the nonimmigrant population are singled out for special scrutiny, particularly Arabs and Muslims, the enhanced powers of immigration authorities have consequences across nonimmigrant populations, including for foreign nationals trafficked to and within the United States.

As noted earlier, U.S. immigration and law enforcement agencies did not historically make a distinction between undocumented migrants and foreign nationals who were trafficked into the United States. In both cases, resolution was typically accomplished through detaining and ultimately deporting foreign individuals who lacked proper immigration documentation and/or who were accused of criminal behavior. The TVPA arguably departs from the status quo in offering the possibility of legal migrant status for individuals identified as victims of "severe" trafficking and authorizing appropriations for prevention-oriented programs and campaigns. But although the U.S. government has claimed that "freeing those trapped in slave-like conditions" and protecting human dignity are the ultimate goals of U.S. anti-trafficking policies (U.S. Department of State 2007a, 2007b), in practice trafficking continues to be approached as a security issue, and the victim-centered provisions of the TVPA come into play only when they complement the Act's security-oriented objectives.

Two interpretations of sex trafficking as a security threat may be identified in the U.S. approach to trafficking. The first interpretation closely matches traditional notions of security, in which political leaders are perceived to have an overriding obligation to ensure the physical safety of the nation state from outside threats. Solidified by the link between trafficking and transnational organized crime, noncitizen migrants are constructed as perpetual outsiders who pose a risk to the state. While citizens are endowed with certain constitutionally guaranteed entitlements, including the right to a presumption of innocence in legal proceedings, whatever rights are accorded to noncitizen migrants by the U.S. government are conditional on the individual fulfilling certain obligations, including adhering to U.S. documentation requirements and refraining from engaging in criminal action. The TVPA does not fundamentally alter the provisional immigration status of trafficked persons or establish rights as *entitlements* for trafficked persons. The TVPA may allow for the reclassification of trafficked persons as "victims" rather than "criminals." But in a reversal of the presumption of innocence, an individual who wants access to protective and social welfare remedies under the TVPA must first prove that she is not a criminal in order to be certified as a victim of severe trafficking by the Department of Health and Human Services (HHS). Those individuals who are unable to convince the authorities that their trafficking experience sufficiently meets the "severe" threshold, and those who do not cooperate with legal proceedings against their traffickers, are unable to escape criminal status and its consequences.

If we accept the government's own statistics, well in excess of 100,000 individuals were trafficked into the United State between 2000 (the year of the enactment of the TVPA) and 2010. As of the end of fiscal year 2009, only 1,995 adult victims had received the necessary certification from HHS to access federally funded assistance in the form of financial aid, food stamps, housing, and medical care.[6] And although the TVPA permits 5,000 T visas[7] to be issued each year to trafficked aliens who have assisted law enforcement authorities and who would suffer "extreme hardship" if they were returned to their home countries, the DHS issued only 1,568 T visas to immediate survivors in the nine years following the TVPA's enactment.[8] The low level of certification and immigration status adjustment is a consequence of several overlapping factors that point to the deficiencies of the TVPA, including the minimal success of immigration and law enforcement agencies in identifying trafficked persons; the considerable discretion accorded to authorities to categorize individuals as deserving or undeserving of assistance; and the inability or unwillingness of trafficked persons to aid law enforcement authorities (Cianciarulo 2007, 827–35; Rieger 2007, 245–48).

The TVPA fails to appreciate the myriad factors that dissuade trafficked persons from cooperating with law enforcement, including the fear of retaliation by their traffickers, distrust of the legal system, and the stigma associated with forced labor, particularly forced sexual labor. By tying victim status and its accompanying *privileges* to the fulfillment of certain obligations under the TVPA, the Act does not satisfy the basic requirements of a truly victim-centered or human rights instrument. Rather than recognizing trafficking persons as individuals endowed with intrinsic rights, it extends rights to victims instrumentally, as a means to another end—namely, the protection of the nation-state through the prosecution of dangerous, transnational actors who arguably threaten to erode the economic, political, and legal authority of the state. The second interpretation of trafficking as a security threat moves away from the traditional focus on guarding the *physical* borders of the state to the threat that trafficking, particularly *sex* trafficking, poses to the state's *moral* security. Ratna Kapur refers to the "cultural panic" that informs responses to trafficking, in which the migrant "Other" is treated "as some form of cultural contaminant who is disrupting a nation's social and cultural cohesion and destroying the authentic fabrics which constitute cultures" (Kapur 2005, 26). The trafficked "Other" is not genderless, but is instead commonly conceived of as a helpless, disempowered female victim. To broach the subject of sex trafficking simultaneously and contradictorily positions individuals trafficked into sexual labor as victims *and* as dangerous actors who pollute and threaten the existing gendered social order.

In *Global Sex,* Dennis Altman has written of the paradox and hypocrisy associated with the American approach to sex. As is particularly clear in the case of pornography, the thriving sex entertainment industry in this country is inseparable from the strong U.S. commitment to both the rule of the market and respect for the right of individuals to freedom of speech and expression. Yet the reality of the sex industry clashes with the generalized sense of American moral righteousness traceable to entrenched puritan values, with religious conservatism manifesting itself in attempts to extend authority over women's bodies and autonomy as a means of safeguarding the family unit widely recognized to be the foundation of American society (Altman 2001, 138–156). Since Altman's book was published, conservatism in the United States surged under the Bush administration, with renewed efforts to patrol women's sexuality taking the form, in part, of a strong moralistic stance against prostitution.

In 2002, President Bush, bowing to the pressure of conservative abolitionist groups and marking a departure from the Clinton administration, adopted a National Security Presidential Directive identifying prostitution as "inherently harmful and dehumanizing" and as a key factor contributing to the problem of trafficking (U.S. Department of State 2004a). Regardless of the fact that trafficking is known to occur both in countries that have and that have not criminalized prostitution, the 2004 TIP report concludes that "where prostitution is legalized, a 'black market' in trafficking emerges, as exploiters seek to maximize profit by avoiding the scrutiny and regulatory costs of the legal prostitution market. Legalized prostitution is therefore a trafficker's best shield, allowing him to legitimize his trade in sex slaves, and making it more difficult to identify trafficking victims" (U.S. Department of State 2004b). As observed by Ronald Weitzer, four advanced industrialized countries that have legalized prostitution—Australia, Germany,

Holland, and New Zealand—have been categorized by the State Department as Tier 1 countries in full compliance with the TVPA's standards, and there is no evidence of trafficking being associated with Nevada's legal brothels (Weitzer 2007, 457). Regardless, the Bush administration rejected the distinction made between "voluntary" prostitution and "coerced" prostitution, contrary to developments at the level of international human rights,[9] and refused domestic and foreign organizations funds for anti-trafficking efforts unless these organizations unambiguously condemn prostitution (U.S. Senate 2003, 11–12)—a policy that remains in place under the Obama administration.

The U.S. debate over prostitution has had immediate implications for the human rights of trafficked persons whose sexual labor is gained through force or coercion. Under the TVPA, "sex trafficking" refers to the "recruitment, harboring, transportation, provision, or obtaining of a person for the purpose of a commercial sex act," while "severe forms of trafficking" additionally require the use of force, fraud, or coercion (U.S. Senate 2000, 1470). This differs considerably from the UN Protocol, which recognizes that trafficking by definition involves the use of force, coercion, abduction, fraud, or deception. The creation of a trafficking hierarchy under the TVPA has, in practice, translated into recognizing only those individuals who were unknowingly, and without consent, trafficked into sexual labor as "true victims" of severe trafficking, while those individuals who may have initially consented to perform sexual labor are not judged sufficiently "innocent" to be deserving of the status and associated privileges of a "victim," regardless of the severity of the conditions under which they were required to labor (Rieger 2007, 248–50). Instead, these individuals are lumped together with their traffickers as illicit actors who endanger American security, values, and way of life.

Sociocultural expectations of appropriate feminine roles and behaviors are among the factors that shape the life circumstances and available opportunities for women and girls across societies, giving rise to gendered risks of being trafficked. Gendered expectations have also, however, informed U.S. responses to trafficking, which prioritize the rescuing of "helpless" women from forced *sexual* labor while making assistance conditional on being identified as both "blameless" and of use to authorities. This leaves the TVPA vulnerable to the criticism that rather than representing a groundbreaking law that promotes the human rights of trafficked persons, it is instead a tool available to the U.S. government to regulate women's sexual autonomy as a means of containing physical and moral threats to the nation-state and extending its global surveillance of, and influence over, other states, thereby advancing its inter/national security objectives.

Conclusion

In exposing the contradictions underlying U.S. anti-trafficking policies, I am not arguing against the need for international standards or action against trafficking. Although cognizant of how representations of trafficking have too often obscured the lived experiences of trafficked persons or have been employed by those in positions of power for strategic purposes, the empirical evidence strongly supports the finding of trafficked labor as a real phenomenon that violates the human rights of hundreds of thousands, if not millions, of individuals each year. But to accept the depiction of anti-trafficking policies as human rights measures when these policies fail to meet minimum human rights standards, and too often exacerbate the vulnerability of trafficked persons, is to erode the meaning and power of human rights. As illustrated by the U.S. government's conditional provision of protective remedies for foreign survivors of trafficking, the rights of noncitizen "Others" are routinely forfeited in the interests of U.S. inter/national security. The sacrificing of human rights has done little, however, to stem the trade in human beings or to advance U.S. security objectives. On the contrary, to approach security as a zero-sum game that warrants the privileging of the welfare of citizens over noncitizens is to ignore how transnational forces have blurred national boundaries and created interdependencies across states.

International human rights norms today shape global perceptions of the legitimacy and authority of states. Although government leaders have mastered the rhetoric of human rights, a shallow approach to human rights too often prevails in government policies and practices. To move beyond a superficial engagement with human rights in the trafficking arena will require radically rethinking notions of citizenship. In a globalized world, today more than ever, individuals confront myriad threats to their human dignity that cannot be remedied by states operating as discrete, self-contained entities. Migration flows in particular are indicative of the fluidity of place and identity, and of the subsequent need to revisit the institutionalized differentiation that marks the obligations of states toward citizens versus noncitizens, a distinction incompatible with the aspiration of the UDHR to envision human rights as held equally by all, regardless of status. Rather than the prevailing practice of attempting to stem trafficking through controlling the movements of illegal migrants, a human rights approach would instead emphasize the factors that compel individuals to seek sanctuary or opportunity elsewhere. Moreover, rather than focusing on legislative changes and the numbers of prosecutions and convictions of traffickers as signifying success in combating trafficking, the principle of indivisibility underlying the international human rights system redirects attention to the structural attitudes, behaviors, and conditions that perpetuate both the appeal of human trafficking as an income-generating strategy and the vulnerability of individuals to being trafficked. Realizing such a dramatic shift in responses to trafficking will perhaps, above all, require the leadership of states that are willing to both fully bind themselves to international human rights standards and subject themselves to the same level of external scrutiny they expect of others.

Chapter 6

Rethinking Gender Violence: Battered and Trafficked Women in Greece and the United States

Gabriela Wasileski and Mark J. Miller

Introduction

Both domestic violence and trafficking in humans pose serious problems worldwide. However, there are differences in the ways in which similarly abused battered immigrant women and trafficked immigrant women are treated by governmental agencies in Greece and in the United States. Trafficking in humans has been securitized worldwide, rather than treated as a human rights violation—that is, framed as an issue linked to international security risk. As a result, countries that do not take legal action to stop human trafficking could face U.S. sanctions such as loss of U.S. military and economic assistance. Under significant international pressure, in 2002 Greece passed a law that criminalized trafficking in humans and took necessary steps for providing protection and assistance to trafficked victims. Nevertheless, domestic violence and battered women remain silent in Greek society, and the availability of services to immigrant victims of domestic violence has eroded. We argue that, due to different issue-framing of victims of trafficking and women who have been battered, the connection of trafficking in humans to national security fosters different legal protection outcomes. Rethinking trafficking to focus on the gender inequities that create private wrongs would foster a rights-based response.

As argued by Alison Brysk's contribution to this volume, gender inequity needs to be viewed as a cause of both domestic violence and trafficking in the two quite dissimilar cases examined in this article. And the Greece–United States comparison underscores the need for rethinking trafficking as rights versus security, as women's rights are human rights. For all the differences between the United States and Greece, it is important to highlight that both states belong to the Organization for Economic Cooperation and Development (OECD), which is widely viewed as the world's club of most prosperous democratic states. These are the states that could change the underlying structural conditions that foster trafficking and domestic violence.

The United States and Human Trafficking Post-1990

The post–Cold War emergence of human trafficking issues in the transatlantic area has often been explained in connection with threats to states' sovereignty—the threat of illegal and unregulated migration (Bravo 2007). The world is in constant flux, and the events of the last few decades, such as the collapse of the Soviet Union and the Communist Eastern Europe bloc, led to increased economic migration and a subsequent increase in forced migration and human trafficking. In other words, the breakdown of states, redrawing international borders, and the technological revolution freed up social forces that underlay civil war conflicts, population and unemployment growth, and globalization that produced a massive wave of population relocation.

Human trafficking is an old issue, but it did not figure importantly in domestic politics and international relations until the post-1990 period (Miller 2001, 2006). Before the 1990s, human trafficking rarely appeared in migration discussions or on international political agendas. It was viewed as a form of human smuggling and a type of illegal migration (Laczko 2002). There was no reliable data available on human trafficking, both because many countries lacked specific anti-trafficking legislation and because human trafficking as a part of clandestine migration is almost impossible to measure accurately (Castles and Miller 2009). Nevertheless, sources such as the International Labor Organization (ILO) and United Nations have reported that an estimated 12.3 million people are held in conditions of forced labor and trafficking for sex slavery at any given period of time (U.S. Department of State 2009).

Several key circumstances surrounding the issue of human trafficking changed, which catapulted the problem onto the international political agenda. Increased media attention and the clarification of the difference between smuggling and trafficking have led to an upsurge in the perceived volume of human trafficking. The framing of the issue of human trafficking has historically occurred around three themes: drawing parallels between human trafficking and slavery; construing human trafficking as a security risk to states' autonomy; and viewing human trafficking as a form of human rights violation (Bravo 2007).

Describing human trafficking as modern-day slavery constitutes influential and evocative wording that draws rapid attention to the need for the public and governments to act to end it. Trafficked victims often lose their rights and personal dignity in order to pay off their "debt" to traffickers through coerced labor and prostitution. Growing numbers of migrants were enslaved by modern-day traffickers, or tricked by schemes offering employment abroad or other prospects of better economic opportunities (Castles and Miller 2009).

Human trafficking as modern-day slavery resonated with memories of the nineteenth-century campaign led by the British. This deeply evocative linkage conjured up memories of a bygone era in the post–Cold War landscape of failed and failing states, organized criminality at the regional and global level, and a novel form of enslavement, particularly of women and children. According to Kevin Bales, modern-day slavery differs from the old form of the transatlantic slave trade in that it entails holding complete power over people rather than just the legal right to own slaves ([1999] 2004). This underscores the significance of the illegality of human trafficking as distinct from slavery in the past.

Framing the violation of human rights in connection with women and children as trafficked victims provided another powerful tool to define human trafficking as an international social problem that needs to be addressed. Women and minors represent the majority of trafficked victims; females constitute 80 percent of all victims (Castles and Miller 2009). While contemporary slavery takes many forms, human trafficking can be thought of as organized crime involving the cooperation of criminal non-state entities crossing several sovereign national territories. States exercise a right to determine who enters and under what conditions they can remain in a territory. However, trafficking in human beings undermines state borders and border controls, usually by illegal entry or engagement in criminal activities. As such, human trafficking is viewed as a threat to state sovereignty (Krasner 2001; see also Hebert, this volume).

The decade of the 1990s also witnessed a perceived upsurge in clandestine or unauthorized migration, which prompted calls for rethinking of security threats. By 1993, Ole Waever and colleagues had formulated a notion of societal security in which immigration and migrant settlement could threaten the social status quo (Waever et al. 1993). Similarly, Huysmans argued that the end of the Cold War shifted attention away from conventional military and nuclear threats to perceived threats arising from asylum seeking and other forms of international migration (Huysmans 2006). Hence, border policing and other instruments of immigration control became reconceptualized as security matters. Not all security analysts, however, viewed aspects of migration as inherently threatening, as international migration can also enhance security, as well as foreign and national security goals (Adamson 2006; Nye 2004).

Nevertheless, by the twenty-first century, human trafficking had been framed to address all the public fears of the post–Cold War period, including the fear of terrorism, a linkage especially evident in the United States after September 11, 2001. Consequently, linking the trafficking phenomenon to security risks, human rights violations, and modern day slavery created an environment in which the United States and other governments around the world would make it a priority to eradicate trafficking in humans.

As a result of the perceived threat that human trafficking posed to state autonomy, in 2000 the member countries of the United Nations established a definition of human trafficking in the United Nations' Protocol to Prevent, Suppress, and Punish Trafficking in Persons, Especially Women and Children that supplemented the United Nations Convention Against Transnational Organized Crime (Bravo 2007). Establishing and defining trafficking in human beings as an international criminal act created an environment propitious for international prosecution of criminals as well as cooperation among state parties (Bravo 2007).

At the same time, the United States enacted the Trafficking Victims Protection Act of 2000 (TVPA)—discussed in chapters (this volume) by Hebert and Gallagher. The fight against trafficking in humans took another step further when President George W. Bush signed the Trafficking Victims Protection Reauthorization Act of 2003 and the Prosecutorial Remedies and Other Tools to End the Exploitation of Children Today Act of 2003, both of which strengthened the tools used by law enforcement authorities to combat trafficking crimes and ensure that victims of trafficking are recognized, protected, and supported. The politics behind this development involved a kind of alliance between Christian fundamentalist organizations and an array of secular interest groups and nongovernmental actors concerned with transnational crime and other "new" security threats.

During the Clinton administration, most of the attention focused on human trafficking centered on human rights violations associated with sexual exploitation of women and children. The emphasis was on the rights of women and the historical dispute over legalized or banned legal prostitution for its connection with promotion of trafficking in humans for commercial sex (Farrell and Fahy 2009). One faction of feminists allied with religious conservatives in an argument that human trafficking primarily involves the sexual exploitation of women and children, and therefore it should be fought through abolishment of legal prostitution. The other point of view sought to treat trafficking from a perspective that legitimates prostitution while strongly opposing coercive and unequal work conditions. Suppression of trafficking gained legitimacy when First Lady Hillary Clinton and Secretary of State Madeline Albright spoke out in opposition to trafficking of women and children (Farrell and Fahy 2009).

The Bush administration took a stand more congruent with the views of fundamentalist Christian organizations, in opposition to the narrow definition of human trafficking supported by the Clinton administration that limited sex trafficking to forced prostitution as opposed to other, potentially more consensual, forms of prostitution. In 2003, President George W. Bush issued a National Security Presidential Directive that, for the first time, linked prostitution and trafficking: "Prostitution and related activities, which are inherently harmful and dehumanizing, contribute to the phenomenon of trafficking in persons" (Office of the Press Secretary 2003).

The attacks in New York City, Washington, D.C., and Shanksville, Pa., on September 11, 2001, served to intensify the securitization of migration issues that became one of the hallmarks of the post–Cold War era. The honeymoon era in U.S.-Mexico relations that had begun soon after the disputed election of President Bush gave way to rancor and disagreement. Large factions of the Republicans in the House and Senate began to oppose key elements of proposed immigration law reforms backed by President Bush (Miller and Gabriel 2008). Hence, the George W. Bush presidency, so marked by the elevation of human trafficking concerns to among the most important national security priorities, ended with securitization of migration issues contributing greatly to the failed comprehensive immigration reforms of 2006 and 2008.

Greece's Response to Human Trafficking Phenomenon

Greece received a major inflow of aliens in the post-1990 period that included many human trafficking cases. Very little had been written prior to the 1990s on southern European immigration, mostly because countries such as Greece had long been viewed as nations of labor emigration with marginal migration inflows into the country—and these were viewed as transit migration to elsewhere. Since the late 1980s and early 1990s, however, there took place a significant reversal in migration direction, and Greece became the EU member state proportionally the most affected by international migration (Castles and Miller 2009).

The geographical location of Greece and its large underground economy are among the key reasons that Greece became an immigrants' magnet virtually overnight. The change in political regime in neighboring Albania, which had long blocked emigration from that very poor society, had profound ramifications for Greece. Hundreds of thousands of Albanians poured into Greece after the collapse of the Communist regime, most of them coming into Greece unlawfully. Large numbers of Albanians continue to arrive in Greece even after the EU and Western effort to stabilize Albania, endow it with democratic governance, and admit it into NATO. In other instances, Greece became a "trap" for immigrants who wanted to migrate to northern EU countries and saw their stay in Greece as temporary (Maroukis 2009). Many asylum seekers have been sent back to Greece from Germany and other European countries pursuant to the European Dublin II regulation under which the state where an asylum seeker first entered the European space is responsible for processing the asylum claim (Pro Asyl and Group of Lawyers for the Rights of Refugees and Migrants in Athens 2007).

Even though the country of origin of many immigrants that are heading toward Greece has evolved, Greece constantly experiences widespread clandestine entry of migrants regardless of the efforts undertaken to strengthen surveillance of coastlines and borders. In addition, it is a venue for trafficking in humans. Greece seems to be a vulnerable country for trafficking because of ongoing undocumented migration and, some would argue, because of legalized prostitution in the country.

Over the last few decades, Greece has transformed its legal system to harmonize with European Union and other international standards (Geddes 2003). As a response to international pressure, significant if grudging changes have been made to Greek migration law and anti-trafficking legislation. Yet Greece continues to lag behind other European countries with respect to the rights of migrants generally and available legal remedies for battered immigrants and victims of trafficking in particular (Karakatsanis and Swarts 2003). Scholars describe the Greek state bureaucracy as corrupt, where rules and legal procedures are inconsistently applied across governmental branches (Karakatsanis and Swarts 2003). In addition, the previous conservative government started taking harsher measures against undocumented immigrants and supported new legislation that made deportation of these individuals easier (Brabant 2009).

Greece's Adoption of the 2002 Anti-Trafficking Law

The creation and enactment of the 2002 anti-trafficking law in Greece was a result of several factors. First, a variety of NGOs led campaigns to pressure the government to address the trafficking issue. Second, Greece faced substantial international pressure when it came under scrutiny as a result of the Trafficking in Persons (TIP) reports (Papanicolaou 2008).

TIP Reports between 2001 and 2003 classified Greece as a Tier 3 country, whose government did not comply with the minimum standards and without an important effort to combat trafficking (U.S. Department of State 2001b, 2002, 2003). However, the 2004 and 2005 reports placed Greece on the Tier 2 Watch List as a result of the Greek government taking law enforcement measures and providing financial assistance for prevention and assistance programs (U.S. Department of State 2004b, 145; 2005). Finally, the country reached a Tier 2 position in the 2006 report as a result of progress in governmental direct cooperation with local nongovernmental organizations (NGOs) in the effort to combat trafficking and the release of significant funding for that battle (U.S. Department of State 2006). Greece's improvement to Tier 2 resulted from a combination of the U.S. pressure for change in anti-trafficking legislation and services and specific initiatives undertaken by the United States. For example, in 2001 the U.S. Embassy in Athens conducted a conference with trafficking in humans as the theme. It also established collaboration with local

NGOs and made available resources for educational exchanges (Papani-colaou 2008).

The anti-trafficking legislation adopted in 2002 was the first important step in combating human trafficking in Greece. However, its promulgation did not automatically translate into guaranteed enforcement. Even with the new anti-trafficking legislation in place, the Greek government fell behind on victims' protection services and prosecution of traffickers. In many instances, trafficking offenders were released from custody on suspended sentences that put trafficked victims in a vulnerable position that could lead to their reluctance to cooperate with criminal justice agencies. In a few highly publicized cases, police officers were found to be complicit in the abuse and rape of immigrant victims (U.S. Department of State 2009; see also Karakatsanis and Swarts 2003). In addition, over the years the government proved unable to provide accurate and satisfactory statistics on trafficking crimes, or those statistics were simply unavailable (U.S. Department of State 2009).

While anti-trafficking legislation in Greece complies with international standards, it offers legal and social protection to trafficking victims only if they are actively engaged in cooperation with the criminal justice agencies. Important gaps remain in terms of assistance to victims, on resources and infrastructure available to them ,and, as mentioned above, statistical data. Thus, although some issues remain underregulated or underdeveloped, human trafficking has received considerable attention in Greek national migration legislation as a result of increased international pressure. As noted, Greece belongs to the OECD and EU; hence Greek politics must become transparent. Greece simply cannot be indifferent to the tremendous pressure to harmonize its legislation with international values and norms.

The phenomenon of human trafficking can also be construed as a gendered violence concern, since the sizable majority of victims of human trafficking are women. Thus, it is insightful to compare regulation on human trafficking with how the issue of battered immigrant women is addressed by national migration policies in Greece and the United States. The migration law of the United States and of many EU countries recognized and addressed the vulnerability of immigrant spouses to domestic violence as a result of either their dependent or undocumented migration status (Van Walsum and Spijkerboer 2007). However, inattention paid to battered undocumented migrants in Greece stands in stark contrast to the attention being paid to human trafficking since 1990.

The situation of battered undocumented immigrant women in Greece is alarming. It is not only that the phenomenon is viewed as marginal in Greek society; battered undocumented immigrants lack any legal or social remedies. In many instances, they are abused or deported. They have little or no access to institutional and economic resources, and they have little or no access to information about the legal system in the country. Unlawful immigrant status puts female immigrants in vulnerable legal, social, and personal situations. It was not until 2006 that specific legislation in Greece defined domestic violence, recognized domestic violence as a crime and provided for certain penalties for offenders, and recognized marital rape as a punishable criminal offense against a person and personal freedom. Moreover, this particular legislation does not address issues of undocumented immigrants at all.

Immigrant women in Greece are frequently employed in domestic work. Since these women often lack necessary work permits as a result of their immigrant status, employment in the informal, or underground, economy is their only recourse. Work in the underground economy typically involves a lack of legal protection from employers' exploitation and no access to welfare benefits. In addition, the long work hours and typically poor working conditions of immigrant women contribute to their social isolation, not only from native populations but also from members of their own community, leaving them with nowhere to go or to look for protection from violence in their homes. These factors exert an influence on whether battered women can decide to leave their batterers, because of their lack of financial resources, welfare benefits, or social network support.

Battered immigrant women who are dependent on their spouses in Greece remain in a difficult situation because the Greek legal system provides only limited support to battered women. The reason behind this reflects the general view that marriage and household issues constitute private matters that should not become public (Chatzifotiou and Dobash 2001). Unlike in the United States, undocumented immigrants in Greece who become victims of violence lack civil legal protections, such as restraining orders, that prohibit any further physical attack from the batterer, or that order batterers to vacate the conjugal residence regardless of who owns the residence. Nor are victims provided monetary compensation for medical and legal fees. In addition, if the woman is an undocumented immigrant or an immigrant who relapses into illegality because her spouse's permit was not renewed—a common problem in Greece—her access to public benefits is reduced, existing only for emergency cases.

The situation of battered immigrant women is worse compared to battered citizen women because immigration policies disadvantage them regarding access to social support and criminal justice agencies. In other words, the immigration status of battered women is in many instances the first and foremost issue with which officials deal. Immigrants are first viewed as aliens, possibly illegal, and only second as victims of violence. In the case of undocumented immigrants, despite a public and legal acknowledgment of the abuse, they can still be subjected to legal provisions such as deportation that have been enacted to control illegal migration. Consequently, an abused immigrant woman, besides fearing the perpetrator, also fears deportation and other legal sanctions related to her undocumented immigration status.

According to immigration lawyers in Athens,[1] undocumented battered women have only three possible legal remedies to adjust their immigration status. First, they can apply for refugee status or to stay legally in Greece for "humanitarian reasons" and "exceptional reasons." The legal grounds for humanitarian reasons could possibly cover undocumented immigrant women who are victims of domestic violence. Law 3386 of 2005 (article 44) specified categories of who could apply for legal residency in Greece for humanitarian reasons. One of the categories is immigrants housed in shelters. However, in reality, the shelters that are run and funded by the state are banned from accepting undocumented immigrants, and shelters that are run by nonprofit organizations, which in most cases lack sufficient resources, qualified staff, and free legal aid, are also of scant help. In addition, the whole legal procedure for applying for humanitarian relief can take years.

The second legal way to adjust undocumented status is to present an "exceptional reason." However, the unclear definition of what constitutes "exceptional reasons" effectively grants huge discretionary power to the three members of the Migration Committee, which reviews such applications and then makes recommendations to the Ministry of Interior's Department of Public Administration and Decentralization. In addition, the crucial requirement is possession of a passport with a valid entry visa to Greece. This requirement ultimately eliminates undocumented immigrants who were smuggled into the country.

The last resort for undocumented battered immigrants is an application for refugee status. But it is almost certain that refugee status will be not granted, as Greece holds one of the last places among EU member states in terms of recognition of refugee status and the granting of other forms of international protection. According to Human Rights Watch (2009), the Greek asylum system grants protection to only 0.05 percent of applicants at initial hearings. In addition, changes to the Greek asylum law in July 2009 eliminated applicants' right to appeal. Nevertheless, the application for refugee status will give a victim of violence at least an opportunity to stay and work in Greece for six months. In addition, like any legal procedure in Greece, it is a very time-consuming procedure. So, it is more likely that this permit would have to be renewed several times before the final decision about deportation. Hence, battered and trafficked migrant women in Greece face much greater challenges than those faced by comparable categories of migrant women in the United States.

U.S. Response to Undocumented Immigrants Who Are Victims of Crime

Unlike in Greece, the U.S. government's enactment of the TVPA created two new nonimmigrant visa categories, effectively giving legal status to trafficked victims and also offering possible protection to battered immigrants. Sec. 1513 (a)(2)(B) reads:

> Creating a new nonimmigrant visa classification will facilitate the reporting of crimes to law enforcement officials by trafficked, exploited, victimized, and abused aliens who are not in lawful immigration status. It also gives law enforcement officials a means to regularize the status of cooperating individuals during investigations or prosecutions. Providing temporary legal status to aliens who have been severely victimized by criminal activity also comports with the humanitarian interests of the United States.

The "T visa" provides legal status for up to 5,000 victims of "severe forms of trafficking in persons" each year under certain conditions, such as willingness to assist in the investigation and prosecution of trafficker (s) and filling out an application for a T visa. The new U visa provides legal status for up to 10,000 victims of domestic violence, rape, trafficking, involuntary servitude, sexual assault, torture, and other offenses. Both of the new visas provide temporary (nonimmigrant) status, work authorization to the victims and certain members of their families, and opportunities to obtain permanent residency status (green cards) after three years under certain conditions (see Table 6.1).

Table 6.1. Number of Petitions of Victims of Trafficking and Battered
Undocumented Immigrants

FY	I-914 T-VISA Approvals / Denials	I-914 T-VISA (Immediate Family Members) Approvals / Denials	I-918 U-VISA Approvals / Denials	I-918 U-VISA (Immediate Family Members) Approvals / Denials
2005	113 / 321	73 / 21	- / -	- / -
2006	121 / 127	95 / 45	- / -	- / -
2007	287 / 106	257 / 64	- / -	- / -
2008	243 / 78	228 / 40	- / -	- / -
2009	313 / 77	273 / 54	5,825 / 688	2,838 / 158

Source: U.S. Citizenship and Immigration Services (USCIS), January 26, 2010.

In other words, the United States in the last two decades developed policies that address protection for victims of domestic violence, and equality in
the workplace—policies that are unrelated to immigration issues. The feminist movement in the United States addressed issues such as violence against
women that led to the development of shelters for battered women and to a
range of legislative reforms and legal protections for victims of domestic violence. A variety of NGOs, politicians, and women's organizations pressed
for protection, and explicitly recognized that victims who were residing illegally could be doubly vulnerable. In 1994, Congress authorized and funded
the Violence Against Women Act (VAWA). The Act included provisions that
granted both undocumented battered immigrants married to U.S. citizens
or to lawful permanent residents the right to apply for legal residency on
their own, rather than depending on their husbands to petition for them. In
2000, Congress extended access to special visas to undocumented battered
immigrant women, regardless of their relationship to their offender. Amendment of the Violence Against Women Act in 2005 extended protection of
battered women by including stalking in the legislation. In addition, VAWA
2005 amended § 384 of the Illegal Immigration Reform and Immigrant Responsibility Act of 1996 (8 USC § 1367). This section prevents the Department of Homeland Security, the Attorney General, and the State Department
from making a deportation based "solely" on information provided by batterers and their family members. Disclosure of information about VAWA

applicants to victim's service providers such as shelters is permitted only with the prior written consent of the immigrant.

The United States addressed the issues of both legal and also undocumented immigrants through its migration policies. Once a victim of crime, regardless of immigration status, enters the system of criminal justice, there are several programs and services available to help crime victims to repair the damage to their lives and property, to obtain justice, compensation, and assistance. In other words, an extensive number of services and sanctuary are provided to these specific crime victims throughout the United States.

How can one account for the sharp contrast in public policies toward trafficked and battered women in the two OECD cases under consideration? Understanding the role of civil society appears key to unraveling the puzzle. According to Edwards (2004), civil society can balance the power of the state as well as the persuasion of the free market. In other words, civil society can affect politics through strategies of institutional cooperation and address as well as solve socioeconomic and political problems. In this era of renewed globalization, civil society is enhanced by and encompasses aspects of global cooperation between charitable foundations, NGOs, media, and, in the idiom of social constructivism, norm entrepreneurs. Strong civil society in the United States led to the establishment of many governmental and nongovernmental organizations dedicated to protecting the legal and human rights of the immigrant community by providing direct legal and social services, referrals, education, and advocacy. In the last two decades, these organizations in the United States came to possess nationally recognized expertise in immigration law, domestic violence, and human trafficking. Independent organizations in the United States that serve to protect immigrant rights have pointed out the inequality and discrimination that migration policies created and, through activism, pushed for reforms of those policies.

In contrast, civil society in Greece is underdeveloped and weak as a result of the excessive influence of the state, political parties, and family institutions (Sotiropoulos and Karamagioli 2006). This pattern of weak civic society engagement had been found in at least one other southern European society in the Mezzogiorno of Italy (LaPalombara 1965). There has been an increase in the number of Greek informal civic activities providing social services to immigrants. However, in many instances, these organizations are overly influenced by the central government. Most NGOs in Athens that provide social services to immigrants are funded through the state. This results in a shortage of resources—including a deficit of qualified staff—and promotes clientelism and favoritism.[2] It seems that nongovernmental organizations depend on state funding because of an absence of a relationship between civil society and the private sector. In addition, widespread and entrenched corruption in Greece led citizens to be skeptical about institutions in general, and this fosters reluctance to participate in civic life (Sotiropoulos and Karamagioli 2006). The Greek state dominates the political agenda. Thus far, the Greek state has demonstrated little inclination to address the issue faced by battered migrant women in particular. Perhaps the reason behind this is fear for the sanctity of family institutions in Greece, inhibiting a much needed response to a prevalent problem of domestic violence. Moreover, overcoming this inhibition might lead to widening of the public agenda to related controversial issues involving immigrants, such as their integration, access to naturalization, and political enfranchisement. Of all EU member states, the Greek public consistently registers the highest degree of hostility toward migrants.

Rethinking Trafficking: From Gender Inequity to Human Rights

Securitization of international migration became a defining feature of the post–Cold War era and helped propel human trafficking to the forefront of domestic and foreign policy agendas. The United States played a key role in engendering a Greek response to human trafficking and related issues that became much more salient as Greece became a zone of immigration, no longer simply a transition area.

The security frame so central to understanding variation in the two countries' responses to domestic violence and trafficking in humans must be replaced with a better understanding of the human rights issues that drive trafficking. There is also a broad need for public policies that use domestic legislation to empower victims, as witnessed in the United States. Greeks and Americans, as well as the citizens of other OECD member states, need to more thoroughly discuss the global inequities that generate both supply and demand for human trafficking.

Chapter 7

Peacekeepers and Human Trafficking: The New Security Dilemma

Charles Anthony Smith

Introduction

In July 1999, the United Nations deployed the Kosovo Protection Force (KFOR) to protect ethnic Albanians in the war-torn province of Serbia. With the adoption of Security Council Resolution 1244, approximately 20,000 UN troops were deployed to Kosovo to protect the civilian population from daily skirmishes between the Kosovo Liberation Army (KLA) and the Federal Republic of Yugoslavia (FRY). Within months, several international human rights organizations began reporting precipitous increases in trafficking for sexual exploitation in the region. An Amnesty International report released in August 2004 reported that human trafficking rings were abducting women from Eastern Europe to be sold into the sex trade that was now thriving in Kosovo. By mid-1999, with over 40,000 troops stationed in Kosovo, brothels had been constructed near military bases, and the previously small-scale market for prostitution was "transformed into a large-scale industry . . . predominantly run by organized criminal networks" (Amnesty International 2004b). The United Nations Development Fund for Women (UNIFEM) soon identified four major areas of increase, all near large force deployments, with most clients reportedly UN peacekeepers.

In studying the effects of humanitarian intervention on the frequency, intensity, and recurrence of conflict, scholars have generated a large and unsettled volume of literature on the desirability and effects of peacekeeping missions (see, e.g., Diehl, Reifschneider, and Hensel 1996; Gilligan and Stedman 2003; Regan 2002; Wilkenfeld and Brecher 1984). Nonconflict externalities such as human trafficking, however, have received relatively little attention. This chapter attempts to remedy the lack of scholarly work in this area by focusing on four case studies: Kosovo, Haiti, and Sierra Leone, where UN forces were deployed in response to armed conflict, and Nepal, where they were not. In the three cases where intervention occurred, significant increases in human trafficking followed, with the magnitude of change directly related to the size of the deployment.

While there may be additional negative externalities, the focus here is whether and to what extent force presence and size affects trafficking for sexual exploitation. I adopt a distinction between smuggling and trafficking made by Graycar (1999). Using the concept of consent as the demarcating element, Graycar suggests that smuggling and trafficking occupy opposite positions on a spectrum, with the degree of consent determining whether a practice is more appropriately considered one or the other. Whereas smuggling is simply the illegal but voluntary movement of people across a border, trafficking is defined here as the forced migration of people against their will through deception, abduction, and involuntary confinement. The importance of this distinction is that trafficking, thus defined, must contain an element of coercion.

Despite the paucity of microlevel data on trafficking for sexual exploitation, the macrolevel trends suggest that human trafficking increases as a result of force deployments. That existing literature has not dealt adequately with this or other negative noncombat externalities is a function of UN missions—if the primary aim of an intervention is to halt conflict, it is natural that the effectiveness of a deployment will be judged on that basis. The aim here is a more complete picture of peacekeeping, one that considers the effect of UN forces during the time they are deployed, not merely after they have gone. The success and desirability of UN-led intervention is contested and ultimately unsettled (Diehl, Reifschneider, and Hensel 1996, 688; Doyle and Sambanis 2000; Fortna 2004; Gilligan and Stedman 2003; Regan 2002; Wilkenfeld and Brecher 1984).

Economic incentives are widely considered the driving mechanism behind the formation of markets in human trafficking (Bales 2005; Salt 2000; Salt and Stein 1997; Schloenhardt 1999). Other theories argue that human trafficking is better understood as an international crime (Strecker and Shelley 2004; Aronowitz 2001; Schloenhardt 1999). In both cases, however, a desire for profit is the primary factor in explaining the creation and expansion of trafficking networks. The economic logic of human trafficking mirrors that of other illicit networks, including those designed to deliver narcotics and weapons—where demand for sex workers outstrips supply, human trafficking networks will emerge (Salt and Stein 1997; Schloenhardt 1999, 214). Alternative approaches to human trafficking focus on the ability of preexisting, transnational criminal networks to profit by satisfying demand for a new good (Caldwell et al. 1999; Ruggiero 1997; Shannon 1999).

Both the literatures on UN intervention and on human trafficking exhibit problems related to the content and availability of data. The abundance of data on force deployment, duration, and the recurrence of armed conflict has meant that researchers often focus narrowly on military outcomes. Important secondary effects of intervention, including the economic changes wrought by the presence of well-paid peacekeepers, are understudied or ignored. By contrast, the human trafficking literature suffers from a lack of adequate data on which to test theories and draw conclusions. Governments that agree to allow peacekeeping forces within their borders often lack the law enforcement and reporting capacity to identify and track the emergence of trafficking networks. Fearing repercussions from the international donor community, they may also be reluctant to disclose such information. Moreover, widespread corruption means that officials with knowledge of such activity may be complicit in the crime or coerced into silence. The resulting lack of reliable data presents serious problems in analyzing the causes of human trafficking and the behavior of trafficking networks.[1]

Recently, the unintended consequences of military intervention, including trafficking for sexual exploitation, have received greater scholarly treatment (see, e.g., Aoi, de Coning, and Thakur 2007; Barth, Hostens, and Skielsbaek 2004; McKay and Mazurana 2004). There is also a large body of scholarship on the relationship between the military and the sex trade industry (Enloe 2000a; Mendelson 2005; Moon 1997; Zimelis 2009). Likewise, Csaky (2008) has explored the sexual abuse of children in a peacekeeping context; Cameron and Newman (2008), along with Klopcic (2004), have similarly investigated the global dimensions of human trafficking. Finally, there are ample case studies of particular UN interventions (see, for example,

Carpenter 2003; Friman and Reich 2007; Tritaki 2003; Vandenberg 2002). The model here combines these disparate bodies of scholarship in a generalizable theory.

The common thread in the human trafficking literature is the premise that an increase in demand for a service in the destination country gives rise to human trafficking networks. Once established, any factor that increases domestic demand for sex workers leads to increases in trafficking rings. An understudied variable in this research is the introduction of a large, relatively well-paid foreign military force. Three general observations about force deployment and prostitution frame the case studies of Kosovo, Haiti, Sierra Leone, and Nepal.

First, history confirms that soldiers and the secondary networks that support them use prostitutes (Elliot 1996; Malone et al. 1993; Turner 1994). Any military presence, then, will result in a demand for prostitution. Second, UN interventions occur overwhelmingly in states where the domestic military is small (Gilligan and Stedman 2003). The intervention produces relatively large increases in the military population. Because of the participation of large numbers of NGOs and private contractors, the total increase in demand will be greater than force numbers alone. Third, the by-product of introducing a large foreign force is the temporary or permanent disruption of local criminal networks. This suppression effect may present opportunities for international human trafficking networks operating in the region. Alternatively, peacekeepers may work with existing and emerging criminal groups. These three observations suggest that UN intervention may lead to an increase in demand for prostitution at the same time barriers to entry in the human trafficking market are reduced.

Two hypotheses can be generated from the above observations. The first is that an introduction of a peacekeeping force into a crisis area should increase the rate of human trafficking by way of the greater demand for prostitution. The second is that the increase in human trafficking should be directly proportional to the size of the occupying force.

To overcome the absence of reliable data on human trafficking networks, I cull three distinct categories of information, mitigating the impact of any one source over- or under-reporting trafficking. While the observable data is necessarily imperfect, this is the best approximation possible of the dependent variable (human trafficking for sexual exploitation) and its relationship to the independent variable (UN intervention). Three primary sources are bolstered with published materials and reports from other nongovernmental organizations.

Amnesty International and Human Rights Watch Reports

Both Amnesty International (AI) and Human Rights Watch (HRW) operate and staff local and regional field offices and employ translators and local residents in the regions in the case studies. AI and HRW are thus likely to quantify and report instances of human trafficking for sexual exploitation. All publicly available material from both organizations for the region and time period is considered. The goal is a reasonable approximation of incidences of human trafficking before and during peacekeeping operations.

The International Organization for Migration

Created in 1951 to aid European countries in dealing with the migration that followed World War II, the International Organization for Migration (IOM) is the largest single organization devoted to the study of international and national migration. With an operating budget surpassing $1 billion, IOM has field offices in 100 countries and researchers who focus specifically on human trafficking. The IOM registers human trafficking via field reports and a specialized database, the Counter Trafficking Module Database (CTMD). However, since the IOM ties reporting and tracking to the outbreak of a conflict likely to alter migration patterns, rather than the introduction of peacekeeping forces, it does not explain increases in human trafficking in terms of UN intervention.

State Department Trafficking in Persons Annual Report

Beginning in 2001, the U.S. State Department has published an Annual Trafficking in Persons Report. The report tracks and categorizes all countries using a three-tier system, with the first tier representing full compliance with the Trafficking Victims Protection Act, the second tier some compliance, and the third minimum or noncompliance (Hughes 2002).

These three data sources, combined, allow a reasonably sound approxima-tion of changes in patterns of human trafficking before and after the introduc-tion of peacekeeping forces. The case studies reflect diversity in geography, conflict type, and magnitude. The cases cover four regions of the world and four conflicts with radically different causes and conclusions. They are rela-tively recent in order to take advantage of new data sources that make devel-oping a proxy variable for human trafficking possible.

Kosovo

Hostilities between the Serbian Military Police, the Yugoslav Federal Army, and the Kosovo Liberation Army (KLA) had reached a critical point by 1998 (Ramet 2001a, 2001b). In March of the same year, the Serbian military police reportedly killed 12,000 Kosovar Albanians, with more than 230,000 displaced as a result of the fighting between Kosovar and Serb forces (Ramet 2001a, 2001b). NATO members authorized a bombing campaign against Serb forces that lasted from March 23 to June 10, 1999. Following the bombing, the Kosovo Protection Force (KFOR) was deployed under NATO authority as part of Op-eration Joint Guardian. The KFOR mandate directed the force to protect the civilian population, oversee the disarmament of KLA and Serb forces, and en-force a ceasefire. By August 1999, the 20,000-troop deployment had doubled to 40,000, and would peak at 50,000; a civilian force of approximately 5,000 deliv-ered logistical and humanitarian support.[2]

The UN force was large relative not only to other peacekeeping missions but also to the local population. At the height of the intervention, KFOR composed 2.4 percent of the Kosovo population. This large force should have greatly increased the demand for sex workers, and thus given rise to human trafficking rings. Given the size of the force, the increase should be relatively large, focused in Pristina, the capital of Kosovo and the headquarters of KFOR and UNMIK (Interim Administration Mission in Kosovo).

Before the NATO bombing campaign and Operation Joint Guardian, both AI and HRW had a significant presence in Kosovo, due to persistent reports of extra-judicial detention by Serb police and other human rights abuses. AI produced thirty-five reports in 1998—the year prior to KFOR deployment—with one devoted exclusively to human rights abuses against women. None of them, however, mention trafficking for sexual exploitation, a pattern that holds for 1996 and 1997 as well. During the same period HRW published twenty-six reports, the vast majority concerning ethnic cleansing and other related crimes. None cite any instances of human trafficking or sexual exploitation. The complete absence of reports regarding trafficking for sexual exploitation during this period suggests that, prior to KFOR, the problem was, at best, a low priority.

With the massive injection of foreign peacekeepers in 1999, rising to a total of 50,000 by March of the following year, the spike in prostitution and the trafficking of women and girls into the Kosovo region was enormous. AI estimated that the number of exploited women and girls increased more than tenfold from 1999 to 2003, from a mere 18 to well over 200 (Amnesty International 2004c). Similarly, the IOM released a report based on interviews with 474 victims of sexual trafficking between 2000 and 2005, with the majority coming from neighboring Moldova and a smaller number from Romania and Ukraine (International Organization for Migration 2000–2005, 3).[3] AI found a clear link between the arrival of peacekeepers and the increase in women trafficked for the purpose of sexual exploitation. According to one report, the arrival of the international community was followed by an "unprecedented" escalation of demand for sex workers, which was then met through international human trafficking (Amnesty International 2004b). AI estimated that from 1999 to 2000, 80 percent of the clients of sex workers were internationals (Amnesty International 2004b). Likewise, HRW cited a "surge" in trafficking into Kosovo and referred to an increase in cases handled by the IOM, which between 2000 and 2001 assisted at least 160 victims of human trafficking (Human Rights Watch 2002).

During this same period, the U.S. State Department referred specifically to Kosovo as it downgraded Yugoslavia to Tier 3 status, a category designated for states who are not complying with the U.S. Trafficking Victims Protection Act. Though Serbia was listed as a Tier 2 country in later years, it was largely due to the passage of a UNMIK regulation outlawing human trafficking (U.S. Department of State 2004b, 173). Indeed, according to a 2005 report, decreasing arrests and prosecutions were the result of more sophisticated trafficking practices, not a reduction in demand or supply. While the UNMIK Trafficking and Prostitution Investigation Unit made seventy-seven arrests and assisted forty-eight victims, the report notes that the decline was likely due to the swift adaptation of "increasingly sophisticated criminal networks" that reacted to stronger enforcement by "shifting the commercial sex trade out of public bars and into private homes" (U.S. Department of State 2005, 195). The total number of raids—2,386—is noteworthy, given Kosovo's population of 2 million;

this means roughly one in every 838 people in Kosovo had some contact with the Trafficking and Prostitution Investigation Unit in 2004.

Against the backdrop of the rapid emergence and proliferation of human trafficking networks, UNMIK created a special police unit in October 2000 with the sole purpose of preventing human trafficking and prostitution. This was followed in 2001 by Regulation 2001/4, which provided assistance to victims, criminalized the trafficking of women, and stipulated stiff penalties for solicitation. Whether the problem had abated significantly by 2005, as is suggested in the IOM report for that year, or whether traffickers had adapted to law enforcement strategy is uncertain. Nonetheless, the enormous increase in human trafficking for sexual exploitation, combined with explicit efforts of UNMIK and other international organizations in stepping up enforcement, strongly validates the hypothesis: Kosovo experienced a significant rise in demand and supply following the KFOR deployment.

Haiti

The crisis that eventually necessitated humanitarian intervention in Haiti began with two contested elections in 2000, including the apparently fraudulent election of Jean-Bertrand Aristide to the presidency. Aristide resigned on February 29, 2004, and promptly fled the country. Per the Haitian Constitution, the president of the Supreme Court, Boniface Alexandre, was sworn in as president. He soon requested that the UN Security Council send troops to Port-au-Prince to quell growing unrest.

The force that arrived following the passage of Resolution 1529 in February faced a severely impoverished nation of 8.7 million that, in the span of one year, had dropped four spots in the United Nations Development Program's Human Development ranking, from 146 to 150. From 2002 to 2003, life expectancy had declined an unprecedented 3.5 years, to 49.1. Infant mortality rates were twice the regional average at 95 per 100 births, and nearly two out of every three Haitians lived below the internationally accepted poverty line. The financial poverty of the average Haitian was mirrored in the country's governance, where a weak and ineffective regime had failed to deliver basic social services and maintain law and order. In this light, the mandate of the Multinational Interim Force (MIF) was relatively modest—to maintain peace, particularly in Port-au-Prince—but was strengthened by the United Nations Stabilization Mission in Haiti (MINUSTAH). Established with the passage of Resolution 1542 in April

2004, MINUSTAH took over all peacekeeping duties in Haiti and grew from an initial 6,700 military personnel to nearly 9,000 by August 2007.

In the years preceding MINUSTAH, AI and HRW reported the declining socioeconomic status of Haiti but did not mention any human trafficking. Haiti's Tier 2 status in the State Department Annual Trafficking Reports for 2001 suggests that human trafficking was present before the MIF deployment. A reclassification to Tier 3 status in 2003 implies that the trafficking problem was becoming more severe, or that the Haitian government was failing to adequately enforce existing laws. A closer look, however, reveals that the State Department was primarily concerned with the internal trafficking of young girls. This was part of a centuries-old tradition whereby parents, unable to care for their children, sent them to work as domestic servants.

In response to these criticisms, the Haitian government established a twenty-person police unit in Port-au-Prince tasked with the prevention of trafficking, and the Ministry of the Interior required border guards to more thoroughly certify documentation at the border. Though an executive order by President George W. Bush in September 2003 moved Haiti back to Tier 2 status, a 2003 report does mention, for the first time, women from the Dominican Republic being trafficked into Haiti as prostitutes (U.S. Department of State 2003). The collapse of the Aristide government in 2004 meant that the State Department lacked a government to evaluate. The 2005 report makes a second mention of trafficking into Haiti from the Dominican Republic, and the 2006 report lists Haiti as a special case due to the collapse of government and the inability to evaluate efforts to stop trafficking. Haiti was likewise classified as a special case in 2007, but the report notes that greater numbers of women are being trafficked into Haiti to serve UN peacekeepers.

HRW and AI reports on the issue, like the Annual Trafficking in Persons (TIP) reports, are mixed. Neither mentions trafficking into Haiti for the explicit purpose of sexual exploitation either before or after 2004. Reports from 2004 onward, however, contain numerous incidences of forced abductions of women and children, widespread rape, and violence against women (Amnesty International 2006a, 2006b). Whether this increase was a result of MINUSTAH or simply a product of the deteriorating security situation that necessitated its creation is not clear; the impact of the UN presence is discussed further in Heather Smith's contribution to this volume. Data from the IOM and U.S. government policy suggest that human trafficking was, at the very least, a problem of growing importance after the introduction of MINUSTAH forces. A joint IOM–State Department conference on trafficking was held in

June 2006 in Port-au-Prince, focusing particularly on raising awareness. A year earlier, the IOM interviewed 1,886 people with varying degrees of involvement in Haitian trafficking networks, including victims, traffickers, middlemen, and leaders of established trafficking rings. Victims overwhelmingly cited poverty and lack of opportunity in their decision to move to Port-au-Prince and become sex workers, and they often worked in bars and brothels. Others were trafficked to Port-au-Prince to become prostitutes against their will, after being promised positions as maids or domestic workers.

A high-profile scandal, first reported in 2007, gives more definitive evidence that UN peacekeepers increased the demand for sex workers. The same year, 114 peacekeepers were expelled from Haiti by the UN after having been found guilty of paying for sex ("UN Ousts Peacekeepers in Sex Case" 2007). A UN committee investigation of the incident was conducted but never made public. Media reports, however, suggest a direct link between peacekeeping forces and increases in prostitution, with one *Los Angeles Times* article noting that young girls had congregated near peacekeeping outposts as early as 2004 (Williams 2007). Evidence from the three primary sources as well as media reports support a strong affirmation of the first hypothesis: there was a measurable increase in human trafficking following the introduction of MIF and later MINUSTAH forces. The support for the second hypothesis—that increases should correspond to force levels—is less clear, most likely because the 9,000 troop deployment represents a much smaller share of the 8.2 million Haitians than the larger KFOR force did in Kosovo.

Sierra Leone

The 1997 conflict in Sierra Leone is most appropriately thought of as a spillover conflict from neighboring Liberia. In March 1997, then-president Kabbah was forced from office in a military coup. President Kabbah's reinstatement one year later was followed by a series of peacekeeping operations first undertaken by the Economic Community of West African States Monitoring Group (ECOMOG) and supported by the United Nations Observer Mission in Sierra Leone (UNOMSIL). The latter of the two operations was replaced in 1999, when the Security Council mandated the creation of the United Nations Mission in Sierra Leone (UNAMSIL).

Troop levels were initially set at 6,000 and increased to a total of 13,000 by May 2000. Fighting continued despite the presence of peacekeepers. Revolutionary United Front (RUF) forces ignored deadlines for disarmament and continued abducting women and children. A tentative ceasefire collapsed entirely in May 2000, when the RUF took more than 500 UNAMSIL soldiers captive. The brazen attack led the Security Council to increase troop levels to a peak of 17,500.

AI and HRW reports from January 1998 to March 2001—the month in which UNAMSIL reached peak troop levels—frequently refer to widespread abduction and sexual exploitation, and implicate the RUF rebels, the Armed Forces Revolutionary Council, and pro-government forces. AI mentions abduction and sexual slavery a combined eighteen times (Amnesty International 1998); HRW gave significantly more attention to the issue over the same period for a total of seventy-one references.[4] Neither organization, however, reported increases in human trafficking as a direct or indirect result of ECOMOG and UNAMSIL forces—an April 2001 report, in fact, notes the complete absence of charges of rape by peacekeepers (Human Rights Watch 2001b).

State Department and IOM Counter Trafficking data corroborate the lack of trafficking networks in areas under the control of foreign troops (U.S. Department of State 2001b). Moreover, in classifying Sierra Leone as a Tier 2 country, the report makes no mention of any increase in commercial trafficking for the purposes of sexual exploitation.

Shortly after UNAMSIL reached maximum strength, human rights organizations began drawing attention to a dramatic rise in prostitution, particularly in Freetown, as a result of the international forces. A joint report compiled by the United Nations High Commission on Refugees (UNHCR) and the UK nonprofit Save the Children in 2002 warned that sexual exploitation had increased precipitously in Freetown, with local residents speaking openly of the change. The joint effort also uncovered evidence that women were being trafficked against their will from neighboring Liberia and Guinea (United Nations High Commissioner for Refugees 2002). The UN acknowledged the problem and on February 28, 2002 pledged to correct it (United Nations Mission in Sierra Leone 2002). Both AI and HRW reports during this period echoed concerns about increases in prostitution and sexual exploitation (Human Rights Watch 2003b).

A reclassification of Sierra Leone in 2004 to Tier 3 status supports the argument that trafficking had increased; indeed, the 2004 Annual Trafficking Report explicitly mentions such an increase and singles out Freetown as a destination of both internal and cross-border trafficking networks. The UNHCR report draws attention to the primary mechanism: an increase in demand created by UN forces, who, critically, were paid large salaries relative to local incomes. Taken together, the similarity between these disparate sources suggests a marked change in the magnitude of the trafficking problem as well as its pattern, with Freetown emerging as the central destination.

Nepal

Located in Asia, a region with well-established and deeply rooted human trafficking networks, Nepal is a "hard case" with respect to our hypothesis (Samarasinghe 2007). Situated in an area that has become a hub for global sex tourism, trafficking networks in Southeast Asia are far more likely to adjust quickly and markedly to increases in demand as a result of armed conflict. If the conflict in Nepal failed to generate a rise in trafficking to the country, we can be relatively more confident that it is the presence of well-paid, international peacekeepers that has driven the formation of trafficking networks in our three previous case studies.

Armed conflict in Nepal began in earnest in 1990, when state-sponsored security forces violently suppressed pro-democracy protests by the Nepali Congress Party (NCP) and a coalition of other leftist groups (British Broadcasting Corporation 2010). In the aftermath of the crackdown, King Birendra was obliged to abolish the Panchayat ruling system and adopt a democratic constitution. In May 1991, democratic elections were held, with the NCP gaining the majority of seats and promptly naming Girija Prasad Koirala as its prime minister. When the Koirala government lost a no-confidence vote in 1994, a communist coalition took power, only to fall apart in 1995 after another no-confidence vote, resulting in the elevation of the new NCP leader, Sher Bahadur Deuba, to prime minister.

Full-scale war came to Nepal on February 13, 1996, when Maoist rebels stormed several government positions. Calling themselves "The People's Army," the guerrillas numbered approximately 5,000. The government declared a state of emergency lasting from February 2000 to August 2002. The government then passed the Terrorist and Disruptive Activities Act and used the new provisions to arrest and detain political dissidents for up to ninety days without a warrant. Maoist rebels retaliated against the repression with a series of abductions and summary executions, and in 2002 Nepal had the highest disappearance rate in the world (Amnesty International 2004d). By December 2003, the death toll had surpassed 8,000, and political instability deepened when Prime Minister Chand resigned in May 2004. Intense lob-bying from the international community resulted in a 2006 peace accord that granted the Maoists positions in the transitional government. The accord proved durable.

Lacking international intervention, the conflict should not produce any new or significant human trafficking networks, and incidences of sexual exploitation should not increase over previous levels for the duration of the conflict. Moreover, since Nepal has historically seen externally oriented flows of forced and voluntary migration to India, its relatively wealthier northern neighbor, any marked changes will be visible in net flows. If international, cross-border trafficking emerges as a direct result of the increase in demand following an injection of peacekeeping forces, there should be no obvious change in levels of human trafficking.

Surveying reports by AI, HRW, the IOM, and the State Department, the theory holds. Between 1999 and 2005, AI published 508 reports on Nepal and the various stages of its civil war. Most are devoted to tracking the scores of civilians and politicians abducted or killed by Maoist and government forces alike. When human trafficking and the sexual abuse of women appear, they are almost exclusively in reference to the outward trafficking of women to India (Amnesty International 2005). There is no evidence to suggest any significant increase in trafficking into Nepal as a result of the conflict. HRW reports from August 2000 to November 2005 similarly support the hypothesis: the single mention of sexual abuse during this period is confined to a note about the plight of Bhutanese refugees (Human Rights Watch 2003a). The exploitation of these refugees, however, is a crime of opportunity and does not represent a demand-driven shift in the flow of trafficked women or indicate an emerging internal market.

The annual Trafficking in Persons (TIP) reports from 2001 to 2007 give a more nuanced picture of trafficking both into and out of Nepal but nonetheless corroborate the AI and HRW data. The most significant difference is that the TIP reports reveal a deep, sophisticated set of networks, particularly for external trafficking. TIP reports in 2003 and 2005 mention an increase in internal trafficking for sexual exploitation from rural areas into larger cities. Possible explanations include a surge in trafficking as a result of a breakdown in law and order during the Maoist insurgency, or a spike in demand as fighters and refugees congregated in urban areas—although not international forces, the latter of these possibilities actually strengthens our hypothesis. The majority of the remaining TIP reports focus on trafficking *from* Nepal into India, China, and the Gulf States; it was estimated that approximately 12,000 Nepalese women were trafficked into India in 2006 alone. Both before and after the conflict, Nepal continued to be a source country for human trafficking. While there is some evidence that internal trafficking patterns changed in response to the civil war, large net outflows persisted.

Conclusion

In Kosovo, Haiti, and Sierra Leone, there are clear signs of increases—dramatic in the case of Kosovo, more subdued in Haiti and Sierra Leone—in trafficking for sexual exploitation as the result of the presence of international peacekeepers. The first hypothesis, that the increase in demand will result in the emergence of trafficking networks, is strongly supported by all three case studies. Prior to the introduction of UN forces in both Kosovo and Sierra Leone, human rights organizations made few references to trafficking problems, if at all. The absence of significant trafficking for the purposes of sexual exploitation in Haiti is less clear but is bolstered by the content of individual IOM, HRW, and AI reports. These documents attribute the patterns to a historical *restavek* system, whereby impoverished families sell their young children to families as domestic servants. Before the MINUS-TAH deployment, there was no mention of sophisticated criminal networks forcibly importing women for the purposes of sexual exploitation. Indeed, despite the vastly different cultural, political, and economic conditions of UN interventions, the theory holds in all three cases considered: an increase in demand, driven by the large influx of well-paid foreign soldiers, resulted in a concomitant increase in levels of human trafficking.

The second hypothesis—that the increase will be determined by the size of the force relative to the local population—is also supported, particularly in the case of Kosovo. A large UN force relative to the existing population, as was the case in Kosovo, elicited a more dramatic rise in trafficking levels. A smaller force, as in Haiti, yielded a smaller increase. In Kosovo, the full-strength deployment of KFOR was followed by a sharp spike in human trafficking for the purposes of sexual exploitation. AI and HRW reports prior to the KFOR deployment identified a mere 18 cases of foreign women being trafficked into Kosovo; after the intervention, that number rose quickly to over 200.

Sierra Leone, where UNAMSIL numbers reached 17,500 at their peak, occupies a middle ground between the relatively large KFOR intervention and relatively smaller MINUSTAH intervention in Haiti. After the 2001 UNAMSIL deployment, there was a large surge and strategic change in trafficking patterns as networks adapted to the UN presence and redirected their efforts to Freetown, the headquarters of the international operation.

As the smallest of the forces considered, the MINUSTAH intervention in Haiti yielded a noticeable but less severe increase in trafficking. The relatively smaller increase was consistent with expectations: the 6,700 troops, which in 2004 swelled to 9,000, accounted for the smallest proportion of the local population of the three cases, with the peak levels representing a mere 0.001 percent of the total population. That the IOM and U.S. State Department nonetheless became concerned about the growing flow of women to Haiti from the Dominican Republican attests to the strong incentives that criminal actors have in satisfying the rising demand for prostitution that accompanies a foreign force.

Scholarly work on individual interventions (see Friman and Reich 2007; Mendelson 2005; Vandenberg 2002) corroborates the hypotheses and gives additional weight to the argument that increases in human trafficking as a result of UN deployments are a systematic feature of interventions, one that occurs regardless of local or regional supply-side constraints. Nepal is the control case and provides counterfactual support. Given the sophisticated and deep networks responsible for the global sex tourism trade in Southeast Asia, any significant increase in demand would have been met by such networks and reflected in trafficking patterns. Critically, the existence of pre-conflict trafficking *out of* Nepal into India and China was not visibly altered by the Maoist insurgency and civil war. The absence of inflows into Nepal during the period suggests that armed conflict is not itself a sufficient condition for the emergence of trafficking networks.

Still, if armed conflict, corruption, and poor governance—staples of weak states and crisis areas—do not necessarily give rise to human trafficking, they surely create fertile ground. The three intervention case studies demonstrate that humanitarian interventions, by their nature, are likely to occur in places where the risk of human trafficking is greatest. It is especially problematic, then, that large deployments of foreign troops inject a demand for sex workers, which in turn acts as a catalyst for trafficking of women for the purposes of sexual exploitation. The paradox of intervention, in this case, is that the chain of abuses suffered by trafficked women, beginning with abduction and leading to rape, forced confinement, and torture, are some of the most severe and deplorable human rights violations that occur in conflict zones. To the extent that UN intervention is justified as a remedy to such ills, there has been surprisingly little research on how to mitigate these externalities of intervention.

A large body of existing literature has illustrated the complex range of factors that affect wartime sexual violence, which include the combatant norms, leadership strategies, and the psychology of group behavior (Wood 2006). Now future research would do well to examine whether the command structure of forces has a measurable effect on the demand for sex workers and resulting increase in trafficking. Other avenues of research might consider whether the composition of international forces—that is, the proportion of soldiers contributed by each country—has any explanatory power. Heather Smith's chapter examines other dimensions of international organizations that may complement these factors.

Finally, these findings suggest that the constituent members of UN peacekeeping forces should reconsider their levels of concern about human trafficking rings. The international community should contribute to research that is more robust by devoting more resources to systematically tracking and reporting human trafficking. Attention to conflict areas by nongovernmental and intergovernmental organizations tends to increase during periods of particular violence and abate afterward. The result is a piecemeal and incomplete understanding of long-term trends in many areas, human trafficking not least among them. More aggressive monitoring would allow not only for a better understanding of how quickly networks emerge and respond to peacekeeping deployments, but also, critically, how these rings behave after the intervention concludes. Human trafficking rings can be easily adapted to deliver whatever contraband may suit the current needs of a world in turmoil. The security of the very states that enable the creation of these smuggling rings is threatened by the international capacity to convert the rings to smuggle other commodities, including illicit drugs or weapons. The establishment and institutionalization of these smuggling rings during UN operations is a new security dilemma that must be taken more seriously, by the UN specifically and the international community more generally.

Chapter 8

The Good, the Bad, and the Ugly: Assessing the Impact of the OAS and the UN on Human Trafficking in Haiti

Heather T. Smith

Introduction

How can global governance contribute to a human rights approach to human trafficking? As the number of international organizations (IOs) has expanded in the post–World War II period, so, too, has their role in global governance. The World Health Organization plays a key role in arresting the spread of infectious disease around the globe. The International Monetary Fund rescues states with loans when they are in danger of economic collapse, and the United Nations (UN) deploys troops to conflict zones to maintain international peace and security. Yet, for all of their positive contributions, we lack an understanding of all the potential shades of IO influence, particularly on human rights conditions in the states they assist. Scholars have long known that IOs can be pathological and dysfunctional and produce unintended outcomes (Barnett and Finnemore 1999). However, the darker side of IO influence has been given little scholarly attention.

This chapter focuses on how rethinking trafficking with a human rights approach also requires rethinking global governance. Brysk's chapter in this volume argues that a human rights approach to trafficking emphasizes both protection and empowerment of trafficking victims. Her analysis argues forcefully for a reconsideration of victimhood—suggesting that a human rights approach to trafficking means expanding our understanding of human rights as claims not only against the state but also against a host of actors "from guerillas to employers to families." This chapter takes up this theme by highlighting IOs as both a source of rights violations and empowerment for trafficking victims. Rethinking trafficking with a human rights approach means expanding our universe of potentially significant actors beyond the state, because IOs have had both considerably positive and devastatingly negative effects on human trafficking. As IOs are tasked with ever expanding responsibilities as part of the fabric of global governance, it becomes of paramount importance to pause and consider their effects on human rights.

I explore the impact of the United Nations and the Organization of American States (OAS) on human trafficking. The institutional design of these IOs differs in ways that make their variation worthy of comparison. The UN is a global IO whose membership consists of nearly all the sovereign countries in the world. With such a large membership, the UN lacks the democratic density that recent scholarly work identifies as essential for IOs to produce positive outcomes (Hansen, Mitchell, and Nemeth 2008; Pevehouse and Russett 2006). The OAS, a regional IO composed of thirty-five Latin American states, has a smaller membership, with a higher democratic density. This variation in their democratic density has considerable implications for the impact these IOs have on human trafficking in Haiti. My study suggests that more-democratic international organizations contribute to a more rights-based approach to global governance.

Haiti is an appropriate case for examining the influence of the UN and the OAS because both IOs have been engaged in Haiti's recent struggles. Notable as the "poorest country in the Western hemisphere," Haiti has endured a variety of challenges—an earthquake in 2010, hurricanes, and coups have exacerbated already crippling poverty. These calamities have weakened the central government and created an opportunity for other actors, particularly international actors, to fill the political vacuum. IOs have emerged as central players in Haitian politics—in some instances their influence has improved conditions in Haiti, while in others IOs actually contribute to violations of human rights.

This chapter rethinks human trafficking by considering the unintended effects of IOs on the likelihood of trafficking. The role of IOs in preventing the spread of disease, limiting conflict, and stabilizing imperiled economies has blinded scholars to the darker effects of IOs on human rights. I argue that UN peacekeepers contributed to an increase in the rate of trafficking into Haiti following their arrival in 2004. UN troops created a demand for trafficking victims that did not exist prior to their arrival. Conversely, the OAS entered Haiti with a strong commitment to human rights and a mandate to curb human trafficking. The influence of the OAS was substantially more positive than the influence of the UN. We must therefore rethink our solutions to human trafficking; IOs cannot be relied upon to benevolently protect human rights. UN peacekeepers patronized those women that were trafficked into Haiti and thus created a market that did not otherwise exist—yet the OAS contributed to positive socialization and reconstructing the rule of law (British Broadcasting Corporation 2006). Rather than conceive of IOs as the solution to human trafficking, this chapter argues that we must examine the identity and opportunity that IOs possess in order to evaluate their impact on human trafficking.

How IOs Affect Global Politics

Scholarly work on the impact of IOs on global politics has been heavily influenced by the Kantian peace literature. More than two hundred years ago Kant argued that a perpetual peace among independent republican states could be created through networks of trade and "institutions of cosmopolitan law" above the states (Bohman and Lutz-Bachmann 1997, 5). Pevehouse and Russet (2006) suggest that densely democratic IOs socialize states to adopt norms of behavior. The European Community, for example socialized the Spanish to democratize (Powell 2001). Densely democratic IOs provide a number of benefits—reducing the likelihood of conflict between members (Pevehouse and Russett 2006), socializing nondemocratic states to adopt peaceful dispute settlement practices (Mitchell 2002), and helping their members settle conflicts peacefully (Hansen, Mitchell, and Nemeth 2008).

The expansive positive contributions of IOs have dominated the literature and developed our collective knowledge on how these actors affect global politics. Membership in preferential trade agreements (PTAs) can increase the impetus to sanction fellow PTA members (Hafner-Burton and Montgomery 2008). Others have challenged the positive outcomes that IOs produce. The traditional critique of IOs, advanced by Mearsheimer (1994/1995), contends that IOs are reflections of state power. As such, they are simply too weak to influence outcomes. There is some limited attention to the negative effects of IOs on global politics. Environmental IOs lack strong monitoring and sanctioning mechanisms and thus may undermine environmental protection (Ringquist and Kostadinova 2005).

For all that we have learned from this growing literature. questions remain. What influences do IOs have on domestic human rights conditions? Do IOs improve human rights in the countries they enter? Under what conditions do IOs undermine human rights? This chapter focuses on the role of the UN and the OAS in Haiti and cannot make bold claims about the full range of these relationships. Instead, I aim to establish the plausibility of my central claim—*democratically deficient* IOs contribute to human trafficking.

Linking IOs and Human Trafficking Outcomes

Do IOs unintentionally promote the development of human trafficking rings? Do the agents of IOs intentionally patronize trafficking victims? Or, are the agents of IOs promoting policies on the ground that decrease the likelihood of human trafficking?

To understand the role that IOs play in affecting human trafficking, I begin with the observation that most IOs and the agents that work for them possess more resources than the individual states they assist. IOs necessarily have an advantage in dealing with impoverished states like Haiti. If the UN sends peacekeepers or the OAS sends observers, the Haitians are likely to grant the intrusion in the hopes that benefits will be forthcoming. Moreover, individual United Nations peacekeepers have more resources than the local populations they work among. IO workers can and do exploit the income gap between themselves and local populations. In 2002, Save the Children and the United Nations High Commissioner for Human Rights reported that women and girls were being trafficked from Guinea and Liberia into Sierra Leone to work as prostitutes in service of UN peacekeepers. By their own admission, UN peacekeepers are among the highest-paying customers for prostitution in Sierra Leone (United Nations High Commissioner for Refugees 2002). In this instance, at the most nefarious end of the spectrum of possible IO effects on trafficking, agents of the IO are responsible for perpetuating the violation of rights, and their presence creates a demand for prostitutes.

IOs need not necessarily play such a negative role. The mechanisms IOs have traditionally employed to pressure states to democratize may also be employed to limit human trafficking. IOs could socialize peacekeepers to refrain from sexually exploitative practices or they could pressure mission executives to punish peacekeepers that patronize prostitutes. IO observers could draw attention to the plight of trafficking victims or hold conferences to teach government officials about how to curb human trafficking. This leads to a range of potential IO effects on human trafficking: perpetuating the violation of rights by patronizing victims, identifying trafficking and publicizing it, pressuring mission heads to punish IO agents that patronize victims, and socializing government officials to arrest the practice.

The impact that an IO will have on trafficking is dependent upon two IO characteristics—identity and opportunity. The identity of the IO refers to the democratic density of the institution. How many members are established democracies? How many members are quasi-democracies or autocracies? Building on Pevehouse and Russett (2006) and Hansen, Mitchell, and Nemeth (2008), I argue that densely democratic IOs have a stronger interest in promoting human rights and liberal-democratic values. Their commitment to democratic ideals at home translates into less tolerance for human rights abuse abroad. Those IOs that are less densely democratic should exhibit lower commitment to these values and be more tolerant of rights violations abroad. The democratic density of the IO is critical because when IOs that are not deeply committed to human rights send peacekeepers into conflict zones, there is a high potential for abuse. Peacekeepers from countries with legal institutions that enshrine human rights should be less likely to go abroad and act in ways that are inconsistent with the values they have learned at home. As the democratic density of an IO decreases, the likelihood that it will either be responsible for or tolerant of human trafficking increases.

The second component that explains IO impact on human trafficking is opportunity. All IOs do not possess an equal opportunity to affect human trafficking. IOs like the UN that send thousands of peacekeepers can have considerable effects on human trafficking in mission countries. Peacekeepers can negatively affect trafficking by creating a demand for prostitutes by directly patronizing sex workers. Alternatively, peacekeepers can function as a domestic police force, working to suppress criminal activity in mission countries. Other IOs—the OAS, for example—do not send troops into conflict zones, so have a more limited opportunity to impact trafficking. Both the UN and the OAS can send observers and pressure government officials to institute anti-trafficking laws. The opportunity to affect human trafficking is greatest where IO agents are on the ground, either promoting positive change or creating a demand for victims. IOs that cannot send troops have a diminished capacity to impact human trafficking.

Relying on the concepts of democratic density and opportunity produces testable hypotheses about the effects of the OAS and the UN on human trafficking in Haiti. The OAS is the more densely democratic IO, yet it possesses a limited ability to impact human trafficking because it cannot deploy troops.[1] The OAS should therefore produce outcomes consistent with its democratic ideals, but the impact of these effects should be limited. The UN lacks the democratic density of the OAS and is therefore more likely to produce negative human rights outcomes. However, these effects should be large because the UN possesses an unparalleled opportunity to deploy thousands of its agents abroad. In short, the OAS should have a weak, though positive, impact on human trafficking, while the UN should have a negative though comparatively larger impact on human trafficking in Haiti.[2]

Politics in Haiti

Haitian politics have been characterized by violence and conflict at least as far back as 1957, when François "Papa Doc" Duvalier won the Haitian presidency and swiftly consolidated his power through a reign of terror. The 2000 presidential and senatorial elections that restored Jean-Bertrand Aristide and his Famnis Lavalas party to power in Haiti were no exception. Despite Aristide's victory in 2000, his early departure from office in 2004 created the crisis that brought the UN and the OAS into Haiti.[3]

The senatorial elections in 2000 were, by most accounts "free, fair, and flawed" (Bohning 2000). Despite a high voter turnout, the method through which the votes were counted violated constitutional rules and privileged Aristide's party (Dupuy 2007; Fatton Jr. 2002; Organization of American States General Assembly 2001). The head of the Provisional Electoral Council, Leon Manus, faced intense pressure and death threats from Aristide to forgo run-off elections for ten Senate seats and award them to Aristide's party. After succumbing to this pressure, Manus fled the country (U.S. Department of State 2001a).[4] OAS election monitors left Haiti and refused to oversee the upcoming presidential elections.

In contrast to the relatively fair parliamentary elections, the 2000 presidential election that restored Aristide to power was deeply flawed. Opposition parties, under the banner of the Democratic Convergence, boycotted the election, leaving Aristide to run against a group of unknown candidates. The Provisional Electoral Council announced that Aristide had won the presidency with 91.5 percent of the vote, with 60.5 percent turnout (U.S. Department of State 2001a). In addition to questioning the turnout reported by the Provisional Electoral Council, the OAS argued that the same faulty vote-counting method used to tabulate Senate votes was used to count presidential votes (Organization of American States General Assembly 2001).

Aristide's Return and Low Levels of Human Trafficking in Haiti: 2000–2004

Upon resuming the presidency, Aristide was immediately met with challenges to his authority. The Democratic Convergence voiced loud opposition to Aristide and Fanmis Lavalas's senatorial victory. Aristide also had to find ways to appease the Bush government and conservative American senators, long openly suspicious of him, to obtain foreign aid that had been withheld pending resolution of the political crisis (Fatton Jr. 2002, 141–46). Political instability, claims of electoral fraud, and aggressive opposition to Aristide's rule constituted considerable problems in Haiti in early 2001. However, prior to the arrival of the UN and the OAS, there is limited evidence of a problem with human trafficking for sexual exploitation between 2000 and 2004.

Neither Human Rights Watch nor Amnesty International issued a report or mentioned human trafficking in Haiti between 2000 and 2004. These NGOs called attention to other human rights violations taking place there during this time but did not highlight problems surrounding the trafficking of individuals into Haiti for the purposes of sexual exploitation.[5] In contrast, the U.S. State Department voiced concerns about human trafficking in Haiti during this same period. What explains the difference? Why did the State Department label Haiti a Tier 2 country in its 2001 Trafficking in Persons Report, a label indicating that there was a human trafficking problem and that Haitian authorities were making efforts to punish the traffickers (U.S. Department of State 2001b)? The State Department was focused on the Haitian *restavek* system—a centuries-old practice of placing young children from poor families to work as domestic servants for wealthier families. The UN estimates that hundreds of thousands of Haitian children are victims of this practice (United Nations High Commissioner for Human Rights 2009). While their plight is tragic, *restaveks* are not trafficked into Haiti from foreign countries for exploitation in the sex industry. The State Department's classification of Haiti as a Tier 2 country in both 2001 and 2002 is a direct result of the *restavek* system but does not constitute the type of human trafficking for sexual exploitation that is the focus of this inquiry.

The U.S. government has been involved in many aspects of Haitian politics for years, restoring Aristide through a unilateral military intervention in 1994, for example. When the State Department's classification of Haiti dropped to a Tier 3 ranking in 2003, again the result of the *restavek* system, the Haitian government responded immediately to U.S. demands. The Tier 3 ranking indicates that Aristide's government was not complying with the minimum requirements of the Trafficking Victims Protection Act, nor attempting to comply. This classification put Aristide among dubious international company, as North Korea, Sudan, Myanmar, and Cuba were also designated Tier 3 countries in 2003 (U.S. Department of State 2003). So when the U.S. government issued Aristide a "work plan" to combat trafficking, he responded by creating a twenty-person anti-trafficking police unit. The Ministry of the Interior also enhanced scrutiny of immigration documents at the border. In response, President Bush issued an executive order upgrading Haiti to a Tier 2 country in 2003 (Bush 2003a).

Despite his somewhat limited success in appeasing the United States by improving anti-trafficking initiatives, a weak mandate resulting from the flawed elections left Aristide vulnerable to domestic opposition. In early February 2004, former members of the Haitian National Police and paramilitary groups coalesced to oppose the government. They attacked police stations and courthouses in the northern Haitian city of Gonaïves, forcing government officials to flee (Organization of American States Inter-American Commission on Human Rights 2005). As the violence and opposition to the government spread to other cities, insurgents threatened to attack Port-au-Prince. On February 29, 2004, Aristide resigned as president and fled to the Central African Republic.[6]

Boniface Alexandre, the president of the Supreme Court, was selected as Aristide's replacement by what Dupuy calls a "U.S. approved 'Council of the Wise'" (Dupuy 2007, 172). Alexandre called on the UN Security Council to deploy peacekeepers to Port-au-Prince to restore order. Dupuy (2007) contends that Alexandre was a figurehead, and real power rested with the council's choice for prime minister, Gérard Latortue. Upon assuming office in

2004, Latortue appointed his cabinet and began finding ways to delay his departure from office (Dupuy 2007, 173).

Between 2000 and 2004 Haitian politics were marred with violence and instability. Aristide's illegal vote-counting methods fomented the opposition of the Democratic Convergence and undermined his mandate to rule. By 2004 violent opposition to Aristide engulfed the country, forcing him to step down as president. Yet for all of the conflict in Haiti between 2000 and 2004, there is scant evidence that it was a destination country for individuals trafficked into sexual exploitation from overseas.

The UN in Haiti

In February 2004 the Security Council adopted Resolution 1529 authorizing the deployment of the Multinational Interim Force (MIF) to Haiti. When the Security Council passed Resolution 1542 in April 2004, MIF became the United Nations Stabilization Mission in Haiti (MINUSTAH). Initially, MINUSTAH was composed of 6,700 UN peacekeepers, but by 2009 there were nearly 9,000 UN peacekeepers in Haiti (United Nations Stabilization Mission in Haiti 2011).

Examining the UN's democratic identity and the opportunities it possesses to affect human trafficking in Haiti sheds light on the various ways IOs can affect human trafficking. With respect to the UN there are two separate identities to consider—the UN and MINUSTAH. Recall that Pevehouse and Russett (2006) found that when states share membership in densely democratic IOs, there is a lower likelihood of militarized disputes between them, and those that do engage in militarized disputes are less likely to escalate to war. Does a strong commitment to democracy among IO members also reduce the probability that agents of the IO will contribute to human rights violations?

The United Nations is the most diverse, representative IO in existence. There are currently 191 members of the UN with varying degrees of commitment to democracy. Figure 8.1 compares composite democratic indicators for the UN, MINUSTAH, and the OAS and demonstrates that the UN is the least democratically dense of the three.[7] These scores are drawn from the Polity IV Project and range from a +10, suggesting that the state is very democratic, through –10, suggesting that the state is very autocratic. The average of all UN member states is only 3.4. This situates the UN in the

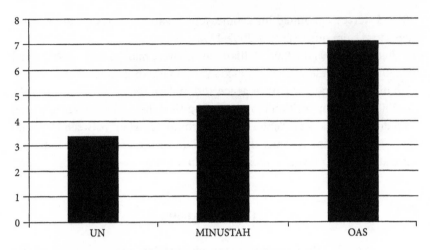

Figure 8.1. Average level of democracy among member states

anocracy category. Vreeland suggests that anocracies have "a mix of institutional characteristics, some democratic and others distinctively authoritarian" (2008, 404). Examples of anocracies include Pakistan, Yemen, and Nigeria. The UN simply cannot be considered a democratically dense IO that will consistently promote liberal, cosmopolitan values.

Though the UN may lack democratic density, this IO can and does act in ways that promote human rights. Did UN members overcome this limitation and take affirmative steps to stop human trafficking between 2000 and 2004, just prior to MINUSTAH's arrival in Haiti? The UN General Assembly passed an important protocol—the Protocol to Prevent, Suppress, and Punish Trafficking in Persons in 2000. The protocol entered into force in 2003 and represents the first global initiative to define human trafficking and emphasize the human rights of trafficking victims. The General Assembly followed the protocol with a series of other resolutions that called attention to the causes and consequences of human trafficking.[8] Though the democratic density of the UN is comparatively low, member states passed numerous resolutions suggesting that the institution was cognizant of the severe human rights violations resulting from human trafficking. Unfortunately, this awareness did not permeate MINUSTAH's mission directives.

MINUSTAH had a slightly higher democratic density than the UN General Assembly at 4.6, also situating MINUSTAH among anocracies. MINUSTAH was composed of troops from fifty-one different countries. The top four troop-contributing countries were Brazil, Uruguay, Nepal, and Sri Lanka. The vast representation of Sri Lanka in MINUSTAH became a serious problem because these troops had not been socialized to standards of behavior that observers might expect of troops hailing from democratic states. Not all troops hailing from democratic regimes will protect human rights, while those hailing from nondemocracies will not necessarily violate human rights. However, the behavior of the Sri Lankan troop contingent in Haiti suggests that they lacked training that would have prevented them from engaging in abuse abroad.

Socialization at home is particularly important with regard to MINUSTAH troops because the UN Peacekeeping Office did not issue instructions to UN peacekeepers regarding sexual exploitation of local populations prior to 2005.[9] MINUSTAH's explicit purpose was to restore order to a country that was rapidly descending into chaos in 2004. The Security Council Resolution authorizing MINUSTAH's deployment identifies the purpose of the mission as stabilizing the country to facilitate the provision of humanitarian assistance (United Nations Security Council 2004). The single mention of human rights in the resolution calls upon Haitians to respect one another's human rights but suggests that preventing human rights violations was not high on the list of MINUSTAH priorities (ibid.).

The ability to send a large, multinational peacekeeping force into conflict zones enhances the UN's ability to impact human rights in mission countries. MINUSTAH was initially composed of 6,700 troops, and those numbers eventually swelled to 9,000. This significant opportunity to impact human trafficking, coupled with a low democratic density and mixed commitment to prevent sexual exploitation (high commitment among the UN General Assembly, low commitment within MINUSTAH), created a dangerous combination and contributed to an increase in the rate of human trafficking into Haiti in 2004.

There is considerable evidence to suggest that: (1) incidences of rape and sexual exploitation of Haitian women and girls coincided with MINUSTAH's arrival in Haiti, and (2) MINSUTAH peacekeepers were, in many cases, directly responsible for patronizing human trafficking victims. Following the arrival of MINUSTAH, Human Rights Watch and Amnesty International began publicizing the widespread abductions of women and girls, including rape and violence (Amnesty International 2006a, 2006b). These reports do not contain explicit references to human trafficking of individuals for the purpose of sexual exploitation, yet they help to establish that sexual exploitation did rise to a level that drew the attention of these NGOs in the years following MINUSTAH's arrival. In 2005 the U.S. State Department classified Haiti as a Tier 2 country, placing it on the Watch List and noting for the first time that women and girls were being trafficked from the Dominican Republic into Haiti to work as prostitutes (U.S. Department of State 2005).

The International Organization for Migration (IOM) surveyed victims, smugglers, intermediaries, and the heads of human trafficking rings in Haiti in 2005. In all, the IOM interviewed 1,886 people in Haiti associated with human trafficking. Some victims were willing to work as prostitutes for a chance to come to the West, others were promised jobs as maids and were held captive and forced to work as prostitutes upon their arrival in Port-au-Prince (International Organization for Migration 2006a). The State Department and the IOM were so concerned about the growing human trafficking problem in Haiti by 2006 that they sponsored a special conference in Port-au-Prince to raise awareness about it (International Organization for Migration 2006b).

By 2007 the State Department directly implicated UN peacekeepers in the sexual exploitation of women and girls trafficked into Haiti from the Dominican Republic: "Dominican women and girls are trafficked into Haiti for commercial sexual exploitation. There are reports that Dominican women are trafficked into Haitian brothels serving UN peacekeepers" (U.S. Department of State 2007a). MINUSTAH mission directors did not offer training to prevent sexual exploitation to the 9,000 peacekeepers they deployed to Haiti. By 2007, this oversight bore tragic consequences—more than 100 Sri Lankan peacekeepers were expelled from Haiti for paying for sex with women and children (United Nations News Centre 2007). The second-in-command as well as two battalion commanders were among the Sri Lankan peacekeepers sent home. The UN Office of Internal Oversight and the Sri Lankan government investigated the scandal, but their findings remain confidential. Other UN agencies have spoken out against growing evidence of sexual exploitation by UN peacekeepers. In 2007, the UN special rapporteur on torture, Manfred Nowak, argued that the UN needed stricter standards for selecting peacekeepers. He suggested that peacekeepers from nations with questionable human rights records might engage in the same crimes abroad that they would at home (British Broadcasting Corporation 2007).

Prior to MINUSTAH's arrival there is no evidence to suggest that women and girls were being trafficked into Haiti to work in the sex industry.

Following MINUSTAH's deployment, these reports increased considerably. This increase is directly related to the arrival of MINUSTAH, a force composed of troops not subject to training on sexual exploitation and many hailing from countries with weak human rights records. Despite the UN's commitment to preventing human trafficking, MINUSTAH lacked a similar commitment and, when given the opportunity, UN peacekeepers patronized trafficking victims, thus contributing to the expansion of the practice in Haiti.

Democracy and the Anti-trafficking Initiatives at the OAS Between 2000 and 2004

In contrast to the UN, the OAS is a densely democratic IO with a strong commitment to promoting democracy and preventing human trafficking. Though more limited than MINUSTAH in its ability to directly affect human trafficking conditions, the OAS held anti-trafficking conferences, organized and funded innovative research on human trafficking in the region, and sent bureaucrats to investigate human rights conditions in Haiti.

OAS member states had a higher democratic density than the UN General Assembly or MINUSTAH in 2004. At 7.1, OAS members are classified as democratic, making it the only IO considered here to be capable of breaking the democratic threshold. The OAS has also aggressively defended democracy in the Western hemisphere since adopting the Santiago Commitment in 1991 (Organization of American States General Assembly 1991). Under the terms of the Santiago Commitment, OAS members may intervene in sovereign member states to defend democracy when it is imperiled. This support for democracy is not rhetorical—immediately following their adoption of the Santiago Commitment, OAS members intervened in Haiti in 1991, in Peru in 1992, and in Guatemala in 1993. While the OAS's democratic identity suggests that its members possess a strong commitment to democracy and human rights, the impact of this IO is curtailed by its inability to deploy troops. Whereas the UN deployed MINUSTAH to Haiti, the OAS sent a bureaucratic mission, the OAS Special Mission to Strengthen Democracy in Haiti. At its peak in 2004, the OAS Special Mission was composed of twenty-three bureaucrats (Stockholm International Peace Research Institute 2010).

The OAS commitment to democracy permeates the institution's approach to human rights and human trafficking. Following the 2000 adoption of the UN protocol, the OAS convened "The Plan of the Third Summit of the Americas." OAS members moved swiftly at the summit to express their concern about human trafficking and their commitment to exchange information to prevent the rights violations associated with the practice (Inter-American Commission on Women Assembly of Delegates 2002).

The Inter-American Commission on Women (CIM), a specialized organization of the OAS, emerged as a key player in shaping the OAS's approach to human trafficking. Though the CIM did not have a physical presence in Haiti, its advocacy drew attention to human trafficking in the region. Following the Third Summit of the OAS, the CIM, the Inter-American Children's Institute, and the International Human Rights Law Institute embarked upon the most comprehensive study of human trafficking in Latin America, titled "In Modern Bondage."[10] The report is pioneering in its scope—relying on field investigations in nine Latin American countries to identify risk factors contributing to trafficking, actors involved in the practice, and evaluations of country response mechanisms.

Langberg (2005) argues that this study sparked debates throughout the OAS and ultimately contributed to concrete changes in the OAS's approach to human trafficking. The report led the OAS to reconceptualize human trafficking as a crime and a violation of human rights (Langberg 2005, 136; Inter-American Commission on Women Assembly of Delegates 2002). Following the publication of the report in 2002, the OAS General Assembly passed two resolutions that instructed various OAS bureaucracies to collect information about trafficking, put on conferences to combat the practice, and establish the "OAS Coordinator on the Issue of Trafficking in Persons, Especially Women, Adolescents, and Children" (Organization of American States General Assembly 2003, 2004). The OAS also created the Anti-Trafficking in Persons Section to support the efforts of the coordinator.[11] Prior to the OAS's arrival in Haiti in 2004, the institution made a strong commitment both to human rights and to combating human trafficking; this commitment informed the OAS's efforts as they entered a country that was rapidly descending into paralyzing violence.

Human Trafficking and the OAS in Haiti: 2005–2007

By 2005 political stability in Haiti was deteriorating rapidly. Latortue's government aimed to pacify the country and disarm the opposition (Dupuy

2007, 179). Disarming Aristide's supporters was a strategy to suppress political opposition. Latortue enjoyed the full economic and political backing of the U.S. government, which he used to partner with the former soldiers responsible for ousting Aristide. Dupuy (2007) argues that Latortue used the same violent tactics that Aristide had used throughout Haiti, but Latortue was more effective in his violence because he had more resources. Civilians, members of the police, MINUSTAH troops, and journalists were among the approximately 15,000 people killed in Haiti between March of 2004 and early 2006 (Dupuy 2007, 189). While Latortue's government was pre-occupied with armed conflict to suppress Aristide supporters and retain power, the OAS worked to limit rapidly accelerating human rights violations and human trafficking into Haiti.

Beginning in 2005, various OAS entities organized conferences to educate the Haitian government about human trafficking. These activities suggest that OAS bureaucrats were actively socializing Haitian authorities about anti-trafficking procedures. The OAS sponsored the Anti-Trafficking in Persons Capacity Building Project in Haiti in October 2005. This conference engaged the Haitian Anti-trafficking Police Unit, training officers about human trafficking and enhancing the capacity of the force. The OAS worked with the International Organization for Migration and the U.S. government in 2006 to run "Together in the Fight Against Human Trafficking in Haiti." In attendance were members of the Haitian police force and representatives from several Haitian government ministries—Women's Affairs, Justice and Public Security, Social Affairs, and Labor and the Ministry of the Interior. Haitian government representatives and members of civil society worked with IO representatives to consider solutions for eliminating human trafficking. In March 2005, the OAS brought representatives from Caribbean governments together to discuss counter-trafficking strategies; Haitian representatives traveled to Washington, D.C., to participate. This was the first time that representatives from Caribbean states met to discuss human trafficking in the region.[12]

The OAS mission and the UN mission in Haiti were not entirely distinct. These actors worked together to stabilize Haiti and to promote free and fair elections (Organization of American States 2004). Despite the OAS's efforts and their collaboration with the UN, levels of human trafficking into Haiti increased after 2004. There is, however, no evidence that OAS bureaucrats patronized sex workers or contributed to their sexual exploitation in Haiti. While UN peacekeepers were being expelled for patronizing prostitutes and

women trafficked into sexual exploitation, the OAS was running conferences, conducting field research, and working to highlight alarming patterns of abuse. The Inter-American Commission on Human Rights (IACHR)
stopped short of directly implicating MINUSTAH in the human rights violations in Haiti following their 2007 visit. However, IACHR Commissioner
Gutierrez Trejo wrote an addendum noting the oversights in the IACHR's
official report:

> The news received and the files lying dormant in the Commission
> record barbaric acts committed by MINUSTAH and the involve-
> ment of this occupying force in cases of systematic violence. It was
> categorically asserted that the occupying forces lent support to those
> perpetrating persecutions, kidnappings, cruel and degrading treat-
> ment, illegitimate deprivation of liberty, and disregard for the physi-
> cal, mental and moral integrity of persons in a context bereft of
> guarantees for the exercise of any rights. In other circumstances, the
> Commission was also told that the occupation force failed to act to
> prevent such acts from being perpetrated. (Inter-American Com-
> mission on Human Rights 2008)[13]

Rethinking Global Governance

There are some important similarities between the UN and the OAS missions to Haiti. In both instances, members of these IOs deployed their agents
in the hopes of stabilizing Haiti. The resolutions approving the deployment
of MINUSTAH and the OAS Special Mission to Strengthen Democracy in
Haiti highlight the good intentions that these IOs possessed prior to their
arrival. Upon arriving in Haiti, the UN and the OAS collaborated on a number of projects such as monitoring elections and promoting stability.

Regardless, these cases reveal that an IO's democratic identity and commitment to combating human trafficking prior their deployment can influence IO
effects on human trafficking. The UN's low democratic density and MINUS-
TAH's weak commitment to human rights undermined their ability to
produce positive human rights outcomes. MINUSTAH peacekeepers were implicated in egregious human rights violations, including patronizing victims of
trafficking for sexual exploitation. The OAS, however, arrived in Port-au-Prince
with a stronger commitment to democracy and an already sustained commit-

ment to curbing human trafficking in Latin America. The OAS made concerted efforts to socialize Haitian authorities about human trafficking, and
though the impact of these efforts was minimal, the OAS, at the very least, did
not contribute to the further deterioration of human rights in Haiti. The diver-
gent effects of these IOs on human trafficking in Haiti are therefore related to
their democratic identity.

Democratic identity alone is still insufficient to explain the differences
in the effects of the UN and the OAS on human trafficking. I have suggested
that the impact of these IOs is also dependent upon their opportunity. The
OAS sent a bureaucratic mission to Haiti, held human trafficking conferences, and sponsored conferences that were attended by Haitian authorities.
The activities of the OAS are consistent with standard IO activities that analysts might have predicted. A few bureaucrats on the ground in Haiti can
slowly change accepted practices and teach the government about effective
legal mechanisms for reducing trafficking, but they are unlikely to have
demonstrably large effects. Without a doubt, OAS efforts were eclipsed by
those of MINUSTAH. The 9,000 UN peacekeepers that made up MINUS-
TAH had the opportunity to make a large imprint on Haitian politics, for
better or for worse. Unfortunately, all the evidence examined above suggests
that MINUSTAH exacerbated already tragic human rights conditions on
the ground in Haiti and diminished the efforts of the OAS to combat trafficking.

One might argue that MINUSTAH was a particularly problematic UN
mission whose composition was not representative of UN missions more
generally. Although MINUSTAH experienced a series of challenges in Haiti,
its composition is actually quite consistent with the other UN missions. The
UN peacekeeping budget derives primarily from the assessments of wealthy
states—in 2010 the United States, Japan, the UK, Germany, and France were
the top five contributors (United Nations Department of Peacekeeping Operations 2010). However, the five countries contributing the highest number
of uniformed personnel to UN peacekeeping missions in 2010 were Bangla-
desh, Pakistan, India, Nigeria, and Egypt (ibid.). Neither MINUSTAH's composition nor the allegations of sexual abuse against its peacekeepers are
unique. Similar claims of abuse at the hands of peacekeepers have emerged
from the UN Mission in the Congo (MONUC), the UN Mission in Sierra
Leone (UNAMSIL), and the UN Mission in Kosovo (UNMIK).[14] Though the
UN cannot easily alter its democratic density, member states can nonetheless
take greater care to train peacekeepers about sexual exploitation in mission

countries, promote awareness through the UN about trafficking more generally, and deploy peacekeeping forces composed of troops from various types of states.

This chapter highlights a tragic trade-off that continues in Haiti—the international community deploys peacekeepers to suppress violence, yet sacrifices the safety and well-being of the victims who are sexually exploited by those peacekeepers. As the international community heaps more responsibility onto institutions of global governance like the UN and the OAS, we must critically assess the effects these actors have on human rights. Whereas the UN arrival in Haiti had devastating effects on human rights, agents from the OAS entered Port-au-Prince with a mandate to eradicate trafficking and to promote human rights. The OAS's influence in Haiti demonstrates that a rights-based approach to global governance is possible but requires careful attention to the power dynamics between IO agents and domestic populations. This chapter demands that we rethink our solutions to human trafficking because IOs cannot be relied upon to intervene on behalf of human trafficking victims.

PART III

From Rescue to Rights

Chapter 9

Making Human Rights Accessible: The Role of Governments in Trafficking and Migrant Labor Exploitation

Christien van den Anker

Introduction

There is a strong basis for the argument that freedom from slavery is a universal right, as it is protected in the Universal Declaration of Human Rights 1948 as well as numerous subsequent treaties that have been ratified widely. Yet in practice, contemporary forms of slavery are widespread, and despite international and state-based action, NGO pressure, and increasing criminal proceedings against employers, the consistent violation of freedom from slavery raises the question: What makes governments reluctant or incapable to protect this right effectively within and across their own borders?

Human rights discourse is traditionally divided over the role of nation-states in their implementation. Everyone acknowledges that human rights are a responsibility of governments toward their own citizens. Yet most human rights advocates also emphasize the role of other governments toward people whose rights are violated by their own governments. It is this cosmopolitan approach to human rights that I draw on for my argument with regard to the normative assessment of the role of governments in combating contemporary slavery and therewith making freedom from slavery accessible as a human right for all (van den Anker 2005).

Despite the abolition of the slave trade in 1807, there are indications that contemporary forms of slavery, including migrant labor exploitation, are occurring on an increasing scale and in industrialized countries as well as in majority rural economies (van den Anker 2007; Craig 2010; Lee 2007). One of the forms of contemporary slavery that has received widespread attention is human trafficking for sexual or labor exploitation. In this chapter I argue that a cosmopolitan approach to human rights would contribute to prevention of trafficking in human beings more effectively than a national approach. I show that national governments are currently complicit in the inaccessibility of human rights for noncitizens, which leaves these people vulnerable to exploitation and contemporary forms of slavery.

In order to show these links between making human rights accessible and ending migrant exploitation and trafficking, let me sketch some of the recent developments in research, policy, and practice around human trafficking and forced labor. Recent research indicates that human trafficking occurs not only in the sex industry but also in a long list of other industries (van den Anker and Doomernik 2006). Some of the industries in Europe in which cases of trafficking were found recently include construction, shipping, agriculture, food packaging, hospitality, domestic work and care, prostitution, and criminal activities such as forced begging (van den Anker and Anti-Slavery International 2006). Another sector with a lot of trafficking and migrant labor exploitation is domestic work (Anderson 2004; Rocha 2009). The international attention for migrant labor exploitation has grown after some highly distressing cases were reported, such as the death of twenty-three Chinese cocklepickers in Morecombe Bay, who drowned due to lack of care by gangmasters. Their families are still paying off the debt to the Chinese facilitators (Morecambe Victims Trust Fund 2009). In the UK the Gangmasters Licensing Authority is now addressing the issue of migrant labor exploitation in the shellfish, agriculture, food packing, and forestry sectors (Balch, Brindley, and Scott 2009; Geddes, Scott, and Nielsen 2007). Yet despite calls from the construction industry, other sectors are not regulated to the same extent.

The debate on trafficking and migrant labor exploitation was focused for a long time on the moral acceptability of prostitution. Yet the question of how to support all trafficked persons needs to address why people's options to enter and leave a job are restricted, and not whether or not it is moral for them to do the work they do (Jordan 2002). Now there is more attention for forced labor and exploitation in other industries, and moral questions are shifting to whether or not migrants for whom an exploitative situation is still an improvement on circumstances they left behind at home have a "right to be exploited" (Szulecka forthcoming).

The most recent international law in the UN system on trafficking in persons refers to both the sex industry and other industries. The Protocol to Prevent, Suppress, and Punish Trafficking in Persons, especially Women and Children, supplementing the United Nations Convention against Transnational Organized Crime, places a duty on governments to harmonize their laws in the area with the so-called Palermo protocol (Ould 2004). More recently, the Council of Europe Convention on Action Against Trafficking in Human Beings uses the same definition as the Palermo Protocol. This convention takes a human rights approach and introduces a thirty-day reflection period for trafficked persons. The Convention on the Rights of Migrant Workers and Their Families is also a relevant instrument in fighting migrant labor exploitation. Yet, this is one of the least ratified conventions in the UN system (Kaye 2003). There are many other human rights instruments being violated in trafficking cases (Weissbrodt 2008; Obokata 2005). International human rights law has therefore assisted in putting migrant labor exploitation on the agenda, but it is still mainly focused on national measures, which, as I will argue below, creates barriers to the accessibility of migrant rights.

International bodies (European Commission Directorate-General Justice) and NGOs (Kaye 2003) increasingly advocate a human rights approach to human trafficking, yet large parts of the media, the police and levels of government still focus on the criminalization of trafficking by prosecuting both traffickers and "illegal" migrants (van den Anker 2006). Despite this focus on criminal justice in trafficking cases, researchers are increasingly noticing that transnational organized crime networks may not play the largest role in the trafficking of human beings (van Liempt 2007; van den Anker 2008).

Human rights are widely viewed as the most basic norm for everyone, notwithstanding residency status. Human rights approaches to trafficking for forced labor are of high importance in preventing trafficked persons from being deported on the basis of migration law violations. In this chapter I will argue that the nationally based mix of social justice matrices as embodied in overlapping restrictive and complex migration, labor, and welfare regimes, creates vulnerability for noncitizens that prevents many of them from accessing their human rights. Although liberal nationalists do not endorse labor exploitation, in practice nationalism is a root cause for the lack of accessibility of human rights for many migrants. Cosmopolitan models of global justice inspire a principled defense of human rights for noncitizens within the borders of nation-states, as well as long-term initiatives to create global equality, which will reduce pressure to migrate as well as enhance safe migration with fair opportunities everywhere.

My argument first assesses the impact of migration regimes, then moves on to labor regimes, and finally to the welfare system. First, in migration regimes, the categorization of different forms of migration (trafficking, smuggling, or legal migration) and the consequent labeling of migrants into migrant workers, victims of trafficking, asylum seekers, refugees, and undocumented, leads to the exclusion of large numbers of migrants who cannot access the protection of their human rights. Although some migrant-rights activists and scholars are critical of the trafficking concept, I argue that as long as this concept is used in a way that shows its connection to the structural factors of the exploitation of migrants, it can be useful to raise wider awareness and increase the political room to address the issue of labor exploitation.

Second, I look at labor regimes as a form of creating accessibility for human rights. A human-rights approach would in theory enhance the equal treatment of exploited persons, whereas due to the current national basis for restrictive and complex labor regimes, these rights are not accessible to all. Moreover, some schools of thought now argue that in working toward implementation of labor rights for all, migrant rights will be protected better, too. In practice, however, migrants are vulnerable in particular ways to exploitation that make it necessary to highlight their cases in order to make human rights accessible to them.

Finally, human rights as expressed in the welfare arrangements in nation-states increasingly exclude vulnerable groups of noncitizens even from basic rights such as housing, health care, and education. Due to the fear of creating a two-tiered system in the decades-old welfare debate, there is currently only destitution for those who fall outside of legalized work or welfare protection. This situation violates the basic human right to an adequate standard of living. The question needs to be asked if the goal of universal access to welfare systems is feasible if the price is exclusion of many noncitizens, or whether a graduation of entitlements is better (van Dam 2009).

A cosmopolitan approach to human rights would in theory resolve the issue of migrant labor exploitation. Yet a cosmopolitan model of global justice as distribution between states paradoxically denies the role of state boundaries and nationalism as factors in the creation of inequality for migrants in the first place. It is cosmopolitanism *within* boundaries that needs to be developed, as well as a vision of the accessibility of human rights wherever people reside or move. This means that cosmopolitanism also needs to engage with the global economic system of production that creates the flows of labor in the current transnational capitalism. Here I argue that a cosmopolitan approach would assist in long-term prevention of trafficking for forced labor and other forms of migrant labor exploitation, especially if we recognize that cosmopolitanism also entails duties toward people without citizenship status within a country. I show that national governments need to acknowledge that their current restrictive and complex migration and labor regimes and their exclusive welfare regimes make them complicit in the withholding of human rights from the most vulnerable people.

Migration Regimes

Complex and restrictive migration regimes contribute to migrants' vulnerability to trafficking and other forms of exploitation. This reduces the protection of human rights in destination countries. It is no coincidence that the growth in trafficking has taken place during a period where there has been an increasing international demand for migrant workers, which has not been adequately acknowledged or facilitated. Lack of regular migration opportunities to take up work in other countries and the fact that many migrants are looking for work abroad as a means of survival, rather than an opportunity to improve their standards of living, has left migrants with little choice but to rely on smugglers or traffickers to access these jobs (Kaye 2003).

The regimes governing migration in Europe have become stricter in how many people they welcome and in what categories of people have free legal access to border crossing (Doomernik and Jandl 2008). The stricter application of the 1951 Refugee Convention and subsequent agreements between European countries about the legitimate treatment of refugees has made access to sanctuary harder to obtain (Seabrook 2009). The consequent culture of disbelief that refugees encounter creates additional vulnerability for them to be labeled as rejected asylum seekers and threatened with deportation or destitution (Khosravi 2010b). The decreasing option to travel through regular channels means more people resort to the services of smugglers (PICUM 2007). Human rights have therefore become less of a reality in traditionally strong welfare states in Europe.

Trafficking is often associated with forced transportation, and sometimes this is true. However, more often migrants decide themselves to travel, either to flee oppression or as part of an employment strategy looking for a job abroad. Without regular channels to do so, they are dependent on the services of others, who may assist them to cross borders for a fee (smugglers) or end up exploiting them in the country of destination (traffickers). The hold over trafficked persons is often a mixture of threat, violence, debt bondage, and deception (van den Anker and Doomernik 2006).

Trafficking is sometimes called an unhelpful concept, as labor exploitation is also high among undocumented migrants, whether or not caused by illegal border crossing or "forced" migration. Without access to the regular labor market, they are forced to take on jobs that no one else wants to do, for less pay and without say over hours or place of work. Often substandard accommodation is part of the deal (Khosravi 2010a). The distinction between smugglers and traffickers is officially very clear: traffickers force people to travel and to work under exploitative circumstances after ending up in the country of destination; smugglers provide a service for people who want to cross borders illegally. In reality these distinctions are not as clear-cut (van Liempt 2010). There may be all sorts of pressures from smugglers on their "clients," and only afterward does it become clear whether labor exploitation is involved. Yet, even if the group responsible for transport and border crossings does not provide a link with exploitative labor, migrants are often vulnerable to exploitation even if they enter the country legally. There is a trajectory of compliance where many migrants are semicompliant with regulations and therefore vulnerable to exploitative employers threatening denunciation to the authorities, which would mean deportation. Many people also move in and out of compliance—for example, when temporary visas run out or students work longer hours than allowed on their student visa (Anderson and Rogaly 2004).

In addition to the restrictive nature of the migration regimes in Europe, their complexity increases vulnerability to exploitation and forced labor. For example, the UK registration scheme (UK Border Agency 2011) for citizens of newly acceded EU-member states such as the Czech Republic, Estonia, Hungary, Latvia, Lithuania, Poland, Slovakia, and Slovenia requires handing over documents to employers, who can then use them to blackmail workers. All the different forms of leave to remain in the UK also mean that people are often unsure what their rights are. And when they seek help—for example, from the Citizens Advice Bureau—they may be registered there in quite some detail but not recognized as victim of trafficking.

Finally, migration regimes have treated trafficked persons and exploited migrant workers mainly as people committing "immigration crimes," that is, they are regularly detained and deported (van der Leun 2010; Vollmer 2010). In several European countries, such as Belgium, the Netherlands, and Italy, there has been for some time the possibility of acquiring a visa to cover a reflection period (Wylie and McRedmond 2010). This is usually tied to then becoming a witness in a case against the trafficker. The European Convention on Action against Trafficking makes such a reflection period Europewide. Some organizations have called for asylum for victims of trafficking on humanitarian grounds, but others are saying the asylum process is too traumatizing. In Ireland, where visas are tied to employers, the Migrants Rights Centre Ireland has successfully campaigned for a bridging visa to allow the exploited migrant to search for a new job. The protection measures for trafficked persons currently are not widely implemented and are often focused on the experiences of sex workers rather than migrant workers in other industries. They lack space and proper models of care. Moreover, the larger numbers of migrant workers who are exploited without ticking the boxes of trafficking for forced labor do not have access to protection. The condition of deportability creates the pressures to accept exploitative work, yet also prevents access to human rights (Khosravi 2010b).

In short, complex and restrictive migration regimes are exacerbating labor exploitation in general and trafficking for forced labor in particular. The categorization of different forms of migration (trafficking, smuggling, or legal migration) and the consequent labeling of migrants into migrant workers, victims of trafficking, asylum seekers, refugees, and undocumented leads to the exclusion of large numbers of migrants who cannot access the protection of their human rights. This shows up as a lack of human rights protection in destination countries that have obligations under international law to guarantee those rights.

Labor Laws

National governments also play a large role in setting the parameters of regimes governing labor practices. Social rights are often understood in a narrow sense as governing access to welfare, yet labor laws are also important for human rights protection. I understand a regime of labor laws to cover both the right to work in a country and the circumstances under which work is done, that is, health and safety, working hours, and so on. Histori-cally, labor rights have been included in the earlier documents as part of human rights doctrine. The Universal Declaration of Human Rights 1948 already includes them; for example, Article 23 gives the rights to work, free choice of employment, just and favorable conditions and protection against unemployment, the right to equal pay for equal work, fair remuneration, and to form or join trade unions. The International Labor Organization (ILO) has played an important role in their specification and implementa-tion. ILO conventions and recommendations cover a broad range of subjects concerning work, employment, social security, social policy, and related human rights (International Labor Organization 2011).

Complex and restrictive labor laws hamper the accessibility of human rights for migrants in several ways. In countries like Ireland, Portugal, and the UK, where visas can be tied to specific employers, migrant workers strug-gle, as they cannot change jobs legally even if they suffer exploitation, be-cause they are no longer entitled to a residence permit without the job the visa was based on. If they are exploited, this means it is very hard to leave; and if they are not, they are more at risk of becoming badly treated as they are in a situation of dependency. Often in trafficking cases, there is multiple dependency on employers combined with social isolation (Migrant Rights Centre Ireland 2006).

Inspections of labor laws governing the circumstances at work are impor-tant to trafficked persons, as they often lead to detection of labor exploitation. However, currently trafficked persons and others who are exploited by em-ployers risk deportation or job loss instead of rehabilitation of the circum-stances under which they work (Migrant Rights Centre Ireland 2006). Sweden is now granting the right to work to asylum seekers. It will be interesting to watch if this has a positive effect on a reduction in the number of cases of labor exploitation. Labor rights illuminate the ways international law, even when translated into national laws, remains dependent on enforcement strategies at the local level. Yet if countries do not appoint enough labor inspectors, labor rights remain inaccessible to migrants who are vulnerable to exploitation.

In some countries, there are reported agreements between the police and employers that not all workers without permits will be taken away in a raid. This illustrates that economic pragmatism is leaving migrant workers vulnerable to exploitation. Political will is of high importance here. The pri-vate sphere of work is especially vulnerable, but so are industries where workers can be isolated in rural premises. There is an important regulatory and enforcement role here for governments, which is currently not adequately implemented. Might this be due to economic pressures, too?

The third leg of this incentive triangle is, then, the sending country, which has an incentive to receive remittances and to avoid investing in return migrants who cut short their earning potential abroad. The role of the governments in sending countries must not be underestimated. The current economic downturn has already resulted in large numbers of migrants returning to countries like Moldova, for example, where they often end up unemployed and in need of state support. The investment of such powerful interests in the existence of labor exploitation means a strong stance is required, with the political courage to follow up violations of what are universal human rights and an important part of any social justice agenda.

Welfare Regimes

Traditionally social rights were seen as most closely tied to welfare regimes. Migrants' access to welfare state provisions depends on two main aspects: how you define the welfare state and what migration status or level of citizenship the person holds. These often depend on position in a family or marital status, too. Researchers are increasingly debating the access to social rights of noncitizens, including people who have been illegalized (Cholewinski 2005; Cuperus et al. 2003; Faist 2009).

Many European countries have sharpened their restrictions to access to welfare provisions (Minderhoud 2004). They have done this by narrowing their conception of what comes under the welfare state to include mainly pensions, child benefit, and collective insurance for disability, long-term illness, and unemployment due to no fault of one's own. In the earlier debates on the merits of a universal or a targeted welfare state, subsidies to housing, health, education, libraries, arts, and other provisions to share access to culture would have been counted under welfare provisions, too. These benefits are now accessible to decreasing numbers of people. Individualization, privatization, and increased surveillance (through database connections, through duties of identification, and by giving social institutions the role of gatekeeper) cause numerous human rights violations for those who are exploited but have no way of demanding redress, as they risk deportation. Undocumented migrants in Sweden are excluded from the wider benefits of the welfare state, and they are at risk of frequent moves and exclusion from education and health care, sometimes resulting in unnecessary death (Khosravi 2010a). This is a clear gap in the fulfillment of social rights.

The effect on vulnerable migrants of their exclusion from welfare provision in both senses is that (1) their isolation increases and therefore the risk of being exploited and (2) the likelihood of finding ways out of an exploitative situation decreases. Being included as workers yet excluded as citizens leaves migrants dependent on their internationally guaranteed human rights. This results in interesting contradictions. The human rights courts have several times decided that states acted unlawfully by using excessive force during deportations and have therefore created a situation where states have sovereignty over who resides but need to respect the human rights of those who do. Lack of access to health care in country of origin is a reason to prevent deportation; so the question needs to be asked how it can be legal that undocumented migrants are excluded from these services in Sweden and other European countries. The Committee on Social Rights of the Council of Europe, which monitors the application of the European Social Charter, ruled that "legislation or practice that denies entitlement to medical assistance to foreign nationals, within the territory of a State Party, even if they are there illegally, is contrary to the Charter" (PICUM 2007).

In summary, restrictive rules of access to welfare in the widest sense leave exploited migrants vulnerable to their employers, as they do not have other options. In the wake of not having access to government resources, migrants are excluded from basic human rights such as access to health care, education, and suitable housing. In combination with the complex and restrictive migration and labor regimes, this leaves many migrants—whether officially trafficked or subject to labor exploitation without ticking the boxes of being trafficked—with limited access to their human rights as protected in international law. There is a wide gap between the obligations of states under international human rights law and the current implementation and enforcement through social policy of welfare regimes. The inaccessibility of social rights for several categories of migrants enhances the vulnerability to contemporary forms of slavery and other forms of exploitation.

Cosmopolitanism and Human Rights

"Cosmopolitanism" is a concept used more widely recently and describes various things for different debates (van den Anker 2010). Here I use the term as the branch of political theory that holds that the scope of morality is global and therefore the boundaries of nation-states should not determine the reach of principles of social justice. Another way of putting it is that cosmopolitans share an assumption of human equality as the basis for moral reasoning about global politics. Debates on global justice, open borders, and global democracy are all places where cosmopolitan positions are taken. Within cosmopolitan circles there are generally three main views. First, global social justice requires global redistribution of resources so that a situation with less economic inequality can be reached (Moellendorf 2009). Within an egalitarian perspective, the ultimate vision is one of a global progressive taxation scheme, but in the absence of the necessary infrastructure, cosmopolitans settle for some global tax, which is paid by governments into a fund for development (Pogge 2008). Another cosmopolitan proposal is the compensation fund for slavery (Van Bueren 2004) or an individual tax on speculative currency transactions, such as the Tobin tax. This is a tax proposed by Canadian economist James Tobin that would prevent the excesses of currency speculation (Dowling 2004).

Second, there are those who argue for open borders or a feasible variation that allows people to move freely and therefore have access to labor markets and the option to send remittances home (Carens 1987; Verlinden 2010). In fact, remittances are now so high on the list of sources of income in some countries that international development funds certainly do not compete—and in some cases nor do foreign investments (Phillips 2009).

Third, there are those who argue for global democracy and institutionalized global citizenship (Marchetti 2008). In Marchetti's view, the democratic deficit has grown due to globalization, and there is a moral argument that all citizens should be included in decisions that have a public scope (ibid., 1). Similarly, transnational migration suggests that a more inclusive system of decision making is required. "Migrants feel structurally excluded, and continuously claim the right of a balanced mechanism through which their entitlements could be weighed with those of the residents in a more legitimate way" (ibid., 81).

These debates have so far generated quite separate literatures, and where they refer to one another, they are often positioned as choices for focus of energies. Yet, it may make more sense to try to develop an integrated vision on them, as this would bring together a comprehensive picture of global governance, including social justice and migration. All three cosmopolitan positions have implications for the realization of the rights of exploited migrants.

This is not to say that there are no useful national measures to be taken. It also does not mean that noncosmopolitans are justifying exploitation. Yet, although liberal nationalists (Miller 2007) do not endorse labor exploitation, in practice nationalism as the basis to construct migration, labor, and welfare regimes is a root cause for the lack of accessibility to human rights for many migrants. This is not only an unintended consequence; there is a moral argument for excluding "others." Miller chillingly asks about the African migrants risking their lives climbing the fences built in Melilla, the Spanish enclave in North Africa: "Surely they must understand that this is not the way to get into Europe. What clearer indication could there be of the proposition that illegal immigrants are not welcome than a double fence up to six meters tall with rolls of razor wire along the top?" (Miller 2007, 3). This type of rhetoric contributes to the justification of the exclusion of migrants even if lives are lost by doing so, which is hardly fitting for a perspective on social justice. This goes against Miller's own commitment to human rights as a basic minimum: "(W)hen human rights go unprotected any agent ... who is able to protect them may in principle bear remedial responsibilities" (Miller 2007, 164).

Cosmopolitan models of global justice are justifications for desired ways of organizing world politics—they are not clear-cut policy solutions. Yet the cosmopolitan principle of equal respect for all provides several ways forward and inspires a principled defense of human rights for noncitizens within the borders of nation-states, as well as for long-term initiatives to create global equality that will reduce pressure to migrate as well as enhance safe migration with fair opportunities everywhere. This tension between cosmopolitan tendencies in the human rights discourse versus nationalist strands has implications for making freedom from slavery an accessible human right for all.

From the perspective of combating trafficking in human beings and migrant labor exploitation, cosmopolitanism can help in several ways. First, it provides a normative and wide-scope perspective from which we can emphasize the need for long-term prevention of trafficking through cross-border and multilateral initiatives on redistribution, social investment, and policy development in areas that enhance trade justice (Manokha 2004). Second, it provides us with a list of principles that would make a difference to the human rights approach to trafficking and migrant labor exploitation. The principles I proposed elsewhere include: respect for the rights of victims; cosmopolitan impartiality (justice for all); respect for the agency of victims; commitment to long-term structural change in the global economy; provision of support to develop viable alternative livelihoods (van den

Anker 2004). These would break through the inherently partly nationalist model of social rights underpinning human rights discourse. The exclusion of "others" becomes unjustifiable in a cosmopolitan model of justice, whether they are "distant others" or living in the same nation-state as the citizens who are within the scope of human rights. Duties for governments are then to develop initiatives that support long-term prevention of trafficking by investing in development, collaborating on global schemes for taxation and debt relief, pushing for global corporate social responsibility and fair trade, and signing up to the UN Convention on Protection of the Rights of Migrant Workers and Their Families. These would also apply to transit countries (Perrin 2010).

One additional angle from which to view cosmopolitanism as relevant to trafficking for forced labor and migrant labor exploitation is global citizenship. Despite some proposals for global democratic institutions that would generate global citizenship in terms of votes and claims, this concept is mostly used as a source of moral duties over and above duties of national citizenship, and it includes solidarity across borders (van den Anker 2002). Yet, there are clearly people who miss out on effective national citizenship and who need solidarity within borders. For example, as discussed earlier in this chapter, in Sweden undocumented migrants are excluded from access to social rights such as education, health care, and housing; they are, however, included in the labor market in practice, which leaves them vulnerable to exploitation without means for redress (Khosravi 2010b). This is true to different extents in other industrialized countries with larger or smaller informal economies and more or less regulation of internal borders. Effective institutionalized global citizenship, as in participation in transnational decision making, would contribute to inclusion of migrants, which would lessen exploitation and increase access to human rights. Moreover, global citizenship in this form could play a role in creating fair opportunities that would lessen the need to undertake risky migration strategies.

Finally, global citizenship as a moral outlook based on hospitality and inclusion of "others" far away or nearby would enhance the accessibility of human rights and social inclusion on all levels of society. This way, persons vulnerable to exploitation due to exclusion would be better protected and would have alternatives open to them. Governments can contribute to making their policies more welcoming to migrants, especially in the most vulnerable categories of undocumented, rejected asylum seekers and trafficked persons. Educating the citizenry on cultural traditions of tolerance and inclusion rather than fighting elections on right-wing anti-immigrant stances would make a big difference to human rights protection.

Conclusion

Developed Western economies (but increasingly also economies in transition and mixed economies) depend on the work of migrant workers. There is a great disparity between the profits these workers generate for these economies, the dependence of whole sectors of economies on the workers, and the level of protection from trafficking and exploitation the benefiting states guarantee for them. In this chapter I argued that the current nationalist models of human rights affecting social policy are lacking not only in practice but also in principle, due to excluding noncitizens. It is the national basis of the mixture of complex and restrictive migration regimes, national labor laws, and limited access to welfare states that leaves migrants vulnerable to trafficking for forced labor and other forms of exploitation. In response to this analysis, I proposed a cosmopolitan approach, which I explained would affect attitudes toward migrants within states as well as beyond them.

I therefore conclude that the best approach toward combating trafficking for forced labor and migrant exploitation in all industries is not just global justice, or open borders, or global democracy. Instead these should *all* be seen as part of one set of principles used as a backdrop for establishing responsibilities for international organizations, states, local authorities, and nonstate actors such as NGOs, businesses, and individuals. Cosmopolitanism means states as well as individuals have duties across borders to assist in making human rights accessible to all at home and abroad. It also means everyone has duties toward people who cannot access human rights due to their migration status. States can make a difference, and they should do so not only to their citizens, but to those who reside in their borders and those who are in need outside of those borders (van den Anker 2010). This means human rights must be accessible to everyone, wherever they reside, and the duty to realize this falls on governments of sending, receiving, and transit countries, toward people residing in their territories as well as toward people vulnerable elsewhere.

Moreover, a cosmopolitan model of global justice limited to redistribution between states paradoxically denies the role of state boundaries and nationalism as factors in the creation of inequality for migrants in the first place. It is cosmopolitanism *within* boundaries that needs to be developed, as well as a vision for the accessibility of human rights wherever people reside or move. This means that cosmopolitanism also needs to engage with the global economic system of production that creates the flows of labor in the current transnational capitalism. National governments need to acknowledge their role in creating the circumstances of injustice in the case of contemporary slavery and related forms of exploitation. They should opt for the creation of the circumstances of social justice for all through every aspect of their governance, but especially in revising migration, labor, and welfare regimes according to human rights principles to make all human rights accessible for all. Only then would they live up to their universal and voluntary obligations of international human rights law, which categorically rules out all forms of slavery past and present.

Chapter 10

Human Rights and Human Trafficking: A Reflection on the Influence and Evolution of the U.S. Trafficking in Persons Reports

Anne Gallagher

Introduction

Until the turn of the present century, the phenomenon of trafficking was of only vague and incidental interest to states and the international community. The traditional concept of trafficking was, by today's standards, extremely narrow: it was generally accepted that only women and children could be trafficked and then only for commercial sexual exploitation. Few states considered themselves directly affected, and at the international level, discussions on trafficking were confined to the margins of the UN human rights system. The changes that have taken place over the last decade are truly astonishing. Trafficking is now the subject of a strong international legal framework. Most states have engaged in substantial legislative, institutional, and procedural reform to take into account new standards and obligations. A unilateral monitoring and evaluation system (the subject of this present chapter) now ensures that the performance of every government with respect to trafficking is subjected to close and critical scrutiny.

The relationship between human rights and human trafficking has been a constant theme in debates and discussions that have surrounded and shaped this new legal and policy environment. Of course, the essential connection between human rights and trafficking is incontestable. Human rights law has, since its earliest days, forcefully asserted the immorality and un-lawfulness of one person appropriating the legal personality, labor, or hu-manity of another. Human rights has battled the demons of discrimination on the basis of race and sex; it has demanded equal or at least certain key rights for aliens; it has condemned and outlawed arbitrary detention, forced labor, debt bondage, forced marriage, and the commercial sexual exploita-tion of children and women; and it has championed freedom of movement and the right to leave and return to one's own country. Despite this distin-guished history, the contemporary response to trafficking has not always been grounded in the firm foundations provided by human rights. For ex-ample, the first treaty on trafficking in more than fifty years, adopted by the UN in 2000, disappointed many human rights advocates by creating a new global prohibition regime in which human rights protections were largely optional (Gallagher 2001a; Chuang 2006). While subsequent legal and policy developments have affirmed the central place of human rights in national, regional, and international responses to trafficking, gaps and weaknesses re-main. It has been shown, for example, that anti-trafficking policies and prac-tices often have a negative and even highly destructive impact on individual rights and freedoms. Of even greater potential significance is the reality that responding to trafficking inevitably involves engagement with controversial and sensitive issues such as labor migration and prostitution. To the extent that common standards and approaches on these issues continue to elude the international community, the global response to trafficking is inevitably partial and compromised.

Concerns about the marginalization of human rights have led to re-peated calls for a "human rights–based approach" to trafficking. A human rights–based approach can best be described as a conceptual framework that is *normatively based* on international human rights standards and that is *operationally directed* to promoting and protecting human rights (Office of the UN High Commissioner for Human Rights [UNHCHR] 2006). Such an approach requires careful consideration of the ways in which human rights violations arise throughout the trafficking cycle, as well as of states' obligations under international human rights law. It seeks to both identify and redress the discriminatory practices and unjust distributions of power that underlie trafficking, that maintain impunity for traffickers, and that deny justice to victims of trafficking.

Under a human rights–based approach, every aspect of the national, re-gional, and international response to trafficking is anchored in the rights and obligations established by international human rights law. The lessons learned in developing and applying a human rights–based approach in other areas, such as development, provide important insights into the main features of the approach and how it could be applied to trafficking (UNHCHR 2006). The key points that can be drawn from these experiences include the following: as policies and programs are formulated, their main objective should be to promote and protect rights; a human rights–based approach identifies *rights-holders* (for example, trafficked persons, individuals at risk of being trafficked, individuals accused or convicted of trafficking-related offenses), their entitlements, and the corresponding *duty-bearers* (usually states) and their obligations; a human rights–based approach works toward strengthening the capacities of rights-holders to secure their rights and of duty-bearers to meet their obligations; and core principles and standards derived from international human rights law (such as equality and nondiscrimination, universality of all rights, and the rule of law) should guide all aspects of the response at all stages.

This chapter uses the U.S. Trafficking in Persons (TIP) Reports as a lens and reference point through which to consider the opportunities and obstacles to securing international acceptance of a genuine rights-based approach to trafficking. Part 1 commences with a brief overview of the history, context, and structure of the reports. Part 2 traces the evolution of the reports over the past decade, with particular focus on recent shifts in scope, tone, and substantive direction and on how these changes have been generally received. Part 3 considers the impact of the reports on the behavior of states, noting the essential difference between compliance and effectiveness and highlighting gaps in knowledge and understanding that hamper our collective ability to identify what works and what does not with respect to trafficking. On the strength of a firm conviction that the reports are here to stay and that there is no credible alternative on the horizon, Part 4 identifies major issues for the future: improving the reports' legitimacy; and their capacity to contribute to a strong and rights-based response to trafficking.

The principal conclusion of the analysis presented in this chapter is that the TIP Reports have a demonstrated capacity for both destruction and genuine innovation. On the negative side, by rejecting international legal standards in favor of criteria imposed by U.S. bureaucrats and politicians, the reports have sidelined international law, including international human rights law— thereby rejecting the core element of a rights-based response. On the positive side, the reports have done more than perhaps any other single initiative to expose the breadth and extent of contemporary exploitation of individuals for private profit; they have shed light on practices and traditions that have too long remained hidden; they have exposed the complicity of public officials in trafficking-related exploitation; and they have compelled many governments who would not otherwise have done so to take action. The recommendations presented in the final part of this chapter reflect the author's conviction that the future credibility and authority of the reports, and accordingly their capacity to effect real and lasting change, rest heavily on the extent to which they can integrate and promote compliance with international rules and standards, most particularly those concerning human rights.

Background and Overview

The U.S. government was at the front line when trafficking emerged (or reemerged) as an issue of global concern in the mid-1990s. At that point, international and domestic U.S. attention was focused squarely on cross-border trafficking for sexual exploitation, particularly of women and girls from central and Eastern Europe and Southeast Asia to wealthy destination countries of western Europe and North America. The Trafficking Victims Protection Act of 2000 (TVPA) was signed into law on October 11, 2000, two months before the adoption of the UN Protocol to Prevent, Suppress and Punish Trafficking in Persons, Especially Women and Children (Trafficking Protocol), the first international treaty on trafficking in more than fifty years. As Chuang (2006) has noted, congressional sponsors of the TVPA believed that the success of efforts to prevent trafficking into the United States depended heavily on the actions of other countries. Accordingly, in addition to addressing many of the glaring gaps and weaknesses in the U.S. legislative framework, the TVPA established a system whereby the efforts of other countries to address trafficking were to be examined and assessed. Specifically, the State Department was required to issue annual reports describing "the nature and extent of severe forms of trafficking in persons" and assessing governmental efforts across the world to combat such trafficking against criteria established by U.S. law. As explored elsewhere by the present author, these reports did not emerge in a legal or policy vacuum but form part of an established tradition of U.S. congressional oversight of the actions of other countries with respect to issues considered to be of particular political significance (Gallagher 2011).

The TVPA, as amended at various points over the past decade, establishes "minimum standards" for the elimination of trafficking as well as criteria for evaluating performance. Governments are required, at a minimum, to: (1) prohibit and appropriately punish trafficking; and (2) make serious and sustained efforts to eliminate such trafficking. In evaluating efforts in this latter regard, the following indicia are stipulated: (1) whether the government vigorously investigates, prosecutes, and punishes trafficking; (2) whether it protects victims and encourages their participation in the investigation and prosecution process; (3) whether it has adopted preventive measures such as public education, birth registration, control of nationals deployed abroad in peacekeeping and similar operations, and measures aimed at preventing forced labor and child labor; (4) whether it cooperates with other governments in investigations and prosecutions; (5) whether it extradites (or is attempting to enable extradition of) traffickers; (6) whether it monitors migration patterns for evidence of trafficking and responds to such evidence in an appropriate manner; (7) whether it investigates, prosecutes, and takes appropriate measures against the involvement of public officials in trafficking; (8) whether the percentage of victims of trafficking that are noncitizens is insignificant; (9) whether the government has taken measures to address demand for trafficking related to commercial sex acts and involvement of nationals in sex tourism; (10) whether it has achieved appreciable progress as measured against the previous year's assessment; and (11) whether it has monitored and provided information to the U.S. government on its national response to trafficking (U.S. Department of State 2010a).

The State Department used the compliance levels of the TVPA to create a system of rankings based on three tiers. Tier 1 is for countries in full compliance with the minimum standards set out above, Tier 2 for countries making an effort but not yet fully compliant, and Tier 3 for those countries that were failing on both counts. Subsequent amendments laid the ground for creation of an additional category, "Tier 2 Watch List," applied to countries that, owing to the severity of the problem or failure to provide evidence of progress, are considered to be on the lower edge of Tier 2 classification. Tier 2 Watch List countries are subject to special scrutiny and, in the absence of a special presidential exemption, are downgraded to Tier 3 after two consecutive years on the Watch List. Under the TVPA and its various amendments, the president is authorized to deny the provision of nonhumanitarian, non-trade-related assistance to any Tier 3 country, that is, any government that does not comply with the minimum standards and is not making significant efforts to bring itself into compliance. In addition, such countries will risk U.S. opposition to their seeking and obtaining funds from multilateral financial institutions, including the World Bank and the International Monetary Fund. The annual TIP Reports are used as a basis for determining whether, and to what extent, sanctions are to be imposed or assistance provided. Sanctions can be avoided through a "national interest" waiver or a determination that a waiver (or partial waiver) is required to promote the purposes of the TVPA or to avoid significant adverse effects on vulnerable populations.[1]

Evolution of the Reports: 2001–2010

The first TIP Report was released in June 2001. It was a slight and somewhat confused document, presenting an obligingly easy target for criticism (Gallagher 2001b). In keeping with the narrower view of trafficking widely accepted at that time, the report's cursory analysis focused heavily on trafficking for sexual purposes, ignoring other egregious forms of exploitation that met both the international and U.S. definitions. The distinction between trafficking and related phenomena such as migrant smuggling was not uniformly understood or upheld. The document confidently cited unverified and unverifiable statistics, declining to acknowledge the complexity of the trafficking phenomenon and the immense difficulties involved in obtaining and synthesizing credible data. Its self-proclaimed "rigorous" evaluative methodology appeared to be little more than a crude information-collection exercise, delegated to untrained embassy officials. Failures to identify sources of information and inconsistencies in applying the evaluative criteria lent weight to claims of a suspect correlation between the general U.S. government attitude toward a particular country and the way in which it judged that country on the issue of trafficking.

While not justifying or trivializing these very significant weaknesses, it is essential to acknowledge that the shallowness and brevity of analysis in that first report were at least partly dictated by what was happening on the ground. In 2001 there were, for example, few national laws against trafficking and almost no recorded prosecutions. Victims were either unrecognized and unprotected or specifically targeted and criminalized. Cooperation between countries on this issue was nonexistent. The international legal framework around trafficking was very new; key definitions and norms were yet to be internalized or even properly understood. Ten years later, the situation is starkly different. The Trafficking Protocol, confirmed as the pre-eminent international legal agreement on this issue, has been ratified or acceded to by 137 countries. The obligations set out in the protocol have been clarified and in some cases extended by subsequent treaties, policy instruments, and interpretive materials. While national implementation of international rules remains uneven and incomplete, there has been considerable progress. Most countries have now criminalized trafficking according to the international legal definition, thereby confirming the expansion of the concept to potentially embrace virtually every situation in which individuals are severely exploited for private profit. Many have gone further, establishing new institutions, structures, and procedures to investigate, prosecute, and adjudicate trafficking cases. Cross-border cooperation is increasingly frequent and better organized. While victims are still regularly denied their rights, most states acknowledge an obligation, at least in principle, to provide those who have been trafficked with some measure of protection and support. The level and speed of change are difficult to exaggerate. In 2000, many states strenuously denied the existence of a problem in which they themselves could be implicated. In 2010, it would be a brave and lonely government that publicly opted out of the undeclared but fully operational "war on trafficking."

The TIP Reports have undergone a similarly dramatic shift. The most obvious and significant changes that can be observed in the most recent reports (U.S. Department of State 2009, 2010a) when compared to their 2001 predecessor include those relating to:

- *Geographical scope:* The first report briefly evaluated 83 countries deemed to be states of origin, transit or destination for "a significant number" of victims of trafficking (generally more than one hundred). The "significant number" threshold was removed in time for the 2009 report, which was tasked to assess *all* countries of origin, transit, and destination, and covered 173 countries as well as 2 additional "special cases" (Haiti and Somalia). Two more states (including, for the first time, the United States) were added in 2010, bringing the total number to 177.
- *Understanding of the trafficking phenomenon:* The reports now reflect a State Department view that movement is not required for

trafficking to occur (CdeBaca 2010). While the legal implications of that view cannot be fully explored within the confines of the present chapter, it appears that the somewhat ambiguous definitions of "trafficking" in both the TVPA and international law are being interpreted in a way that maximizes their potential application to situations of private exploitation. The broader narrative focus of the reports has expanded beyond the cross-border trafficking of women and girls for sexual exploitation to embrace a wide range of trafficking end-purposes, including forced labor, bonded labor, debt bondage, forced marriage, forced begging, exploitative adoption, child sex tourism, child soldiering, and organ removal. Individual country narratives continue to focus primarily on cross-border trafficking into sexual exploitation. However, internal exploitation and end-purposes of trafficking other than sexual exploitation are now routinely identified.

- *Level of country analysis:* Individual country assessments now address all minimum standards and criteria through two to three pages of analysis (with a significantly greater amount of space being dedicated to the first U.S. assessment presented in 2010). The information provided in the narrative appears to generally support the grading awarded, and there is some effort to explain the tier movement. A graph indicates tier movement over the life of the reports.

- *Introduction of thematic analysis:* The reports now include sections that outline major forms of trafficking and consider contentious or cross-cutting issues such as the role of parents in child trafficking, the detention of adult victims in shelters, trafficking in government procurement, and the relationship between trafficking and domestic violence. The 2010 report takes thematic analysis one step further by introducing standards and principles in relation to certain aspects of the national trafficking response—for example, legislation and the provision of shelter.

- *Use of data and statistics:* While limitations on data are now obliquely acknowledged, the reports continue to include secondhand information that is not fully referenced or cited. In 2009, for the first time, the State Department declined to provide its own estimate of the global scope of trafficking, drawing instead on data provided by the International Labor Organization (ILO). The 2010 report uses, without attribution or explanation, the same ILO estimate to extrapolate estimates of trafficking prevalence and victim identification rates. Country reports no longer cite estimated numbers of victims, although, as noted above, unverified estimates provided by others are still quoted without qualification. Governments are required, under threat of downgrading, to provide data and other information to State Department officials on investigations, prosecutions, convictions, and sentences. There is still little acknowledgement of the unreliability of much of the official information so provided.

- *Methodology:* Recent reports claim, and to a limited extent reflect, a more rigorous methodology for information collection and analysis. A system of outreach and consultation was recently established, providing interested and informed parties with the opportunity to contribute their views and insights. It is unclear how this new system operates in practice and to what extent it influences the direction of country assessments.

- *Approach to prostitution:* Since their inception, the reports have regularly conflated trafficking with prostitution. They have also been used as a vehicle for advancing what many have perceived to be an aggressive U.S. government campaign against prostitution (Berman 2006; Chuang 2006; Soderlund 2005; Weitzer 2007). The 2009 reports began to modify this approach while maintaining a strong focus on prostitution as the site of much trafficking-related exploitation. The 2010 report went a step further, stating that "prostitution by willing adults is not human trafficking regardless of whether it is legalized, decriminalized, or criminalized." However the same report notes that, as required under the TVPA, the reports evaluate the efforts of those countries with legalized prostitution to reduce demand for commercial sex "as part of its assessment of the countries' serious and sustained efforts to eliminate severe forms of trafficking in persons."

- *References to international law and standards:* The Trafficking Protocol is cited increasingly often, and country narratives now note whether the state under assessment is party to the protocol. Other relevant treaties are generally not referred to in either thematic anal-

yses or country narratives. Human rights concepts of central importance to trafficking, such as discrimination, are rarely mentioned.
There is no reference to human rights obligations or to violations of
established legal rights. A table of ratifications of a small number of
relevant treaties is provided. In 2010 an estimate was provided of
countries that had yet to convict a trafficker "under laws in compliance with the Palermo Protocol."

Public response to the TIP Report echoes, as least in part, the developments
outlined above. The initial focus of concern, within and outside the U.S.
government, was on the technical quality of the reports. Their empirical
basis was questioned and serious weaknesses identified with regard to both
methodology and data (U.S. Government Accountability Office [USGAO]
2006). As the State Department has worked to address these issues, such
criticisms have waned. Inclusion of the United States in the country assessments cuts off a major source of disparagement, as does the increased focus
on trafficking for labor exploitation and the more nuanced consideration of
the link between trafficking and prostitution. More fundamental grievances
remain unresolved. The very existence of the report continues to anger
those who object to the United States' appointing itself supervisor and arbi-
ter of a complex international issue that remains both contested and controversial. Any reform falling short of the reports' abolition will be unlikely to
shift the views of its harshest critics.

It should come as no surprise that recent changes to the TIP Reports have
not been universally welcomed. For those who consider the campaign
against trafficking to be principally about prostitution and sexual exploitation, the gradually increased focus on trafficking for labor exploitation
and the 2010 affirmation that trafficking is not the same as prostitution
represent a betrayal of the TVPA and of U.S. leadership on this issue
(Horowitz 2010). Significantly, only the TVPA is cited as an authority for
such criticisms. International law, including international human rights
law, is clear on the point that the end-purposes of trafficking extend well
beyond sexual exploitation. International law also affirms that states remain free to regulate adult prostitution as they see fit, subject to constraints imposed by human rights law. It is tempting to point out that the
failure of the reports to align themselves more closely with international
norms and standards provides dangerous ammunition to those who seek

to manipulate the campaign against trafficking to suit narrow political and ideological agendas.

Compliance and Effectiveness

In what way—and to what extent—has the reporting system established under the TVPA changed the behavior of states? More specifically, to what extent has the United States secured compliance with its stipulated minimum standards? The issue of compliance is a complex one, and the limited research undertaken thus far (Freidrich, Myer, and Perlman 2006; USGAO 2006; Wyler and Siskin 2010) provides little useful guidance on this point. There is an understandable temptation, to which the State Department itself has yielded (USGAO 2006; Warren 2010), to use movement within the grading system as evidence of impact. A country that has advanced from Tier 3 to Tier 1, for example, may be identified as having responded to the pressure or threat of sanctions as well as to the "naming and shaming" effect that accompanies highly public negative assessments of this kind (Friman 2010). However, such an approach ignores the myriad of political and other factors that affect a particular country's grading in a particular year as well as the many internal and external influences, beyond the reports, on that country's response to trafficking. Ratification of the UN Trafficking Protocol, for example, may be the primary impetus for a state to criminalize trafficking. The protocol may also have contributed to the internalization of norms that are simultaneously being advocated through the TIP reporting process. Pressure from neighboring states could lead to changes in willingness to engage in cross-border cooperation. The provision of technical assistance through a bilateral aid program could enhance criminal justice capacity to investigate and prosecute trafficking cases. The presence or absence of strong victim-support agencies will likely have a significant bearing on the rate of victim identification as well as the extent to which states have moved to protect and assist those who have been trafficked.

It is individual states that can most accurately assess the effect of the TIP reporting process on their own behavior. However, states cannot be relied upon to provide helpful or honest insight in this regard. There is little discernible benefit to be gained by a government admitting that a particular initiative or response was prompted by a criticism, assertion, recommendation, or grading contained in the TIP Report. Most countries provide no official comment or reaction. Some respond positively to an elevation in their assessed status (Government of Mauritius 2009). Others, often those identified as belonging to Tier 3, release statements disagreeing with the State Department assessment (Agence France Presse 2009; Garcia 2006; Singapore Ministry of Foreign Affairs 2010). A few protest, perhaps too strongly, that they are immune to the reports ("Malaysia 'Immune'" 2009). Of course, if one lowers the evidentiary threshold, there is considerable anecdotal information available to support the contention that the TIP Reports have had a significant impact on the way in which individual countries have responded to trafficking. The present author has elsewhere examined several examples to illustrate this contention—as well as to underline the many ways in which attribution can be complicated (Gallagher 2011).

That analysis revealed that the TIP Reports have exercised a strong, if not decisive, influence on the way in which states have responded to trafficking. However, beyond this largely intuitive conclusion, it remains difficult to assess the extent to which changes can be directly or indirectly attributed to the reports and the political process of which they form a central part. The problem is partly one of timing. The mechanism established under the TVPA commenced almost immediately after adoption of a hugely influential international treaty on trafficking—one that created legal obligations that, in many respects, echoed the minimum standards established by the TVPA. The Trafficking Protocol generated a range of institutions, instruments, procedures, and initiatives that have played some role in helping to shape national trafficking responses (Gallagher 2009). Other potential influences on national responses to trafficking include the availability of considerable development assistance funds from the United States and other Western donors for law reform, capacity building of criminal justice agencies, and victim protection and support; increasingly active and informed civil society groups; and the advocacy efforts of a wide range of international governmental and nongovernmental organizations. Further complicating attribution is the likelihood that the TIP Reports exercised some influence over these other forces as well—prompting donor governments to develop assistance programs, for example, and shaping the way in which priorities were identified.

The conclusion on compliance is therefore less than satisfying. For any individual working with or within national governments on this issue, the

power of the TIP Reports is indisputable. However, that instinctive conclusion should be tempered by the knowledge that the reports are still just
one component of the international landscape around trafficking, reflecting,
reinforcing, and feeding off other initiatives and other actors. Future research could usefully focus on the interplay between the TIP Reports and
these other components and players. A closely related aspect that deserves
further examination concerns motivation: what exactly is driving states'
response to the TIP Reports? Are the actions of states in this area simply
the product of a rational cost-benefit calculation of national interests? If
so, what are the factors shaping that perception of self-interest? Consider-
ations of reputation and of consequences (such as sanctions) may both
play a part, but it is evident that their relative importance will differ from
country to country and perhaps even from time to time. To what extent is
compliance affected by the perceived legitimacy (or illegitimacy) of the
TIP reporting process itself? It is not unreasonable to infer that there will
be a relatively greater willingness to accept and internalize rules that are
considered to be clear and fair and emanating from accepted processes
(Cleveland 2002; Raustiala and Slaughter 2002). To the extent that the TIP
reporting mechanism is considered intrusive, unfair, and out of step with
international norms, its ability to capitalize on a "legitimacy effect" will
inevitably be compromised. It follows that a normative convergence between the national and international, explored in more detail in the following section, will likely contribute to improved compliance in both
arenas.

Of course, *compliance* is not the same as *effectiveness*. It is one thing to
try to understand the extent to which state behavior is influenced by the TIP
Reports and complies with the specific standards therein. Ascertaining the
degree to which the reports actually have an impact on the underlying problem of trafficking is another proposition altogether and one that appears to
be well beyond current levels of knowledge and understanding. In 2006, the
U.S. Government Accountability Office found that "there is little or no evidence to indicate the extent to which different types of efforts—such as
prosecuting traffickers, abolishing prostitution, increasing viable economic
opportunities or sheltering and reintegrating victims—impact the level of
trafficking" (USGAO 2006). A report released by the same agency a year
later confirmed this grim finding (USGAO 2007). It is not to the credit of
the United States, nor indeed to the many governments, intergovernmental
organizations, NGOs, and other actors operating in the crowded and well-

resourced arena of "counter-trafficking," that this situation remains un-changed and virtually unchallenged.

Toward the Future: Improving Legitimacy and Promoting Human Rights

Ten years after their inception, the TIP Reports seem to be here to stay. Sup-port for the reports has, under a series of very different administrations, re-mained uncommonly constant, and there is nothing to indicate that this will change in the coming years. If one accepts that public scrutiny of trafficking-related exploitation is a good thing, and that monitoring of state responses to trafficking can potentially operate to address such exploitation, then the as-sured future of the TIP Reports should be reason for optimism. The dearth of credible alternatives lends additional weight to that position. Several examples serve to illustrate this point. In 2009, the UN Office on Drugs and Crime (UNODC) released its monumental Global Report on Human Trafficking. The report was billed as providing "an unprecedented view of the available information on the state of the world's response to trafficking, including near-comprehensive data on national legislative and enforcement activity" (UNODC 2009). While it contains some interesting information on criminal-ization, the criminal justice response, and assistance to victims, the UNODC Report's usefulness as a source of knowledge, or even of advocacy, is severely constrained. Methodological and analytical weaknesses are revealed most starkly in several of the report's more bizarre conclusions: that almost 80 per-cent of trafficking is for sexual exploitation, for example, or that women com-prise the overwhelming majority of traffickers. These claims are not "fact" in any sense of the word, reflecting nothing more than current reported patterns of investigations and prosecutions. It is disingenuous in the extreme to pres-ent those patterns as free of distortion and as representative of the actual global situation. Despite these and other significant weaknesses, the UNODC Report has been subject to virtually no critical review or analysis.

Another much more important theoretical rival for the TIP Reports is the reporting mechanism established under Article 32 of the UN Convention Against Transnational Organized Crime (UNCTOC), the parent treaty of the Trafficking Protocol. While the "Conference of Parties" (COP) for that convention was not originally mandated to deal with trafficking, that omis-sion was remedied in 2004 when COP functions of monitoring, information exchange, and cooperation were extended to the Trafficking Protocol. The COP is thus now empowered to request and receive information on states parties' implementation of the protocol and to make recommendations to improve the protocol and its implementation. A review of the voluminous and highly repetitive documentation produced for the COP and its various working groups confirms that the self-reporting procedure is a relatively crude mechanism for promoting or measuring compliance. Reporting rates are low, and the information received from governments is uneven, shallow, and often ambiguous. There is no opportunity to seek clarification from, or for dialogue with, states' parties. The analytical compilations of responses prepared by UNODC (the overstrained and underresourced COP secretariat) provide, at best, a highly generalized picture of compliance patterns and trends and do not amount to even a cursory review of state party performance (Gallagher 2010).

It is unclear whether recent efforts to improve this situation, including the establishment of a dedicated trafficking–in-persons working group within COP, will bear fruit. In truth, the prospect of states parties to the Organized Crime Convention and its Trafficking Protocol being made subject to a rigorous oversight mechanism—or even a procedure capable of evaluating their performance of key obligations—appears to be remote. States involved in the review of current arrangements have made clear that while they are willing to consider establishing a mechanism that is "transparent and efficient," there are limits on what would be acceptable. For example, the focus of any such mechanism should not be on compliance per se, but rather on helping to develop national policies for implementation as well as technical assistance and international cooperation initiatives (UN Conference of the Parties 2009). In what appears to be a direct reaction to the TIP reporting mechanism, states parties have also declared that any oversight mechanism established under the convention must also be "non-intrusive, impartial, non-adversarial, non-punitive and flexible. In addition, it should not criticize or rank States or regions but rather contribute to problem solving. It should furthermore respect the sovereignty of States" (UNCOP 2009, 4). Regrettably, that emphatically deferential view, echoed in a recent G77 Statement to the UN Crime Commission (Group of 77 plus China 2009), appears to be shared by those who, had it not been for the experience of the U.S. mechanism, might have been expected to support a more rigorous approach to monitoring state parties' international legal obligations with respect to trafficking (Global Alliance Against Traffic in Women [GAATW] et al. 2009).

The above analysis makes abundantly clear that, at least at the present, the TIP Reports are not *displacing* a potentially superior alternative—or performing a function that could be better discharged by the international community. Without the reports, our collective knowledge of trafficking-related exploitation would likely be less; individual governments would likely have greater control over the flow of information that properly belongs in the public domain; and even the most egregious failure on the part of a state to deal with trafficking-related exploitation would likely come at little reputational or other cost. For the committed multilateralist, such conclusions are cause for sober reflection. However, a belief in and commitment to strengthening the international system is not incompatible with a desire to see the kind of changes in the TIP Reports that would allow them to play a greater role in exposing exploitation and calling states and others to account.

The following paragraphs focus on three areas for strengthening of future reports: maximize their legitimacy; acknowledge and monitor risks to human rights; and identify good practices and promote rights-based responses to trafficking.

Maximize the Legitimacy of the Reports

The relationship between legitimacy and compliance has already been noted. In short, the more legitimate the TIP Reports are (or are perceived to be), the easier it will be to seek and secure positive changes in state behavior. Legitimacy is an ephemeral concept that, in the present context, is the product of a broad range of factors of varying relevance. The extent to which the reports are perceived to be a fair and accurate reading of the actual situation is obviously critical, and it is in this area that substantial progress has been made. Even those who continue to complain about political hubris and self-righteousness generally agree that individual country assessments are "thorough and largely consistent with facts as observed, reported by the media and examined in other comprehensive reports on the same issue" (Baroud 2009). It is essential that the higher standards secured over the past several years continue to be maintained. At the same time, expectations should be grounded in an understanding that the reports are political creatures, produced through a political process and serving specific political ends. From this perspective it is naïve to expect that country narratives will always be able to maintain an objective distance from the two sharp ends of U.S. foreign relations. Vital allies will likely need to underperform more flagrantly than less valued ones to be bumped off Tier 1. Extreme political and ideological opponents of the United States may never be moved from Tier 3, no matter what they do to try to conform to the TVPA minimum standards.

QUALITY AND USE OF DATA

While there has been some retreat from the reports' earlier tendency to cite unverified and unverifiable data and statistics, this could be taken further through a frank admission of the well-known problems and pitfalls associated with quantifying the extent of the trafficking problem (Ali 2010; Feingold 2010; Savona and Stefanizzi 2007; USGAO 2006) and the limits of current knowledge. Such an admission could operate as a counterweight to the current unhealthy and unhelpful fixation on numbers and statistics that appears to be an endemic affliction of intergovernmental agencies, NGOs, researchers, and academics working in this area. It may also help to stem the widespread manipulation of data to serve narrow policy goals or organizational requirements. An open acknowledgment of limitations should extend to the information contained in the report itself. The reporting and ranking process is not "scientific" or "objective" in the sense that an assessment of national creditworthiness or literacy rates could (or should) be. Attempts to present the assessments and the resulting rankings in this way creates what has been aptly called "an imaginary of concreteness" (Warren 2010), obscuring the reality that the quality of information sources varies considerably, as does the capacity of U.S. officials to verify and correctly interpret certain data. It also hides the elusiveness of trafficking itself: we do not yet fully understand, for example, when or how exploitative work morphs into trafficking, or when a migrant worker in a difficult situation becomes a victim of trafficking. A document such as the TIP Report should not be presented as a definitive statement of fact that can be relied upon by, for example, national refugee determination agencies in deciding whether or not a victim of trafficking has a valid claim for asylum (Dorevitch and Foster 2008; Saito 2007). A caveat contained in the introduction to the annual Narcotics Control Report—"Although the Department strives to provide accurate information, this report should not be used as the basis for determining legal rights or obligations under U.S. or foreign law" (U.S. Department of State 2010b, 3)—could provide a useful template in this regard.

CONVERGENCE WITH INTERNATIONAL NORMS AND CRITERIA

More than anything else, improving the legitimacy of the TIP Reports will require the U.S. government to work actively to link the criteria by which states are assessed to relevant international legal norms, including human rights. The development of a robust international legal framework around trafficking has been a recent and remarkable success story of international law (Gallagher 2009). The vast majority of states are now parties to one or more treaties that set out, with an unprecedented level of particularity and detail, their obligations with respect to the prevention of trafficking, the protection of victims, and the prosecution of perpetrators. Those instruments are supplemented by a raft of widely accepted international human rights treaties dealing with matters that are directly relevant to trafficking and national responses—including the rights of children, the rights of women, rights relating to work and freedom of movement, and prohibitions on forced labor, child labor, forced marriage, and enslavement.

There is significant normative convergence between these international rules and the minimum standards laid down by the TVPA and subsequently elaborated on by the State Department. However, as Chuang (2006) has previously noted, this does not reach a point of full symmetry. For example, there are important differences between the U.S. definition of "trafficking in persons" and that which has been accepted in international law (Gallagher 2010). The reports' prohibitionist stance with respect to prostitution (reflected in the TVPA definition) is at odds with international law, which does not require states to criminalize prostitution. The TVPA criteria also fail to reflect rights and obligations that do not relate solely or specifically to trafficking but are nevertheless critical to an accurate assessment of the legality and quality of national responses. The right to a fair trial and the obligation to provide access to remedies are just two of many examples. Even in situations where differences between the TVPA standards and international law do not have a great practical impact, the very fact of such differences serves to underline the unpalatable and intrinsically unreasonable reality that states are being judged—not with reference to the international rules that they have helped to develop and have freely accepted—but against criteria established unilaterally by the U.S. government.

Acknowledge and Monitor Risks to Human Rights

Abundant evidence is available to support a contention that measures taken in the name of addressing trafficking can have an adverse impact on individual rights and freedoms. Throughout the world, trafficked persons are routinely detained in jails, immigration centers, and shelter facilities (Gallagher and Pearson 2010). Victims of trafficking are commonly prosecuted for status offenses such as prostitution, illegal immigration, or illegal work (GAATW 2008; UN Special Rapporteur on Trafficking in Persons 2009). Some states have used the threat of trafficking to justify legislative, administrative, or other measures aimed at preventing individuals from emigrating in search of work (Oishi 2005; UN Special Rapporteur on Violence Against Women 2000). Victims of trafficking in danger of reprisals or retrafficking are forcibly repatriated, sometimes on the strength of information contained in the TIP Reports (Dorevitch and Foster 2008; Saito 2007). Assistance and support to victims is often conditional on their agreeing to cooperate with authorities (GAATW 2007, 2008; UN Special Rapporteur on Trafficking in Persons 2009). Anti-trafficking raids and rescues (increasingly conducted by foreign vigilantes, including some supported by the U.S. government and prominent U.S. philanthropists) raise troubling ethical and legal questions that have yet to be properly addressed (Agustin 2007; Soderlund 2005; Thrupkaew 2009). Like trafficking itself, the negative fallout from interventions is often highly gendered. The detention of victims of trafficking in shelters and welfare facilities, for example, is invariably directed against women and girls, compromising not just the right to freedom of movement but also the prohibition on discrimination (Gallagher and Pearson 2010). Invariably, emigration restrictions justified with reference to the anti-trafficking imperative are discriminatory in both intent and impact, being limited to a group defined by its sex (always female) and often also age (Oishi 2005; UN Special Rapporteur on Violence Against Women 2000).

It is not only trafficked persons caught up in the anti-trafficking imperative who are at risk when responses are inappropriate or interventions go wrong. The danger that suspects' rights will be trampled on in the "war against trafficking" is not a remote one. Even those states most attached to the rule of law may be tempted to compromise the rights of individuals suspected of certain high-profile crimes, including organized crime and migrant smuggling, with which trafficking is often associated. External and internal pressures on criminal justice agencies to be seen to be responding to trafficking present an additional risk factor that has a particular resonance in the present context. Such pressures can have especially unfortunate consequences in states with underdeveloped criminal justice systems, where rules of evidence and procedure already fall short of international standards (Gallagher and Holmes 2008). Unfair trials, distorted targeting of offenders (for example, of low-level "enablers," such as recruiters or transporters, rather than those directly involved in exploitation), and disproportionate penalties are a reality of the criminal justice response to trafficking in many of the countries in which the present author has been working.

The 2009 report was the first to prominently highlight negative impacts of anti-trafficking responses such as victim detention and criminalization. The 2010 report continued a focus on these two issues, articulating "core principles for shelter programs" and "10 troubling governmental practices," including penalization of victims, ill-conceived raids of worksites or brothel districts, and emigration/immigration restrictions enacted in the name of addressing trafficking "for an entire country or nationality" (but curiously, not on the basis of sex). Unfortunately, this new and welcome attention to negative impacts is almost never continued through to individual country assessments. The likely explanation for this failure is that the broader danger of "collateral damage" inherent in many anti-trafficking interventions does not figure at all in the TVPA minimum standards or evaluative criteria. In other words, it is only through its introductory narratives that the State Department has been able to flag these critical issues. It is essential for the credibility of the national assessments that some way be found to not only affirm that state responses to trafficking must not violate established rights or obligations but also to examine state practices against this standard. That will require careful and consistent attention to international norms that relate to matters such as the prohibition on discrimination, the right to freedom of movement (including the right to leave one's country and to return), the prohibition on arbitrary detention, the right to a fair trial, the right to seek asylum from persecution, and the obligation to provide access to remedies for violations of human rights. It is these basic and universally accepted norms that provide essential criteria against which state responses to trafficking should be monitored and evaluated.

The process of preparing the reports should also be informed by an understanding that some states will manipulate the political momentum against trafficking to pursue other policy objectives such as immigration control or repression of a particular social or ethnic group. To date, acknowledgment of this reality has been confined to the narrative sections of the report. Individual country assessments should seek out and clearly identify instances (and, where appropriate, perpetrators) of negative impacts and make specific recommendations with respect to this issue. The reports can also do a great deal more to promote the rule of law and the right to a fair trial. A nuanced and refined analysis of the quality of the national criminal justice response to trafficking would view quantity of prosecutions as only one of many positive indicators of performance. It would draw on a sample of cases to identify: (1) the degree to which end-exploiters are targeted and prosecuted; (2) outcomes (sentences, victim compensation, asset confiscation, etc.); and (3) situations in which trafficking-related prosecutions have not met international criminal justice standards. The State Department's own *Country Reports on Human Rights Practices* could be an important source of information on the quality of the national criminal justice response and its capacity to protect basic rights. Qualitative analysis of this kind should be extended to other aspects of the trafficking response, such as victim protection and assistance. This could involve, for example, assessing the nature, level, and impact of support provided to victims rather than simply the number of shelters or available shelter places.

Identify Good Practices and Promote Rights-Based Approaches

Despite its links to some of the oldest of all human rights laws, trafficking presents unfamiliar challenges to states and to the international community. The *crime* of trafficking, for example, is essentially a new one. Many states are developing their criminal justice responses on the run, often under political pressure and principally through trial and error. While communication between national criminal justice agencies is improving on this issue, there is still very little cooperation or cross-fertilization of ideas across national borders. Victim support is another new area. There is now a strong collective experience of providing services to victims of domestic and sexual violence. However, there is much less understanding of the particular challenges involved in supporting and protecting those who have been trafficked. The field of anti-trafficking at the international, regional, and often even national levels is crowded and competitive. While such an environment can foster innovation and excellence, it can also lead to duplication of experience and effort, contradictory standards, and closed circles of knowledge.

The TIP Report is potentially a powerful vehicle for the dissemination of common standards, experiences, and good practices in the area of human trafficking. The breadth and depth of the State Department's information base makes it uniquely situated to help identify what "works" (and, equally, what does not) in relation to the three main areas of anti-trafficking activity: protection of victims, criminal justice responses, and prevention. While such efforts may have crumbled on shallow foundations only a short time ago, the present situation is very different. There is, for example, much greater clarity today about the core elements of an effective criminal justice response to trafficking: a solid legal framework; a front-line law enforcement capacity; specialist investigators; victim and witness support; committed prosecutors and judges; and a capacity to exchange intelligence, evidence, and suspects with other countries (Gallagher and Holmes 2008). As noted in the 2010 report, there is now sufficient collective experience in drafting and implementing specialist trafficking in persons laws to enable the identification of some basic principles of a good law. Other areas of anti-trafficking activity that would be suitable for exploration of good practices and articulation of common standards, including those related to human rights, include: victim identification; access to remedies; protection from further harm (reprisals, retrafficking, etc.); securing victim privacy; addressing vulnerabilities to trafficking; identifying and addressing trafficking-related corruption; legal status including temporary residence permits; addressing the special rights and needs of trafficked children; victim repatriation and reintegration; exercise of criminal jurisdiction (including extraterritorial jurisdiction); sanctions; and assets confiscation (including use of assets to compensate victims).

Conclusion

A human rights approach to trafficking will never be accidental. It will never be a by-product of another approach or another set of policy preferences. As noted in the introduction to this chapter, a human rights–based approach requires explicit articulation. It also requires commitment: an affirmation of the central importance of international human rights standards and a careful application of the rights and obligations imposed by those standards.

The U.S. Trafficking in Persons Reports have exercised a profound influence over the way in which states and others understand and respond to trafficking and to the many forms of exploitation with which it is associated. Each and every state, irrespective of its relative power, position, or adherence to a particular treaty, is now subject to close and continuing scrutiny. A verdict, with potentially serious consequences not generally available under international law, is then pronounced. Governments work hard to prepare themselves for this annual examination and, almost without exception, appear to care very deeply about the outcome. While one may prefer a different, more inclusive, and more equitable political reality, these developments should nevertheless be welcomed, not least because of the lack of a credible alternative. The international machinery available to expose the many ways in which individuals exploit each other for private profit, to identify government toleration of or complicity in that exploitation, and to evaluate national responses is weak and highly compromised. The external compliance machinery created through the TIP Reports explicitly recognizes that governments bear a responsibility to prevent trafficking and related exploitation, to end the current high levels of impunity enjoyed by traffickers, and to protect and assist victims. Attempts to persuade governments to take these obligations seriously deserve support and encouragement.

However, the United States can use the report to do much more. Along with its capacity to influence positive change, the report has demonstrated an alarming power to exacerbate negative impacts of anti-trafficking interventions, to nurture destructive and polarizing debates on seemingly intractable issues such as prostitution, and to damage the coherence and authority of an important and widely accepted international legal regime. The failure of the report to align itself with international standards also prevents the articulation and promotion of a genuine rights-based approach to trafficking. These are serious risks. They deserve to be openly acknowledged and carefully managed. The U.S. Congress and the State Department have thus far shown a remarkable willingness to adapt the reporting process to take account of new understandings and new policy preferences. Their continued commitment in this regard will be required if the United States is to consolidate its leadership position in the global effort to identify and eradicate trafficking.

Chapter 11

The Anti-slavery Movement: Making Rights Reality

Kevin Bales and Austin Choi-Fitzpatrick

Introduction

How we end slavery is the 27-million-person question. What does the re-thinking of this volume tell us about how to end slavery and trafficking—and how can we integrate this with the knowledge and practice of the anti-slavery movement in the field? In this volume, the contributions rethinking the roots of trafficking suggest we must address interlocking dynamics of domination: gender, consciousness, political economy, and international relations.

When we look at what supports slavery around the world, things seem a little discouraging. Apparently all we have to do is end world poverty, stop all corruption, keep people from being greedy, slow the population explosion, end the environmental destruction and armed conflicts that impoverish countries, convince the big lenders to cancel international debts, and get governments to keep the promises they make every time they pass a law. How tough is that? Yet the response from the field is surprisingly hopeful: if ever there was a tipping point when slavery can be brought to a full stop, it is now.

Many of the world's trends are moving in the right direction for the eradication of slavery, but we are going to have to provide the brainpower and the economic muscle to make it happen. International debts are being canceled. The population explosion is slowing down. The struggle against environmental destruction has never been so fierce. The number of people living in extreme poverty has actually fallen from 1.5 billion in 1981 to 1.1 billion in

2001 even as the world population increased, and there are clear plans to significantly reduce extreme poverty by 2015 and then end it by 2025.[1] There are a number of ways to get governments to enforce their own laws; some involve carrots, and some involve sticks. Stopping any armed conflict is going to be tough, but if you reduce poverty and corruption, and increase good governance, the likelihood of conflict also falls.

The positive trends in our economies and cultures, the growing acceptance of human rights, and the relatively small part that slavery plays in our world economy mean slavery is ripe for extinction. Slavery is a big problem, but not as big or as intractable as global warming or global poverty—27 million is a lot of people, but they are just .0043 of the world population. Slave-made products and services are worth about $13 billion a year, exactly what Americans spent on Valentine's Day in 2010. The UN estimates that human traffickers make $32 billion in profits annually—but these sums are tiny drops in the ocean of the world economy. No industry or big corporation, no political party, no state or country or culture is dependent on slavery. No government or business would collapse if slavery ended today. The cost of ending slavery is just a fraction of the amount that freed slaves will pump into the global economy. For those of us in the world's richer countries, the cost of ending slavery would be so small we would never notice it.

The things we have to do to end slavery in America are somewhat different from what we have to do in India or Ghana or Thailand. Like a lot of crimes, slavery takes on the coloration and culture of its surroundings. Slavery is tangled up in both local and global economies. Ending slavery means attacking it at all levels: local police, the United Nations, industries, churches, and governments will all have to play a part. The chapters in this volume that analyze response suggest that there are systematic flaws in the current U.S. approach, other Organization for Economic Cooperation and Development (OECD) countries that host migration like Greece, and even many UN operations. But even here, the wider experience of the anti-slavery movements suggests new possibilities for more effective response from above and below—and a way to implement van den Anker's call for cosmopolitan rights.

Civil Society: Mobilization at the Grass Roots

It is easy to think about slavery in a simple way, as evil slaveholders and innocent slaves, a crime that is truly black and white in its moral contrast.

Often, from this viewpoint, slaves are victims who need to be rescued—helpless, dependent, a little pathetic, and, we expect, grateful for a chance at freedom. What this view misses is the resilience and strength of people caught in slavery, their endurance, intelligence, and compassion. Some slaves are so beaten down that it is hard to get up. Others have been denied the knowledge of their own rights and freedoms. But a tiny seed of knowledge can grow into a powerful, unstoppable push to freedom. If we are going to help this push to freedom, we need to recognize and respect the power in every person in slavery, especially when slaves join together and make a decision to struggle together for their own freedom.

Social movement organizations and nongovernmental organizations (NGOs) are crucial in this effort. They help get the word to the rest of the world about both the sorrows and struggles of those living in slavery and those working for freedom (Bob 2005). These groups are also connected to broader networks of abolitionists, donors, governments, and a host of other actors. Perhaps most significantly, these organizations are able to serve as hubs for critical knowledge about the utility of specific strategies and the analysis of particular conditions. For a slave, feeling oppressed is one thing; knowing that around the world there are efforts to end this exploitation is quite another. Social movement organizations and NGOs are critical conduits for knowledge, economic resources, movement strategy, and international pressure—importantly this conduit flows both ways, with grassroots struggles teaching the rest of the world critical lessons about human courage and solidarity.

The model of solidarity and empowerment our human rights approach to trafficking suggests can already be seen in some of the successful campaigns of the broader anti-slavery movement. An example of this courage and solidarity can be found in the dusty backwaters of Bihar, India, where the Progressive Institute for Village Enterprises (PGS) works with stone breakers. These workers have often been entrenched in debt bondage for generations, forced to work on land they do not own, secured through leases they do not control in order to break rock they cannot sell. As members of the Kol caste, they are near the bottom of India's discriminatory hierarchy. Grinding poverty and a lack of alternative means of employment quickly drive workers back into this system. In the late 1990s, community organizers worked with workers from the village of Sombarsa and together they set out to secure a lease for the workers, defying local elites who had monopolized the leasing system. When the villagers started to meet to strategize this approach, the community organizers were abused, only deepening the villagers' resolve. As one man put it, "On the basis of what they said and what we thought among ourselves, we started walking the path" (Bales 2007, 66). To everyone's surprise, 3,500 people attended this first meeting. Goondas (petty local criminals) came, beating those in attendance. Those in attendance struggled back and began throwing building stones at their attackers, killing one of the Goondas. For this, eight villagers were placed in jail, the village was ransacked, then burned to the ground. At least one child died in the hazing.

In the wake of this violence, a local self-help group took the villagers in and slowly they began rebuilding. Unable to return to their homes, they resettled at the edge of Sonbarsa, in a small unincorporated area they called *Azad Nagar*, "Land of Freedom." After a year of struggle with local elites, they gained access to their own lease, effectively freeing them to leave their conditions of indebtedness and pursue their own employment.

Watching and listening as communities make the collective and conscious decision to throw off slavery, standing with them in the moment of crisis, and seeing what works and what fails during the first slow and careful steps toward autonomous life shows us the essential ingredients of a sustainable future. If a community of ex-slaves, individual migrants who have been trafficked, or at-risk individuals is going to survive in freedom, these are the best guarantees:

- *Immediate access to paid work:* Ideally, this should yield income ex-slaves generate themselves, doing jobs they know, not handouts. The residents of Azad Nagar are working as stone breakers—only this time under their own terms, and with their children's opportunities in mind.
- *Building up savings:* For the poor and vulnerable, assets can be the difference between a problem and a catastrophe.
- *Access to basic services:* Having a school means the children stay out of work today and build up human capital for tomorrow; a clinic within a reasonable distance means small illnesses do not become debilitating, and simple vaccinations save lives; access to clean water near the home will literally add hours of productivity to the lives of ex-slaves and marginalized people struggling to survive beyond indebted labor.

- *Working with the earth:* While slaves are often forced to participate in environmental destruction, building a sustainable community in freedom means sustaining the natural environment as well; similarly, environmental degradation at home is linked to high risk for trafficking.
- *"Rights-based development":* For the enslaved and at-risk, participation and partnership in development projects are crucial.

Likewise, every effort must be made to avoid and overcome dependency in anti-slavery coalitions:

- *Reliable funding:* Indigenous anti-slavery groups need the same stability that they are helping ex-slave communities to build.
- *Flexibility:* Funders should keep in mind that the goal is freedom, not a "successful" project that delivers less than that.
- *Assemble the tool kit for legal empowerment:* Every anti-slavery group needs a good understanding and the ability to use whatever anti-slavery tools and laws exist.
- *Critical thinking, critical funding:* Increase the level of understanding and trust between the workers on the ground and the funders in their offices to the point that working together they are faster, smarter, lighter, quicker, and more powerful than slaveholders.

First a Seed, Then a Tree, Then a Forest

Helping individuals reach a tipping point against slavery in one community is achievable, but we know less about how to translate that experience in one village to a whole state or region. How do we build organizations and coalitions that will have a wider impact? First, successful community-based solutions need to be *scaled up* as much as possible. To do that, anti-slavery groups and their funders have to always think about incubating new strategies and then multiplying them. Once a successful strategy is tested, it should be proactively offered to the world as a freely available "open-source" program.

Second, anti-slavery groups need to join together and *cooperate*, forming a wider movement with a shared identity. This can be tough since groups often feel themselves to be in competition for recognition and resources. Being human beings, even altruistic anti-slavery workers can have egos that make them want to be leaders or respond to praise in ways that are not healthy. It is important to remember that some grassroots workers chosen for special attention by the media have had their lives and their effectiveness severely disrupted by demands far in excess of their workload, jealousy from other workers, and increased visibility to slaveholders and their thugs.

Third, scaling up successful anti-slavery programs also means shifting more of the responsibility to the government. The *creation of government accountability*, for law enforcement and for provision of preventive and rehabilitative services, needs to be *intrinsic* to anti-slavery strategies. To end slavery and trafficking, the culture and purpose of government must be for human rights rather than sectional interests.

Governments: Carrying the Biggest Stick

Slavery is a crime in every country. Governments have *already* taken the collective decision to stop it; now it is just a matter of bringing political will and resources to bear. Admittedly, sometimes it is hard for a country to face up to slavery. No government, no society likes to admit that slaves live inside its borders, feed its economy, and suffer terrible violations of their rights. This leads to split personalities when it comes to slavery: countries denounce it to the world, unable to look it in the face at home. It is denial, and if the majority of those in power practice that denial, it is deadly.

Nearly every country will need to build a unique set of responses to slavery. These responses will have many common elements, but the precise mix will vary from country to country. First, we should analyze what role specific governments play in the political economy of slavery; for example, do they facilitate international sex trafficking or enable domestic plantations with child labor? Answering these questions requires distinguishing between political capacity and political will. Japan, for example, has the resources it needs to eradicate slavery (mainly sex trafficking) very quickly inside the country, but it has an extreme shortage of the political will necessary to get the job done. A poor country like Ghana may have the best will in the world to respond to forced and child labor in rural areas, but not enough money to take on the slaveholders. On the other hand, Burma has almost no resources to fight slavery, but that is not their problem. In Burma, the military dictatorship *is* the main slaveholder—and their crimes against their own people are vicious and terrible. A democratically elected government exists in Burma (Myanmar)—locked away by the dictatorship. When the heroes of the legitimate government finally come to power and the corrupt dictatorship falls, slavery in Burma will be on the way out.

In the rich countries of the global North, slavery can be reduced to almost nothing very quickly; it is primarily a matter of priorities and resources. In Eastern Europe, the Middle East, South America, and many of the countries of Southeast Asia, governments will face a very tough struggle with the *corruption* that feeds on slavery and fuels it in turn. There is a clear link between poverty, corruption, and slavery. This is one of the toughest jobs we face in ending slavery, but the payoff will go beyond the freedom brought to slaves. Rooting out slavery and the corruption that enables it will dramatically improve lives for almost all citizens in a whole range of countries and should be supported by the countries of the rich North.

Stop Looking for the Quick Fix

Every politician and government official (and concerned citizen) needs to come to an understanding that slavery, human trafficking, and their eradication are multidimensional. There has to be a constellation of governmental responses and strategies that address the many facets of the problem; otherwise success will be elusive. Slavery is a legal problem, obviously, but it is, to a greater or lesser extent in every country, also a problem of economic development, migration, gender, prejudice, corruption, and political priorities and will. There is no quick fix for slavery—not busting up brothels, not buying people out of slavery, not passing laws (without making sure they get enforced). The fact is that any country that can build a highway or a health service or a school system can assemble the minds needed to think through the mix of factors that support and enable slavery inside their borders. If they need advice, that is available as well.

A Robust Legal Response Is Crucial

In too many countries, freed slaves or migrants are treated as illegal aliens, second-class citizens, or worse. Any law that decriminalizes victims also needs to be explicit on one key point—the consent of the victim to exploitation is irrelevant to enforcement. International law is clear: a person cannot legally hand themselves over to slavery, and national laws must be equally clear on this point. A human rights approach reminds us that slavery is a crime against humanity, and that means it affects all of us, and it is our mutual responsibility to enforce it—because without global enforcement, it spreads. It is a small but crucial extension of the legal response to assemble dedicated anti-slavery enforcement teams. Labor inspectors should have the right to look at all industries, no matter how informal, for evidence of forced labor. A promising example of this can be seen in Brazil's use of mobile anti-slavery teams. These teams, while underresourced, are able to investigate cases and prosecute perpetrators in remote locations across the country.

Protect and Support Freed Slaves and Migrants

In addition to decriminalizing the victims of slavery and trafficking, governments need to provide for their rehabilitation and support. Freed slaves need help to get back on their feet, to build the strength and confidence to testify against slaveholders. This help—from social service agencies or the government itself—should be given no matter where the freed slave has come from. Several of the contributors to this volume emphasize that protection for trafficking victims must be delinked from their participation in prosecution of traffickers who may still threaten them or their home communities.

Raise Awareness and Promote Prevention

Despite being a hidden crime, slavery can be remarkably visible in many parts of the world. It is the duty of governments to work with other groups and produce public awareness materials that focus on the crime of slavery as well as discouraging the demand that leads to slavery. Public awareness campaigns should also raise awareness of enticements and recruitment methods used by slaveholders. One critical lesson from Nepal is that slaves are deprived of information. One of the strongest chains they bear is the one that holds them back from knowledge. Knowledge can be, literally, liberating. Nepali *Kamaiya*, Ghanaian fishing slaves, and Indian bonded workers all have said that they never knew that their enslavement was illegal until they learned it from their liberators.

Use Diplomacy, Trade, and Aid to End Slavery

Foreign aid from rich countries should be thought through with an anti-slavery focus, some of it targeting the underlying economic desperation that engenders slavery. Trade policies should reflect the idea that slave-made goods should be taboo on the world market. Trade financing can be linked to demonstrable efforts to remove slavery from local as well as international markets. At present this is not the case. The Department of Labor (DOL) is moving in this direction but, as Hebert and Gallagher demonstrate in their chapters in this volume, anti-trafficking sanctions imposed by the United States are applied selectively and do not effectively remove the profit motive. Recent criticism has also been leveled against the DOL's List of Goods Produced by Child Labor or Forced Labor (U.S. Department of Labor 2009), as it overlooks the role of corporations, risks condemning entire industries pockmarked by slavery, and does not account for the complexity of supply chain manufacturing.

Address the Root of Global Migration

Most wealthy countries need workers but also fear the changes that large numbers of immigrants will bring. Real leadership and a deeper understanding are desperately needed on this issue. One area of confusion is the way that human trafficking and slavery fit into questions of immigration. It is important to recognize how restrictive immigration policies, combined with desperation to survive and improve their lives, make the poor vulnerable to human trafficking, as van den Anker's chapter explains. We can address the illegal flow of slaves into our countries by addressing the reasons life is not livable in their home countries, as well as facing up to the economic demand for people to fill jobs in richer countries. This brings the circle back to high-level diplomatic conversations.[2]

Focus on the Outcomes

The outcome of human trafficking is to place a person into slavery. The outcome of slavery is that person coming under the complete control of a slaveholder, with violence normally used to ensure that control. Because of a partial understanding or in response to a particularly sensational case, many countries adopt laws that only focus on one segment of enslavement, such as forced prostitution. Likewise, it is necessary to focus on the outcomes of eradication, specifically freeing people from slavery and their reintegration into normal life. That seems obvious, but more than one country has equated passing laws with getting the job done. The laws are needed, but they have to be enforced to have an effect—and linked to attention to the various forms of exploitation.

For an example of how badly things can go wrong when laws, or enforcement, are missing, one need look no further than Japan. Thousands of women have been brought into Japan for enslavement in prostitution. Many if not most of those women can identify the men who trafficked them, yet Japan arrests a handful of perpetrators each year. The key law against prostitution in Japan is one that punishes solicitation, so it is prostitutes, not the men who use them, who are arrested and punished. But in reality, the government does little to suppress this illegal business. In fact, many of its actions actually support the illegal sex trade that gives rise to trafficking. For more than twenty years the government has opened the country to human traffickers through a rapidly increasing number of "entertainer visas." The visa is supposedly given to singers and dancers who will be giving performances in theaters and nightclubs. In reality, no effort is made to track the whereabouts of these workers, their conditions, or their rates of exploitation. On the street, Japanese police are "tolerant" of organized crime. In the report on human trafficking to Japan written for the Organization of American States, the researchers noted that local women's groups trying to help trafficking victims report that "policemen return women, who came to seek help [at the *koban*], to the traffickers." While there is a system of *koban* in the rural areas as well, the report goes on to note: "For women who are working in remote areas of Japan, such as the isolated islands in Okinawa, it is almost impossible to escape" (Organization of American States 2005, 28).

Intergovernmental Actors

Slavery is global. As we think through how to end it, we need to find ways to use those organizations that are global in scope. Globalization is an active process, and it offers the chance of a truly universal, global consensus on human rights. That universal consensus includes an end to slavery. Yet the contributions in this volume show that some international organizations contribute to the problem, while others help build the solution. What can the anti-slavery experience show us about the sources for global governance for emancipation?

The United Nations

The United Nations' approach to slavery is rooted in Article 4 of the Universal Declaration of Human Rights, which simply and clearly states that no one should be held in slavery. Additionally, upon its formation, the UN inherited the League of Nations 1926 Convention to Suppress the Slave Trade and Slavery, a strong and comprehensive instrument that was then reenacted in 1956. Furthermore, Article 8 of the International Convention on Civil and Political Rights guarantees freedom from slavery and servitude. More recently (2000) the United Nations has adopted the Trafficking Protocol which, as Hebert points out in her chapter, obligates state parties to pass legislation criminalizing trafficking, strengthen border controls, train law enforcement, and ensure travel documents are not easily replicated (UN Trafficking Protocol 2000, Articles 5–12). As Gallagher points out in her chapter, while a stunning number of countries have criminalized trafficking and "many have gone further, establishing new institutions, structures, and procedures to investigate, prosecute, and adjudicate trafficking cases," it is unclear whether the protocol will gain an oversight mechanism sufficient to monitor state compliance. Of course, all conventions have a reporting mechanism, but what matters is whether cases are referred to an inspectorate and whether the supervising entity has the power to simply report or actually investigate.

With these complexities in mind, it comes as no surprise that the United Nations suffers terribly from the distance between dream and reality. That distance is seen over and over when something bad happens in the world and people ask: "Why isn't the UN *doing* something about that!?"—not realizing that the UN isn't *allowed* to do much of anything. Much could be said about the major changes needed to foster real democracy within the UN, as Heather Smith emphasizes in this volume. Yet we really cannot wait; we must use the United Nations because slavery is a global problem needing the organization's global reach. The good news is that a number of mechanisms are already at work in the UN that can be applied to slavery. Of course, any success requires cooperation from the Security Council. Thus, we argue that the Security Council of the UN should do these five things:

- *Appoint a Special Representative of the Secretary General on Slavery*: This representative should be given the mandate to review and report on the state of global slavery and to prepare plans, materials, and proposals for a Security Council meeting devoted to contemporary slavery.
- *Hold a meeting of the Security Council devoted to slavery*: This meeting would have clear-cut goals and would be the first step in making the UN a global leader in ending slavery. With the materials and plans for the meeting prepared by the special representative, and discussed in advance with the permanent members, the meeting will confirm the UN's commitment to ending slavery. The Security Council would then back up that commitment in three easy, noncontroversial ways:
  - *First, the permanent members, and any of the elected members of the Council, could make public, significant contributions to the representative's budget.* Remember that the work of a special representative ultimately has to come from national governments. When the permanent members make a matched contribution, it will make clear that they are taking the problem seriously.
  - *Second, on the recommendation of the special representative, the Security Council would appoint a committee of experts to review the existing conventions on slavery and recommend how to unify and clarify these conventions, as well as coordinate and improve the UN's programmatic response to slavery.* Given a year to report, this group would return with new, precise definitions of

slavery and human trafficking that could be put to the General Assembly, as well as an action plan to bring the eradication of slavery into the work of all the departments of the UN, from the Food Program to the Space Program.

○ *Finally, the Security Council would establish a commission to determine how the existing UN inspection mandate could be applied to slavery.* When that commission came back with a resolution to form an inspectorate for the slavery and human trafficking conventions, then there would, at long last, be teeth in the UN's work on slavery.[3]

The International Labor Organization

The International Labor Organization was set up in 1919, at the same time as the League of Nations, but unlike the League, it survived. In its constitution, the ILO aims to bring dignity to all workers and promote safe working conditions, reasonable hours, adequate wages, no child labor, and social security in old age. It aimed to accomplish this by bringing together three key actors: governments, workers (often represented by labor unions), and employers (likewise represented by employer or business associations). When the United Nations was set up in 1946, the ILO became its first specialized agency. The ILO has been a leader in exposing the modern enslavement of children and adults, though for most of its existence the ILO was a species of permanently lame duck.

In spite of having little power, the ILO has been the seat of two significant advances in the past twenty years. One grew from a campaign against child labor that culminated with child workers from around the world marching into the ILO annual conference in Geneva and exuberantly pressing their case to the normally stuffy bureaucrats.[4] The result was a new Convention on the Worst Forms of Child Labor, which clearly specified child slavery and helped to dramatically expand, with crucial support from then-President Bill Clinton, an international program to eliminate child labor. This program has been spending more than $50 million a year for that past five years, and the results show that when resources are at least adequate, significant progress can be made. The ILO's most recent major report on child labor made a very bold assertion. The title of the report was "The End of Child Labor: Within Reach"—which seems pretty far-fetched when one considers the pervasive and historically constant reality of children working all over the world. But the

ILO workers had watched the resources and expertise go in, and the results come out. From 2000 to 2005, damaging child labor (we are not talking about kids with paper routes, lemonade stands, or Saturday jobs here) fell by 11 percent, and the number of children in the most dangerous kinds of work fell 33 percent in the five-to-fourteen age group. In a world focused on a "war on terror," this astounding change went unnoticed, but for literally millions of children, a new life was beginning. The ILO led this transformation with its shoelaces tied together in ways that are explained below. The important thing is how relatively inexpensive the outcomes were, and how the lessons of this work can be brought over to the eradication of slavery.

The requirement to be a passive recipient of reports also began to shift in 1998, when the ILO issued its Declaration on the Fundamental Principles and Rights at Work. One of the four "fundamental principles" was "no slavery," and this opened the door to lobbying by Anti-Slavery International for a relatively innocuous but radical proposal that a team be created to take *positive action* against slavery. This idea was taken up, and the ILO Special Action Program to Combat Forced Labor was set up in 2001. Under the leadership of Roger Plant, a man not ready to wait for slavery to end on its own, the ILO conducted an in-depth investigation of slavery worldwide. This effort was backed by action projects testing ways to bring slavery to an end. The result was a global report on forced labor published in 2005 that helped to bring the subject to the notice of governments. Like the report on child labor, this remarkable report passed the public relatively unnoticed, but it forms the basis for Plant's hard-nosed advocacy with recalcitrant governments. Crucially important is that the research is so clearly documented that it can be repeated in a few years—and we will have our first chance to see what changes are occurring, for better or worse, in global slavery. The ILO's Special Action Program is one of the most effective activities of the UN system, yet it runs on a tiny budget of about $16 million a year, the largest part of which, some $11 million, is spent on direct support to the victims of slavery. It is an indication of where slavery ranks in the priorities of the UN that the program receives less than .0008 percent of the UN's budget.

World Trade Organization and the World Bank

Operating in parallel to the United Nations are two organizations with an equally global reach: the World Bank and the World Trade Organization

(WTO). Many of the things needed to end slavery, and demolish the poverty and corruption that support it, can be done more easily with the support of these international financial institutions. But at the moment, the systems of international finance are sometimes neutral, sometimes positive, but sometimes working against freedom for slaves. Unlike the UN, the World Bank and the WTO were never tasked with the job of ending slavery. Their assigned job is to facilitate and regulate the global economy. Something they do share with the UN is their imperfection, but if we decide to wait for the perfect organization, we will wait forever. The crucial question is: how can we use the World Bank and the WTO, the tools we have today, to end slavery?

One answer is that we can use "conditionality" as a tool to pressure aid-receiving countries to take slavery seriously. Conditionality concerns the conditions applied to loans given out by the Bank, rules about how to repay the loan, accountability, and where and how the loan will be used. The fundamental issue is not *whether* the World Bank should apply conditionality—it already does—but rather *what* the guiding principles for these conditions should be. In fact, adjusting "conditionality" is also a good way for the Bank to address slavery. Specifically, this can be done through: taking existing standards for protecting workers and applying them as conditions for loans; globalizing the World Bank's currently limited rule that funds be spent in a way that supports core labor standards; and doing more to ensure that "conditional cash transfers" (CCTs) do not support slavery, but instead complement local anti-slavery efforts.

Today any country should be able to stop importing goods made by slave labor under Article XX of the GATT treaty. This article says a country can block trade in order to protect "human life" or "public morals." Slavery is clearly a threat to human life and public morals, but the trick is in the enforcement. Since the WTO was set up to regulate trade, its mechanisms are clumsy when it comes to protecting rights. To enact a ban on slave-made goods, a country that is a member of the WTO has to jump through a number of hoops. The first is that it should wait to enact a ban until the WTO has instructed the offending country to bring its laws and actions into line with the regulations. A second hoop is to show that a product was clearly linked to slavery. It is not good enough to ban coffee from one country because human rights are being violated there; you have to show that buying that coffee leads directly to human rights abuses. For the ban to stick, there has to be a necessary and essential link between the product and the violation. When it comes to slavery, this can be clear. Since the workers have no choice, their lives are under threat, and they are used to make a specific product, the link can be demonstrated through both logic and evidence.

Businesses: Ending the (Product) Chain

Slavery in the food we eat, the clothes we wear, and the cars we drive is an ugly blot on our lives. We think of it as well as a big problem of business. In fact, while it is a serious problem *for* business, it is really a problem *of* government. It is a strange fact that in the United States we have laws and regulations dating back more than one hundred years, and tested all the way to the Supreme Court, that mandate the power of government to control any business that uses any slave-made products or commodities. These laws have tended to be forgotten in the rush to make new laws concerning crimes like human trafficking that focus on the victim, but what they make clear is that any goods with slave input are contraband and forbidden in the United States. What's more, the Supreme Court has ruled that these laws do not stop at our borders or when noncitizens practice the slavery in other countries.

The Thirteenth Amendment and Slavery in the Global Economy

It was the Thirteenth Amendment to the U.S. Constitution that abolished slavery in the United States. While the Thirteenth Amendment ended legal slavery, current research shows how it has been applied to other types of slavery since the Civil War (Wolff 2002). Over time the Supreme Court applied the amendment to changing industrial contexts, and Wolff argues that it can be equally applied to modern slavery in the global market.

After the end of legal slavery, bondage put on new disguises. These masks included the Chinese "coolie" system and a kind of illegal debt-based slavery backed up by local police called peonage. Through a series of cases the Supreme Court has established precedents allowing justice to move forward despite mutations in the forms slavery takes. For Wolff (2002) these rulings lead to three key points about the anti-slavery law enshrined in the constitution. The first point is that, according to the Thirteenth Amendment, no U.S. citizen can own a slave, no matter where that slave is located. No U.S. citizen can be either a master or a slave. The second point is that the law forbids any business (operating within or outside of the United States) that *supports* slavery. The third point is that the Thirteenth Amendment also applies to industrial markets for slave labor. Corporate contact with slavery can happen in three ways: an American company can directly subject foreign workers to slavery; the company can hire someone else to subject the workers to slavery; or the company can profit from slavery that it had no part in creating. The Supreme Court has ruled that, however it happens, if companies profit from slavery, then they are in violation of the Thirteenth Amendment.[5] The Thirteenth Amendment would also support the passage of state laws prohibiting slave-made goods from being sold, and allowing the seizure of such goods. Under existing rulings, even a city government could pass ordinances that would treat slave-made goods in the same way as a controlled substance and confiscate vehicles, shops, and any other means of transporting and distributing the prohibited items.

Prohibiting the Profits and Products of Slavery

The rulings of the Supreme Court concerning profiting from slavery are clear. The 1864 *Slave Trade Cases* held that it was illegal for an American company to profit from slavery, no matter where that slavery occurred. There is a strong historical logic to this; in many ways, the slave trade was the first truly globalized market in human history. The slave trade of the past and human trafficking of today, by their nature, transcend borders.[6] Even in 1864 the Supreme Court recognized the fundamentally international nature of the crime, and ruled that circumstantial evidence of slavery was sufficient to bring a charge. The Court said that since slavery was so repugnant, a trader or businessman, such as a ship builder or outfitter, should avoid any possible activity—anything *necessarily suspicious*—that could tie them to the slave trade.[7]

Today, a number of "traders" (companies) could be identified as engaged in legitimate commerce but whose business is "necessarily suspicious." The most obvious companies are those that might directly exploit slave labor within the United States—agricultural labor contractors, operators of exotic dance clubs, escort services, and restaurants—all businesses where slavery has been found. Such violations can already be prosecuted under existing labor laws,[8] but the importance of this ruling is to extend responsibility to those companies that profit from slavery that occurs *outside* the national borders (within national borders, this activity could fall under state definitions of *prohibited articles* or *controlled substances*). On one hand, this points to transportation, as it did in the original *Slave Trade Cases*—the ships, aircraft, and vehicles used to carry victims of human trafficking. On the other hand, it also points to companies that are trading in the goods (and services) produced by slaves.

"Hot Goods" Law

Another legal tool, the "hot goods" law, allows any U.S. Labor inspector to seize goods, foodstuffs, or commodities, including goods that have "any part or ingredient thereof" tainted by illegal labor exploitation, or even if the product's wrapping or packaging was made with slavery or child labor. The rule that a good can be seized if "any part or ingredient thereof" is made with slave labor means that a shipment of packaged apple pies can be seized if the apples were originally picked by slave labor. The law covers the goods all the way along their path of distribution and stops just before the final consumer, so the shipment of pies can be grabbed at any time from the orchard to factory to distribution center to local shop, but no one can confiscate the pie in your refrigerator. If the same rule applied for slave-made goods from overseas, then chocolate made with a portion of slave-made cocoa, shirts produced with a portion of slave-made cotton, or cell phones assembled with a portion of slave-mined coltan could be seized.

What this brief and exploratory legal history boils down to is this: if the trade in slave-made goods is supporting slavery, and if U.S. companies are knowingly profiting from this trade, then the *Slave Trade Cases* should apply. What's more, the Supreme Court ruled that strong circumstantial evidence is good enough. Finally, we have a lot to learn from the application of the hot-goods law to cases of slavery. If we really wanted to get tough on slavery, the law is there, waiting for us to pick it up and swing it.

But What About Consumers?

We must remember that there are proven ways to build the cooperation that makes supply chain management possible without hurting poor people or businesses around the world. This is important, because if America suddenly and rigidly enforced its existing laws and the door slammed on imports of every country with slavery, the resulting economic havoc would likely increase slavery, at least in the short run, and it would certainly harm many farmers, workers, and businesses in other countries who have nothing to do with slavery and hate it as much as we do. The logical way forward is to work and organize by economic sector, bringing together the companies that use pig iron, or sugar, or coltan, or cotton, or whatever product we know is marked with slavery. It is the nature of the modern global market that most companies will be buying from many of the same sources and can trace their product chains to the same regions, mines, and even specific factories. The Kimberly Process for certifying diamonds as conflict-free represents a precedent for such an effort. The cost of investigating a product chain can be expensive for a single company, but cheap if the expense is spread across a number of companies. When government comes into the partnership, it becomes possible to give incentives for cleaning up a product chain. The federal government, for example, could allow companies to deduct half the cost of their product chain investigation from their corporate taxes. In this way, businesses are helped to clean up, and the government has fewer busts to make and fewer shipments to seize. The tax break could also apply to funds spent to free and rehabilitate slaves and to set up the mechanisms for monitoring and certifying commodities and products.

There is another role for the federal government that is very low in cost but very high in effectiveness, similar to the human rights campaign tactic of "naming and shaming." Given that slavery is unlawful in the United States, and that businesses must avoid even the imputation of profiting from slavery, then a small unit, possibly within Customs Enforcement or the Justice Department, should be set up and empowered to call businesses together. Off the record, officials could make clear the legal responsibilities of each company, and then pose a choice—either the businesses could collectively decide to engage in an agreement to monitor and clean up their product chains, or they could let the government investigate their products and risk seizure and forfeiture. There is no reason such an office could not learn something from Brazil, and list on their website those companies that choose to cooperate with each other and the government to investigate their supply chains, and those that have not yet developed a plan to ensure that their supply chain is clean.

Finally, it will take a little while for consumers to fully comprehend the slavery in the goods they buy, but when they get it, watch out. They will be asking, as many are asking today, why there are not slave-free agreements in industries such as those using cotton, sugar, coffee, pig iron, or coltan.

Baby-boomers are not going to want their retirement funds invested in industries that do not check their product chains for slavery. Smart businesses understand that to end slavery we have to bridge that gap between human rights objectives (like ending slavery) and business objectives (like making a profit). In the villages of northern India, slaves had to come to a collective conscious decision that they were going to reject slavery and face danger and risk in the push for freedom. In the great urban villages of North America and Europe, consumers have to do the same. The popularity of fair trade coffee suggests that consumers will opt for ethical options when such goods are clearly marked and reasonably priced.

International Development: End Poverty, End Slavery

With slavery festering in the mix of poverty and corruption, and freedom growing with education and economic autonomy, it makes sense to pull together the work that is attacking poverty with the movements that will end slavery. The largest numbers of slaves are in the developing world, exactly where billions are being spent to reduce poverty, improve health and education, and increase the quality of life. Putting aside factors like international debt repayments and unfair trade subsidies that suck out resources, economic development has been pouring money into the global South for decades. Why would linking development and slavery make anything better? As it turns out, new research suggests that one of the reasons economic development is taking so long is precisely *because* we have not taken on slavery. It seems that ending slavery may be one of the best things we can do to make a serious dent in poverty.

In a number of statistical trials, it was the amount of slavery that best explained differences in human development between countries (Smith 2009, 10). Other factors also play a role, but in predicting human development, the amount of slavery seems to be more important than the extent of democracy, the level of national debt, the amount of civil conflict, or the level of corruption. Obviously, slavery ruins the lives of slaves, but if this research is true, then it turns out that slavery is a major cause of depressed economies, low literacy levels, and shorter life spans, for *all* citizens in poor countries.

By this measure, it may be that not only does combating poverty help to end slavery, but combating slavery helps to end poverty. Maybe this should have been clear to us from other evidence. The long history, both before and long after 1865, of low education levels, shorter life spans, doubtful democracy, and poor economic development in the states of the American Deep South certainly reflects the legacy of slavery.

The more we have worked with and watched grassroots anti-slavery organizations around the world, the more we have come to believe that organizing communities to break out of slavery or to drive out human traffickers or slaveholders is a powerful inoculation against many of the toughest problems faced in community and economic development. First and foremost, development that is lodged in ending slavery does not run the risk of further entrenching and hardening the existing disparities of power. When the aim is to help people who live under threats of violence to escape slavery, or to best protect children who are vulnerable to being snatched away, you rarely need to carry out surveys to make sure you are achieving your goals. When people in slavery are coming to freedom, it is a pretty sure indicator that you have reached the people most in need. It also turns out that rescuing and bringing back enslaved children is a highly successful way to engender trust with communities that so far have had no reason to trust outsiders. What's more, it is hard to do good anti-slavery work and not bring benefits to other people who are equally at risk. If the returning child slave needs access to a decent school and the teacher is not in attendance or midday meals are not being served, improving the school for that child benefits all the other kids as well, including those at risk for overseas trafficking.

All evidence points to the fact that a deep engagement with poor communities helps to achieve a key goal held by development organizations, making sure that local people "own the process." When ex-slaves feel ownership of change and development, new groups emerge, ranging from milk cooperatives to social movements. Such groups may be tiny and informal, but they are likely to reach out to others. They instinctively look for allies, people and groups who will protect them when slaveholders fight back or corrupt officials deny justice. When one of the first outcomes of a development project is freedom, you can bet the participants have a strong vested interest in holding on to it. Human development is also essential to maintain freedom. In practically every case of someone falling back into slavery, the key cause is the lack of the economic and food security that is the aim of most development work.

The bottom line is that when it comes to poverty, slaves are the champions. They own nothing, not their labor, not even their own children. Their past, present, and future belong to someone else. There is no choice in this poverty; it is bounded by violence and pain. Sometimes, for slaves, even destitution looks worth a gamble. We do not have to end global poverty to end slavery, but ending the poverty of slaves is crucial to securing their freedom. And it turns out that ending slavery can have a significant impact on poverty, not just for the slaves, but also for the rest of their community, slave and free. A great deal of thought, theory, and practice focuses on ending poverty, rather less on how to end slavery. What is becoming clear is that these two goals should be harnessed together; their combined strength is greater than the sum of the parts.

Conclusion: The Beginning of the End of Slavery

We know that ending slavery is possible, that it is within our grasp. Every country has banned it, every faith has condemned it, and every thinking person hates it. If there is a cause that can unify humanity, it is the end of slavery. We would want to end this crime even if it meant great sacrifice, but, in fact, ending slavery costs little. Whether it takes ten or twenty or even thirty billion dollars, the cost is a small fraction of what we spend on the most trivial of our entertainments. Share this cost among us all—citizens, businesses, and governments—and over twenty-five years, it is little more than pocket change. Yet today the importance of slaves is not economic. Rather, they are important to our moral universe. The act of abolition will not only free the slaves, it will free us all.

Rethinking trafficking means rethinking our power and purpose. It means shifting our focus from sex to slavery. The notion of human trafficking has resonated with the general public, practitioners, and scholars. The next step is to begin focusing with precision on the center point of exploitation, the act of enslavement. It means shifting our focus from coercion to the broader problem of domination. Coercion must remain at the center of our analysis of slavery as a social relationship, but our work must challenge systems of domination within social, economic, legal, and political fields. The response to such domination is rights. Finally, then, rethinking trafficking requires shifting our focus from abolition to emancipation, from rescue to rights, and from protection to empowerment. It is in this struggle for dignity, rights, and recognition that our common humanity comes into its sharpest focus.

Notes

Chapter 1

1. This can also be seen in Kevin Bales's recent description of slavery as a "chain around the brain." While his intention seems intended to resonate with popular conceptualizations of earlier forms of slavery, it also underscores a more psychologically oriented element of coercion. This is true of a larger literature on the Stockholm Syndrome in such exploitation as well.

2. At this point in an individual's experience, we can ask which identity is primary, that of victim or of worker. Furthermore, we can ask who is in the position to determine this primary identity.

3. This is not to say that no attention is given to the conditions upon return. Efforts are made to ensure that the survivor is safe from retrafficking or the recommencement of abuse. What I highlight are the broader socioeconomic contexts.

4. For an alternative account, see Singh and Tripathi (2010).

Chapter 2

1. Unlike most professional historians, who tend to view extended historical research as an end in itself, recent treatments of contemporary slavery have primarily concentrated upon historical events that are held to be of most relevance to current concerns. This underlying essentialism is by no means unfounded or illegitimate, since there are many occasions where it can be necessary to foreground particular issues and events in order to simplify, exemplify, and/or prioritize, but it also invariably runs the risk of leaving other relevant materials out of the equation. This theme also extends to the relationship between theory and history. See Quirk 2008.

2. Recent examples include Brown and Morgan 2006; Campbell 2004; Campbell, Miers, and Miller 2009; Clarence-Smith 2006; Davis 2004; Eaton and Chatterjee 2006; Mirzai, Montana, and Lovejoy 2009; Spaulding and Beswick 2010; and Toledano 2007.

3. For a snapshot of global trends in this period, see Drescher 2009, 372–411; and Quirk 2009, 40–45, 73–91.

4. In this context, West Africa incorporates territories from Senegambia to Cameroon, and is bounded in the interior by the Sahara.

5. Lovejoy (2005, 3) recently revised this estimate upward to "in excess of two million and perhaps more than 4.5 million," but I have retained the earlier figure in order to provide consistency with a latter estimate from 1936.

6. On definitions, see Meillassoux 1991; Miers and Kopytoff 1977; and Rossi 2009, 1–25. For information on interviews with former slaves, see Klein 1998, 243–46; O'Hear 1997, 21–45; and Wright 1993.

7. European engagement with West Africa predates the conquest of the "New World," but the tenor of their overall strategic and economic relationships was substantially different in both continents. See Eltis 2000, 137–192.

8. On the broader relationship between anti-slavery and colonialism in Africa, see Cooper 2000; Grant 2005, 11–37; and Miers 1975, Part II.

9. This line of argument is most developed when it comes to legal abolition in the British Caribbean. See Drescher 1977 and Eltis 1987.

10. See, for example, Brantlinger 2003, 46, 73, 75, 90–93, 96, 121–22, 124–30, 158; Cooper 1996, 23–56; and Falola 2009, especially 55–78.

11. For a similar exercise, albeit one not directly concerned with slavery, see Hill 2005.

12. For a similarly selective timeline, see King 2004, 96–105.

13. Smith briefly discusses slavery in Africa and the rise of Islam, but no information is provided on how they were abolished (2007, 141–44).

14. Recent works where the history of slavery and abolition has been overlooked include Batstone 2007; Waugh 2006; and Kara 2009. For a more nuanced example, see Bales, Trodd, and Williamson 2009, especially 191–98.

15. For a critique of this approach, see Quirk 2006, 579–80.

16. For selective anti-slavery case studies, see Clark 2007, 37–60; Keck and Sikkink 1998, 8–32; Klotz 2002, 49–76; Ray 1989, 405–39.

17. Recent histories of human rights have tended to offer extended discussions of the early campaign against transatlantic slavery, while saying little about developments elsewhere in the late nineteenth and early twentieth centuries. See Hunt 2007 and Ishay 2008. A broader perspective can be found in Lauren 2003.

18. See, for example, Brooks 2004 and Martin and Yaquinto 2007. For a broader historical perspective, see Howard-Hassmann 2008.

19. The key starting point here is Bales [1999] 2004.

Chapter 3

1. The full texts of the Sexual Offenses and Asylum and Immigration Acts are available at www.legislationline.org/?tid=178&jid=54&ijid=0&less=true.

2. The full text of the Canadian legislation is available at www.legislationline.org/?tid=178&jid=11&less=true.

3. British newspapers also tend to have a partisan bias (Hallin and Mancini 2004). But since there is a clear partisan consensus on direction of public policy toward human trafficking, we should not expect the conservative *Times* of London to be any more critical of the sitting Blair government than the Labor-oriented *Guardian* or *Independent*.

4. The search criteria used was: (traffic!) w/3 (human or persons or women or girls or children or sex! or labor!). The "!" signifies a wild card. In this case, Lexis would search for articles with the term "traffic" or "trafficking." The "w/3" instructs Lexis to include articles where the second term is within three characters of the first term.

5. After extensive pretesting by me and my research assistants, two assistants divided the articles roughly in half and were then responsible for coding those articles. The articles were coded once more by the author. When there were disagreements between me and a coder, it was typically on the questions asking about sources, causes, and solutions. Rather than choose from the list of options provided, coders tended to write out answers in open-ended form. I performed the coding of open-ended responses and collapsed them into the choices already provided.

Chapter 5

1. My use of the female pronoun throughout the chapter is not intended to replicate the common conflation of "trafficking victim" with "woman." Rather, it is employed in a generic sense, though in a way that serves as a corrective to the normalized use of the male pronoun as a universal referent.

2. The State Department established this as the threshold for inclusion in the tier system in its 2002 TIP Report. See U.S. Department of State 2002.

3. Although TIP Reports have been released by the TIP Office since 2001, it was not until 2003 that states failing to comply with TVPA standards faced potential sanctions. See U.S. Department of State 2003.

4. The remaining four Tier 3 countries subject to sanctions during this period are Cambodia, Equatorial Guinea, Liberia, and Venezuela.

5. Many non-governmental sources argue that this figure is conservative, and questions have surfaced about the research methodology behind the government's statistics. See Cianciarulo 2007, 826.

6. The 2008 TIP report noted that 1,379 victims had received certification from the HHS up to the end of fiscal year 2007. An additional 616 individuals were granted certification during the 2008 and 2009 fiscal years (U.S. Department of State 2008, 2009, 2010a).

7. A T visa is a nonimmigrant category that allows trafficking victims temporary residence in the United States during the investigation and prosecution of their case when they are determined to face "unusual and severe harm" in their home country (U.S. Attorney General 2002).

8. The 2008 report noted that 1,008 T visas were issued to immediate survivors up through the end of fiscal year 2007. An additional 560 T visas were issued to survivors during the 2008 and 2009 fiscal years (U.S. Department of State 2008, 2009, 2010a).

9. For example, the UN Declaration on the Elimination of Violence Against Women (DEVAW) recognizes only "trafficking in women and forced prostitution" as forms of violence that threaten women's human rights.

Chapter 6

1. Information based on a field study in Athens, Greece, during September and October 2009, funded by University of Delaware.

2. Information based on a field study in Athens, Greece, during September and October 2009, funded by University of Delaware.

Chapter 7

1. For a more in-depth discussion on the challenges of such limitations, see Laczko and Lee 2003; Laczko 2002; Bales 2005, 136–38.

2. KFOR was preceded by the ill-fated Kosovo Verification Mission (KVM), a team of 1,500 troops sent by the Organization for Security and Cooperation in Europe. Following KFOR's conclusion, UNMIK was established. Both of these, however, were much smaller than KFOR and with narrower mandates.

3. For a discussion on the theoretical distinction between forced and voluntary prostitution, see Doezema 2000 and Samarasinghe 2007, among others.

4. Derived July 1999 to April 2001from the Human Rights Watch website at www .hrw.org/doc?t=africa&c=sierra.

Chapter 8

My sincere thanks to my research assistants, Margaret Williams and Jacob Owens, as well as the International Affairs Department at Lewis & Clark College, for providing partial funding to support this research.

1. Parish and Peceny (2002) suggest that by 2002 the OAS system was composed almost exclusively of liberal states, determined to promote democracy.

2. There is one methodological hurdle to overcome—measuring shifts in the rate of human trafficking. Governments often lack the capacity or the political will to report arrests for human trafficking. To overcome this data limitation, I rely on a dataset

developed by Smith and Smith (forthcoming). This dataset measures annual rates of trafficking in specific countries using two indirect and one direct measure of the practice: (1) annual NGO reports, (2) U.S. State Department reports, and (3) the number of trafficking victims assisted in the country by the International Organization for Migration.

3. It is important to note that 2004 was not the first year that either the UN or the OAS had a presence in Haiti. For an excellent overview of the OAS in Haiti throughout the 1990s, see Shamsie 2004.

4. Fatton Jr. (2002, 120) argues that Fanmis Lavalas employed illegal vote-counting methods despite its control of the Senate in order to obtain a super-majority.

5. Between 2000 and 2004 AI issued a series of reports that highlighted politically motivated killings in Haiti, a lack of press freedom, violation of human rights by prison guards, government interference in the judiciary, summary executions carried out by Haitian national police, and violence perpetrated by illegal armed groups (Amnesty International 2000, 2001, 2003, 2004a). Human Rights Watch echoed these concerns (2001a, 2004).

6. Aristide's 2004 departure is controversial—Aristide claimed that he was kidnapped in a coup sponsored by the U.S. government (Dupuy 2007, 171–75).

7. Polity scores are drawn from 2004, the year that the UN sent MINUSTAH and that OAS bureaucrats arrived in Haiti.

8. The General Assembly passed resolutions A/RES/55/67, A/RES/57/176, A/RES/58/137, and A/RES/59/166 between 2000 and 2004.

9. In November 2005 the UN Conduct and Discipline Team was established under the auspices of the UN Department of Peacekeeping Operations. Since 2005, upon arrival in mission countries all UN peacekeepers are required to undergo mandatory training to prevent sexual exploitation and abuse. For more information on this training, see the UN Conduct and Discipline Unit's home page: http://cdu.unlb.org/UNStrategy/Prevention.aspx.

10. Both the CIM and the Inter-American Children's Institute are part of the OAS system. The findings of the study were published in International Human Rights Law Institute 2002.

11. The Anti-Trafficking in Persons Section of the OAS was created under the authorization of OAS Resolutions 1948 and 2019.

12. For more on all of these conferences, see the OAS's Anti-Trafficking in Persons Section website: www.oas.org/dsp/atip_Detail.asp.

13. Gutierrez Trejos's statement is included at the end of the IACHR's Report following its visit to Haiti in 2007.

14. On Kosovo and Sierra Leone, see Smith and Smith forthcoming. On the Congo, visit the UN's Conduct and Discipline Unit's home page: http://cdu.unlb.org/AboutCDU.aspx.

Chapter 10

This chapter is a revised and extended version of the article "Improving the Effectiveness of the International Law of Human Trafficking: A Vision for the Future of the US Trafficking in Persons Reports" (Gallagher 2011). Thanks to Angela Ha for editorial assistance. The opinions expressed in the chapter are those of the author and should not be taken to represent, in whole or part, those of the organizations with whom she is or has been associated.

1. In 2009, seventeen countries were placed in Tier 3. In September of that year, the U.S. president determined that two of these countries would be sanctioned without exemption (Cuba and North Korea, both already under sanction) and that a further six (Burma, Eritrea, Fiji, Iran, Syria, and Zimbabwe, most of which were already under sanction) would be partially sanctioned. Sanctions against the remaining eight Tier 3 countries (Chad, Kuwait, Malaysia, Mauritania, Niger, Papua New Guinea, Saudi Arabia, and Sudan) were subject to a national interest waiver (Wyler and Siskin 2010). In 2010, thirteen countries were placed in Tier 3. At the time of writing, no determination had yet been made about sanctions against these countries.

Chapter 11

1. The eight Millennium Development Goals (MDGs)—which range from halving extreme poverty to halting the spread of HIV/AIDS and providing universal primary education, all by the target date of 2015—form a blueprint agreed to by all the world's countries and all the world's leading development institutions. They have galvanized unprecedented efforts to meet the needs of the world's poorest. However, it has to be said that at the beginning of 2007, the world was already falling behind on the timetable to achieve these goals. The plan to end extreme poverty by 2025 is explained in Sachs 2005.

2. The aim would be that origin countries and destination countries could solve this problem together by registering and regulating those who help people find work overseas, acting to protect their citizens working abroad, and making sure that migrant workers have a clear understanding of the realities of both working abroad and the risks of human trafficking.

3. We recognize that some of this capacity is spread across a number of offices. Yet our call is for a single commission whose target is the UN inspection mandate writ large.

4. Convention 182 on the Worst Forms of Child Labor, adopted June 1999, came into force in November 2000. Note that the international and UN definition of "child" is a person under the age of eighteen.

5. It is important to note that the Thirteenth Amendment, along with every other statute condemning slavery, is regarded as *jus cogens* (compelling law), and for that reason overrides any commercial or economic interests.

6. Note, for example, the origin of the word "slave"—extensive slave-raiding and taking in areas of what is now Eastern Europe by groups in what is now Germany fed hundreds of thousands of victims into the slave markets of ancient Rome. So extensive was this trans-European trade that the word "slav," meaning the Slavic people captured into slavery, became synonymous with, and then acquired wholly, the meaning "slave."

7. "It does not seem unreasonable, since it is the paramount interest of humanity that the traffic in men be, at all events, arrested, to require of the trader, who engages in a commerce, which, although not unlawful, is necessarily suspicious from its theatre and circumstances, that he *keep his operations so clear and so distinct in their character, as to repel the imputation of prohibited purpose*" (The Slavers (Kate) 1864, our emphasis).

8. U.S. Constitution. §§ 1581–1594. See, e.g., *United States v. Bibbs*, 564 F.2d 1165 *(involuntary servitude in agriculture)*; *United States v. Bradley and O'Dell*, 390 F.3d 145 *(involuntary servitude in tree removal service)*.

Bibliography

Abbott, Karen. 2007. *Sin in the Second City: Madams, Ministers, Playboys, and the Battle for America's Soul*. New York: Random House.

Abdullah, Ibrahim, and Patrick Muana. 1998. "The Revolutionary United Front of Sierra Leone." In *African Guerillas*, ed. Christopher Clapham, 173–78. Oxford: James Currey.

Adamson, Fiona B. 2006. "Crossing Borders: International Migration and National Security." *International Security* 31(1): 1165–99.

Adas, Michael. 1989. *Machines as the Measure of Men: Science, Technology, and Ideologies of Western Dominance*. Ithaca, N.Y.: Cornell University Press.

Adelman, Madelaine. 2003. "The Military, Militarism, and the Militarization of Domestic Violence." *Violence Against Women* 9: 1118–52.

Agence France Presse (AFP). 2009. "Malaysian Outcry at U.S. Trafficking Blacklisting." June 16.

Agustin, Laura Maria. 2005. "Migrants in the Mistress's House: Other Voices in the 'Trafficking' Debate." *Social Politics: International Studies in Gender, State and Society* 12(1): 96–117.

———. 2007. *Sex at the Margins: Migration, Labour Markets and the Rescue Industry*. London: Zed Books.

Ali, Habib Mohammad. 2010. "Data Collection on Victims of Human Trafficking: An Analysis of Various Sources." *Journal of Human Security* 6(1): 55–69.

Allain, Jean. 2006. "Slavery and the League of Nations: Ethiopia as a Civilized Nation." *Journal of the History of International Law* 8: 213–244.

Althaus, Scott. 2003. *Collective Preferences in Democratic Politics*. New York: Cambridge University Press.

Altman, Dennis. 2001. *Global Sex*. Chicago: University of Chicago Press.

Amnesty International. 1998. "Sierra Leone: 1998—A Year of Atrocities, Sierra Leone: AI Recommendations to the Contact Group on Sierra Leone, New York, 1999." Press Release, November 1.

———. 2000. "Haiti: Amnesty International Urges UN Not to Abandon Haiti." AMR/36/009/2000, December 4.

———. 2001. "Haiti: Human Rights Challenges Facing the New Government." AMR/36/002/2001, April 18.

———. 2003. "Haiti: Abuse of Human Rights: Political Violence as the 200th Anniversary of Independence Approaches." AMR/36/007/2003, October 8.

———. 2004a. "Haiti: Amnesty International Calls on the Transitional Government to Set Up an Inquiry into Summary Executions Attributed to Members of the Haitian National Police." AMR/36/060/2004, June 3.

———. 2004b. "Kosovo: Facts and Figures on Trafficking of Women and Girls for Forced Prostitution in Kosovo." Press Release, June 5.

———. 2004c. "Kosovo: Trafficked Women and Girls Have Human Rights." Press Release, June 5.

———. 2004d. "Nepal: 'Disappearance'/Fear of Safety." January 19.

———. 2005. "Nepal: Children Caught in the Conflict." July 26.

———. 2006a. "Haiti: Open Letter to the President of the Republic of Haiti, Rene Garcia Preval, Regarding Amnesty International's Recommendations for the Protection and Promotion of Human Rights." AI Doc 36/011/2006, October 2.

———. 2006b. "The Call for Tough Arms Control: Voices from Haiti." AI Doc 36/001/2006, January 1.

———. n.d. "Protecting the Human Rights of Women and Girls Trafficked for Forced Prostitution in Kosovo." AI Index: EUR 70/010/2004.

Anderson, Bridget. 2004. "Migrant Domestic Workers and Slavery." In *The Political Economy of New Slavery*, ed. Christien van den Anker, 107–17. Basingstoke: Palgrave.

Anderson, Bridget, and Ben Rogaly. 2004. *Forced Labor and Migration to the UK*. Study prepared for COMPAS in collaboration with the Trades Union Congress.

Anderson, Bridget, and Martin Ruhs. 2007. *The Origins and Functions of Illegality in Migrant Labor Markets: An Analysis of Migrants, Employers and the State in the UK*. Oxford: COMPAS.

Andrijasevic, Rutvica. 2007. "Beautiful Dead Bodies: Gender, Migration, and Representation in Anti-Trafficking Campaigns." *Feminist Review* 86(1): 24–44.

Aoi, Chiyuki, Cedric de Coning, and Ramesh Chandra Thakur. 2007. *Unintended Consequences of Peacekeeping Operations*. New York: UN University Press.

Aradau, Claudia. 2008. *Rethinking Trafficking in Women: Politics Out of Security*. New York: Palgrave Macmillan.

Armstrong, Elizabeth, and Mary Bernstein. 2008. "Culture, Power, and Institutions: A Multi-Institutional Politics Approach to Social Movements." *Sociological Theory* 26(1): 74–99.

Aronowitz, Alexis A. 2001. "Smuggling and Trafficking in Human Beings: The Phenomenon, the Markets that Drive It and the Organizations that Promote It." *European Journal of Criminal Policy and Research* 9: 163–95.

Australian Government. 2009. *Australian Government Anti-People Trafficking Strategy*. Australian Government fact sheet, June. Available at www.ag.gov.au/www/ministers/RWPAttach.nsf/VAP/(966BB47E522E848021A38A20280E2386)

~056+June+17+Human+Trafficking+Fact+Sheet.pdf/$file/056+June+17+Human
+Trafficking+Fact+Sheet.pdf, accessed January 2011.

Australian Government, Attorney-General's Department. n.d. "People Trafficking."
Available at www.ag.gov.au/www/agd/agd.nsf/Page/People_Trafficking, accessed
July 2009.

Baguioro, Luz. 1999. "Manila Senate Ratifies Pact with U.S." *Straits Times* (Singapore),
May 28.

Balch, Alex, Paul Brindley, and Sam Scott. 2009. *Gangmasters Licensing Authority Annual Review 2008.*

Baldwin-Edwards, Martin. 2004. "Statistical Data in Immigrants in Greece: An Ana-
lytic Study of Available Data and Recommendations for Conformity with European Union Standards." A study conducted for Migration Police Institute
(IMEPO). Athens: Mediterranean Migration Observatory, UEHR, Panteion University.

Baldwin-Edwards, Martin, and Katerina Apostolatou. 2009. "Greece." In *Statistics and
Reality: Concepts and Measurements of Migration in Europe*, ed. Heinz Fassmann,
Ursula
Reeger, and Wiebke Siever, 235–64. Amsterdam: Amsterdam University Press,
IMISCOE-Reports.

Bales, Kevin. [1999] 2004. *Disposable People: New Slavery in the Global Economy*, 2d
ed. Berkeley: University of California Press.

———. 2005. *Understanding Global Slavery: A Reader*. Berkeley: University of California Press.

———. 2007. *Ending Slavery*. Berkeley: University of California Press.

Bales, Kevin, and Zoe Trodd, eds. 2008. *To Plead Our Own Cause*. Ithaca, N.Y.: Cornell University Press.

Bales, Kevin, Zoe Trodd, and Alex Kent Williamson. 2009. *Modern Slavery: The Secret
World of 27 Million People*. Oxford: One World.

Barnett, Michael, and Martha Finnemore. 1999. "The Politics, Power, and Pathologies
of International Organizations." *International Organization* 53(4): 699–732.

Baroud, Ramzy. 2009. "Beyond Politics: People for Sale in a Hungry World." *Al Jazeera
Magazine*, June 28. Available at http://english.aljazeera.com/news/articles/39/
Beyond-politics-People-for-sale-in-hungry-world.html, accessed January 2011.

Barrett, Stanley, Sean Stokholm, and Jeanette Burke. 2004. "The Idea of Power and the
Power of Ideas: A Review Essay." *American Anthropologist* 103(2): 468–480.

Barth, Elise Fredrikke, Karen Hostens, and Inger Skjelsbaek. 2004. *Gender Aspects of
Conflict Interventions: Intended and Unintended Consequences*. Oslo: PRIO.

Batstone, David. 2007. *Not for Sale: The Return of the Global Slave Trade and How We
Can Fight It*. New York: Harper Collins.

Beeks, Karen, and Delila Amir, eds. 2006. *Trafficking and the Global Sex Industry*.
Lanham, Md.: Lexington Books.

Bennett, D. Scott, and Allan C. Stam. 2004. *The Behavioral Origins of War*. Ann Arbor, Mich.: University Michigan Press.

Bennett, W. Lance. 1991. "Toward a Theory of Press-State Relations." *Journal of Communication* 40(2): 103–25.

Bennett, W. Lance, Regina Lawrence, and Steven Livingston. 2007. *When the Press Fails: Political Power and the News Media from Iraq to Katrina*. Chicago: University of Chicago Press.

Berdal, Mats, and Spyros Economides, eds. 2007. *United Nations Interventionism, 1991–2004*. New York: Cambridge University Press.

Berman, Jacqueline. 2006. "The Left, the Right and the Prostitute: The Making of U.S. Antitrafficking in Persons Policy." *Tulane Journal of International and Comparative Law* 14(2): 269–94.

———. 2003. "(Un)Popular Strangers and Crises (Un)Bounded: Discourses of Sex-Trafficking, the European Political Community and the Panicked State of the Modern State." *European Journal of International Relations* 9(1): 37–86.

Bilateral Safety Corridor Coalition (BSCC). 2011. Home page, www.bsccoalition.org/index.html, accessed January 2011.

Blanchard, Peter. 2008. *Under the Flags of Freedom: Slave Soldiers and the Wars of Independence in Spanish South America*. Pittsburgh: University of Pittsburgh Press.

Bob, Clifford. 2005. *The Marketing of Rebellion: Insurgents, Media, and International Activism*. Cambridge: Cambridge University Press.

Bohman, James, and Matthais Lutz-Bachmann. 1997. Introduction. In *Perpetual Peace: Essays on Kant's Cosmopolitan Ideal*, eds. James Bohman and Matthais Lutz-Bachman, 1–22. Cambridge, Mass.: MIT Press.

Bohning, Don. 2000. "Voter Turnout High in Haiti Despite Risk." *Miami Herald*, May 22.

Bose, Sumantra. 1994. *States, Nations, Sovereignty: Sri Lanka, India, and the Tamil Eelam Movement*. Thousand Oaks, Calif.: Sage.

Brabant, Malcolm. 2009. "Greek Police Flatten Migrant Camp." BBC News, July 12. Available at http://news.bbc.co.uk/2/hi/8146597.stm, accessed April 2010.

Brantlinger, Patrick. 2003. *Dark Vanishings: Discourses on the Extinction of Primitive Races, 1800–1930*. Ithaca, N.Y.: Cornell University Press.

Bravo, Karen E. 2007. "Exploring the Analogy Between Modern Trafficking in Human and the Trans-Atlantic Slave Trade." *Boston University International Law Journal* 25(2): 207–95.

British Broadcasting Corporation (BBC). 2006. "Fears Over Haiti Child Abuse." BBC News, November 30.

———. 2007. "UN Requires 'Better' Peacekeepers." BBC News Online, July 28. Available at http://news.bbc.co.uk/2/hi/europe/6920867.stm, accessed January 2011.

———. 2010. "Timeline: Nepal." *BBC News Online*, August 4. Available at news.bbc.co.uk/2/hi/south_asia/1166516.stm, accessed January 2011.

Brooks, Roy. 2004. *Atonement and Forgiveness: A New Model for Black Reparations.* Berkeley: University of California Press.

Brown, Chris, and Philip Morgan, eds. 2006. *Arming Slaves: From Classical Times to the Modern Age.* New Haven, Conn.: Yale University Press.

Brysk, Alison (ed.). 2002. *Globalization and Human Rights.* Berkeley: University of California Press.

Brysk, Alison. 2005. *Human Rights and Private Wrongs: Constructing Global Civil Society.* New York: Routledge.

———.2009. "Beyond Framing and Shaming: Human Trafficking, Human Security, and the International Human Rights Regime," *Journal of Human Security,* Fall 2009.

Brysk, Alison, and Gershon Shafir, eds. 2004. *People Out of Place: Globalization and the Citizenship Gap.* New York: Routledge.

Bush, George W. 2003a. "Presidential Determination with Respect to Foreign Governments' Efforts Regarding Trafficking in Persons." Presidential Determination 2003–35, September 9.

———. 2003b. *Statement by His Excellency Mr. George W. Bush, President of the United States of America: Address to the United Nations General Assembly September 23, 2003.* Available at www.un.org/webcast/ga/58/statements/usaeng030923.htm, accessed July 2010.

Caldwell, Gillian, Steve Galster, Jyothi Kanics, and Nadia Steinzor. 1999. "Capitalizing on Transition Economies: The Role of the Russian Mafia in Trafficking Women for Forced Prostitution." In *Illegal Immigration and Commercial Sex: The New Slave Trade,* ed. Phil Williams, 42–73. London: Frank Cass.

Cameron, Sally, and Edward Newman, eds. 2008. *Trafficking in Humans: Social, Culture, and Political Dimensions.* New York: UN University Press.

Camp Arirang. 1996. Produced and directed by Diana S. Lee and Grace Yoongkung Lee. National Asian American Telecommunications Association. Videocassette. 28 min.

Campbell, Gwyn, ed. 2004. *The Structure of Slavery in Indian Africa and Asia.* London: Frank Cass.

Campbell, Gwyn, Suzanne Miers, and Joseph Miller, eds. 2009. *Children in Slavery Through the Ages.* Athens: Ohio University Press.

Carens, Joseph. 1987. "Aliens and Citizens: The Case for Open Borders." *Review of Politics* 49(2): 251–73.

Carment, David, and Patrick James. 1998. "The United Nations at 50: Managing Ethnic Crises, Past and Present." *Journal of Peace Research* 35(1): 61–82.

Carpenter, Michael. 2003. "The Modern Slave Trade in Post-Communist Europe." *Center for Slavic and East European Studies Newsletter* 20(1): 5–8, 15.

Casselman, Ben. 2004. "Three Stories a Day? How Young Reporters Learn to Skim." *Columbia Journalism Review* (May/June).

Cassese, Antonia. 1995. *Self-Determination of Peoples: A Legal Reappraisal.* Hersch Lauterpacht Memorial Lectures. Cambridge: Cambridge University Press.

Castles, Stephen, and Mark J. Miller. 2009. *The Age of Migration: International Population Movements in the Modern World*. New York: Guilford Press.

CdeBaca, Lou. 2010. "A Decade in Review, a Decade Before Us: Celebrating Successes and Developing New Strategies at the 10th Anniversary of the Trafficking Victims Protection Act." March 18. Available at www.state.gov/g/tip/rls/rm/2010/138532 .htm, accessed January 2011.

Chaddock, Gail Russell. 2000. "Congress Takes Aim at Modern-Day Slavery." *Christian Science Monitor*, October 18.

Chapkis, Wendy. 2003. "Trafficking, Migration, and the Law." *Gender & Society* 17: 923–37.

Chatterjee, Indrani. 1999. *Gender, Slavery and Law in Colonial India*. Oxford: Oxford University Press.

Chatzifotiou, Sevaste, and Rebecca Dobash. 2001. "Seeking Informal Support: Marital Violence Against Women in Greece." *Violence against Women* 7(9): 1024–50.

Choi-Fitzpatrick. n.d. "Let My People Go: Salvation Schemas Among Evangelical Abolitionists, 1830 and 2010." Under review.

Cholewinski, Ryszard. 2005. *Irregular Migrants: Access to Minimum Social Rights*. Strasbourg: Council of Europe.

Christopher, Warren. 1996. "Commemorating Human Rights Day." Remarks made at a ceremony commemorating Human Rights Day at the U.S. Department of State, Washington, D.C., December 16. *U.S. Department of State Dispatch* 7 (51).

Chuang, Janie. 2006. "The United States as Global Sheriff: Using Unilateral Sanctions to Combat Human Trafficking." *Michigan Journal of International Law* 27(2): 437–94.

Cianciarulo, Marisa Silenzi. 2007. "Immigration: Modern-Day Slavery and Cultural Bias: Proposals for Reforming the U.S. Visa System for Victims of International Human Trafficking." *Nevada Law Journal* 7: 826–40.

Cicero-Dominguez, Salvador. 2005. "Assessing the U.S.-Mexico Fight Against Human Trafficking and Smuggling: Unintended Results of U.S. Immigration Policy." *Northwestern University Journal of International Human Rights* 4 (2). Available at www.law.northwestern.edu/journals/jihr/v4/n2/2, accessed January 2011.

Clarence-Smith, William Gervase. 2006. *Islam and the Abolition of Slavery*. Oxford: Oxford University Press.

Clark, Ian. 2007. *International Legitimacy and World Society*. Oxford: Oxford University Press.

Cleveland, Sarah H. 2002. "Norm Internalization and U.S. Economic Sanctions." *Yale Journal of International Law* 27(1): 1–102.

Cockburn, Alexander. 2006. "Nick Kristof's Brothel Problem." *The Nation*, February 13, 2006, 8.

Colley, Linda. 1992. *Britons: Forging the Nation 1707–1837*. New Haven, Conn.: Yale University Press.

Conklin, Alice L. 1997. *A Mission to Civilize: The Republican Idea of Empire in France and West Africa, 1895–1930*. Stanford, Calif.: Stanford University Press.

Cooper, Andrew, and Thomas Legler. 2001. "The OAS Democratic Solidarity Paradigm: Questions of Collective and National Leadership." *Latin American Politics and Society* 43(1): 103–26.

Cooper, Frederick. 1980. *From Slaves to Squatters: Plantation Labor in Agriculture in Zanzibar and Coastal Kenya, 1890–1925*. New Haven, Conn.: Yale University Press.

———. 1996. *Decolonization and African Society: The Labor Question in French and British Africa*. Cambridge: Cambridge University Press.

———. 2000. "Conditions Analogous to Slavery; Imperialism and Free Labor Ideology in Africa." In *Beyond Slavery: Explorations of Race, Labor, and Citizenship in Postemancipation Societies*, ed. Frederick Cooper, Thomas Holt, and Rebecca Scott, 107–50. Chapel Hill, N.C.: University of North Carolina Press.

Cotton, James, ed. 2004. *East Timor, Australia and Regional Order: Intervention and its Aftermath in Southeast Asia*. New York: Routledge, Curzon Press.

Council of Europe. 2011. Committee on Social Rights website, www.coe.int/t/dghl/monitoring/socialcharter/ecsr/ecsrdefault_EN.asp, accessed January 2011.

Cox, Caroline. 2007. "Fighting Slavery in Africa." In *Creating the Better Hour: Lessons from William Wilberforce*, ed. Chuck Stetson, 239–56. Macon, Ga.: Stroud & Hall.

Craig, Gary. 2010. *Child Slavery Now*. Bristol: Policy Press.

Crawford, Timothy. 2001–02. "Pivotal Deterrence and the Kosovo War: Why the Holbrooke Agreements Failed." *Political Science Quarterly* 116(4): 499–523.

Critchell, David. 2003. "Inside the Teen-Hooker Factory." *Rolling Stone*, October 16, 2003, 78+.

Csaky, Corinna. 2008. *No One to Turn To: The Underreporting of Child Sexual Exploitation and Abuse by Aid Workers and Peacekeepers*. London: Save the Children UK.

Cuperus, Renâe, Johannes Kandel, Karl Duffek, Rene Cuperus, eds. 2003. *The Challenge of Diversity: European Social Democracy Facing Migration, Integration and Multiculturalism*. Innsbruck: Studien Verlag.

Curran, James. 2005. "What Democracy Requires of the Media." In *The Press*, ed. Geneva Overholser and Kathleen Jamieson, 120–40. New York: Oxford University Press.

Curtin, Phillip. 1964. *The Image of Africa: British Ideas and Action, 1780–1850*. Madison: University of Wisconsin Press.

Davis, David. 2006. *Inhuman Bondage: The Rise and Fall of Slavery in the New World*. Oxford: Oxford University Press.

Davis, Robert. 2004. *Christian Slaves, Muslim Masters: White Slavery in the Mediterranean, the Barbary Coast, and Italy, 1500–1800*. Houndmills: Palgrave.

Dearing, James, and Everett Rogers. 1996. *Agenda-Setting*. Thousand Oaks, Calif.: Sage.

Demleitner, Nora V. 2002. "Immigration Threats and Rewards: Effective Law Enforcement Tools in the 'War' on Terrorism?" *Emory Law Journal* 51(3): 1059–94.

Derrick, Jonathan. 1975. *Africa's Slaves Today*. New York: Schocken Books.

DeStefano, Anthony M. 2008. *The War on Human Trafficking: U.S. Policy Assessed*. Rutgers, N.J.: Rutgers University Press.

Diehl, Paul, Jennifer Reifschneider, and Paul Hensel. 1996. "United Nations Intervention and Recurring Conflict." *International Organizations* 50(4): 683–700.

DiNicola, Andrea, Andrea Cauduro, Marco Lombardi, and Paolo Ruspini, eds. 2009. *Prostitution and Human Trafficking: Focus on Clients*. New York: Springer.

Doezema, Jo. 2000. "Loose Women or Lost Women? The Re-emergence of the Myth of White Slavery in Contemporary Discourses of Trafficking in Women." *Gender Issues* 18(1): 23–50.

———. 2010. *Sex Slaves and Discourse Masters: The Construction of Trafficking*. London: Zed Books.

Donnelly, Jack. 2003. *Universal Human Rights in Theory and Practice*. Ithaca, N.Y.: Cornell University Press.

Doomernik, Jeroen, and Michael Jandl, eds. 2008. *Modes of Migration Control and Regulation in Europe*. Amsterdam: Amsterdam University Press.

Dorevitch, Anna, and Michelle Foster. 2008. "Obstacles on the Road to Protection: Assessing the Treatment of Sex-Trafficking Victims Under Australia's Migration and Refugee Law." *Melbourne Journal of International Law* 9(1): 1–46.

Dowling, Emma. 2004. "Strategies for Change: The Tobin Tax." In *The Political Economy of New Slavery*, ed. Christien van den Anker, 201–16. Basingstoke: Palgrave.

Doyle, Michael, and Nicholas Sambanis. 2000. "International Peace Building: A Theoretical and Quantitative Analysis." *American Political Science Review* 94(4): 779–801.

Drescher, Seymour. 1977. *Econocide: British Slavery in the Era of Abolition*. Pittsburgh: University of Pittsburgh Press.

———. 1987. *Capitalism and Antislavery*. Oxford: Oxford University Press.

———. 2002. *The Mighty Experiment: Free Labor Versus Slavery in British Emancipation*. Oxford: Oxford University Press.

———. 2009. *Abolition: A History of Slavery and Antislavery*. Cambridge: Cambridge University Press.

Dumett, Raymond. 1981. "Pressure Groups, Bureaucracy, and the Decision-Making Process: The Case of Slavery Abolition and Colonial Expansion in the Gold Coast." *Journal of Imperial and Commonwealth History* 9(2): 193–215.

Dumett, Raymond, and Marion Johnson. 1989. "Britain and the Suppression of Slavery in the Gold Coast Colony, Ashanti and the Northern Territories." In *The End of Slavery in Africa*, ed. Suzanne Miers and Richard Roberts, 71–118. Madison: University of Wisconsin Press.

Dupuy, Alex. 2007. *The Prophet and Power: Jean-Bertrand Aristide, the International Community and Haiti*. Lanham, Md.: Rowman and Littlefield.

Eaton, Richard, and Indrani Chatterjee, eds. 2006. *Slavery and South Asian History.* Bloomington: Indiana University Press.

Edwards, Brian. 2000. "Lap of the Gods." *Index on Censorship* 1.

Edwards, Michael. 2004. *Civil Society.* Cambridge: Polity.

Ehrenreich, Barbara, and Arlie Russell Hochschild. 2004. *Global Woman: Nannies, Maids, and Sex Workers in the New Economy,* 2d ed. New York: Owl Books.

Elliot, L. 1996. "Child Prostitution: A Case Study in the Military Camps in Liberia." Paper presented at National Institute of Health International Conference on Aids, July 7–12. Available at gateway.nlm.nih.gov/MeetingAbstracts/102218066.html, accessed January 2011.

Eltis, David. 1987. *Economic Growth and the Ending of the Transatlantic Slave Trade.* Oxford: Oxford University Press.

———. 2000. *The Rise of African Slavery in the Americas.* Cambridge: Cambridge University Press.

Eltis, David, and David Richardson. 2008. "A New Assessment of the Transatlantic Slave Trade." In *Extending the Frontiers: Essays on the New Transatlantic Slave Trade Database,* ed. David Eltis and David Richardson, 40–41. New Haven, Conn.: Yale University Press.

Enloe, Cynthia H. 1993. *The Morning After: Sexual Politics at the End of the Cold War.* Los Angeles: University of California Press.

———. 2000a. *Bananas, Beaches, and Bases: Making Feminist Sense of International Politics.* Sacramento: University of California Press.

———. 2000b. *Maneuvers: The International Politics of Militarizing Women's Lives.* Los Angeles: University of California Press.

Entman, Robert M. 1993. "Framing: Toward Clarification of a Fractured Paradigm." *Journal of Communication* 43(4): 51–58.

———. 2004. *Projections of Power: Framing News, Public Opinion, and U.S. Foreign Policy.* Chicago: University of Chicago Press.

EUbusiness. "EU Report Blasts 'Unreliable' Greek Economic Statistics." January 12. Available at www.eubusiness.com/news-eu/greece-economy.28d, accessed April 2010.

European Commission Directorate-General on Justice, Freedom and Security. 2004. *Report of the Experts Group on Trafficking in Human Beings.* Brussels.

Express. 2009. "Reception Centres Key to Immigration Problem in Greece." July 17. Available at www.express.gr/index2.php?option=ozo_content&perform=view&id=190561, accessed January 2011.

Faist, Thomas. 2009. "The Transnational Social Question: Social Rights and Citizenship in a Global Context." *International Sociology* 24(7): 7–35.

Falola, Toyin. 2009. *Colonialism and Violence in Nigeria.* Bloomington: Indiana University Press.

Farr, Kathryn. 2004. *Sex Trafficking: The Global Market in Women and Children.* New York: Worth.

Farrell, Amy, and Stephanie Fahy. 2009. "The Problem of Human Trafficking in the U.S.: Public Frames and Policy Responses." *Journal of Criminal Justice* 37(6): 617–26.

Fatton Jr., Robert. 2002. *Haiti's Predatory Republic: The Unending Transition to Democracy*. Boulder, Colo.: Lynne Rienner.

Fegley, Randall. 2010. "Bound to Violence: Uganda's Child Soldiers as Slaves." In *African Systems of Slavery*, ed. Jay Spaulding and Stephanie Beswick, 203–28. Trenton, N.J.: Africa World Press.

Feingold, David A. 2005. "Human Trafficking." *Foreign Policy* (September/October): 26–31.

———. 2010. "Trafficking in Numbers: The Social Construction of Human Trafficking Data." In *Sex, Drugs and Body Counts: The Politics of Numbers in Global Crime and Conflict*, ed. Peter Andreas and Kelly M. Greenhill, 46–75. Ithaca, N.Y.: Cornell University Press.

Flournoy, Craig. 2004. "Red Dawn in Dallas." *Columbia Journalism Review* (May/June).

Flowers, R. Barri. 1998. *The Prostitution of Women and Girls*. Jefferson, N.C.: McFarland.

Fortna, Virginia. 2004. "Does Peacekeeping Keep Peace? International Intervention and the Duration of Peace After Civil War." *International Studies Quarterly* 48(2): 269–92.

Fragomen, Jr., Austin T. 1997. "The Illegal Immigration Reform and Immigrant Responsibility Act of 1996: An Overview." *International Migration Review* 31(2): 0438–60.

Frederick, John. 2005. "The Myth of Nepal-to-India Sex Trafficking: Its Creation, Its Maintenance, and Its Influence on Anti-Trafficking Interventions." In *Trafficking and Prostitution Reconsidered: New Perspectives on Migration, Sex Work, and Human Rights*, ed. Kamala Kempadoo, 127–47. Boulder, Colo.: Paradigm.

Free the Slaves, and the Human Rights Center of the University of California, Berkeley. 2005. "Hidden Slaves: Forced Labor in the United States." *Berkeley Journal of International Law* 23.

Freidrich, Amy, Anna Myer, and Deborah Perlman. 2006. "The Trafficking in Persons Report: Strengthening a Diplomatic Tool." UCLA School of Public Affairs Applied Policy Project, May 8. Available at www.spa.ucla.edu/ps/research/J-Traffic06 .pdf, accessed January 2011.

Friman, H. Richard. 2010. "Numbers and Certification: Assessing Foreign Compliance in Combating Narcotics and Human Trafficking." In *Sex, Drugs and Body Counts: The Politics of Numbers in Global Crime and Conflict*, ed. Peter Andreas and Kelly Greenhill. Ithaca, N.Y.: Cornell University Press.

Friman, Richard, and Simon Reich, eds. 2007. *Human Trafficking, Human Security, and the Balkans*. Pittsburgh: University of Pittsburgh Press.

Gallagher, Anne T. 2001a. "Human Rights and the New UN Protocols on Trafficking and Migrant Smuggling: A Preliminary Analysis." *Human Rights Quarterly* 23(4): 975–1004.

———. 2001b. "Book review: *Trafficking in Persons Report* (U.S. State Department, United States of America, July 2000)." *Human Rights Quarterly* 23(4): 1135–41.

———. 2006. "Recent Legal Developments in the Field of Human Trafficking: A Critical Review of the 2005 European Convention and Related Instruments." *European Journal of Migration and Law* 8(1): 163–89.

———. 2009. "Human Rights and Human Trafficking: Quagmire or Firm Ground? A Response to James Hathaway." *Virginia Journal of International Law* 49(4): 789–848.

———. 2010. *The International Law of Human Trafficking*. Cambridge: Cambridge University Press.

———. Forthcoming 2011. "Improving the Effectiveness of the International Law of Human Trafficking: A Vision for the Future of the U.S. Trafficking in Persons Reports." *Human Rights Review*.

Gallagher, Anne T., and Paul Holmes. 2008. "Developing an Effective Criminal Justice Response to Human Trafficking: Lessons from the Front Line." *International Criminal Justice Review* 18(3): 318–43.

Gallagher, Anne T., and Elaine Pearson. 2010. "The High Cost of Freedom: A Legal and Policy Analysis of Shelter Detention for Victims of Trafficking." *Human Rights Quarterly* 32(1): 73–114.

Gans, Herbert J. 2005. *Deciding What's News: A Study of CBS Evening News, NBC Nightly News, Newsweek, and Time*, 25th Anniversary Edition. Chicago: Northwestern University Press.

Garcia, Gabriel. 2006. "The State Department Human Trafficking Report: Raw Ideology Rather than Bona-fide Research." *Council of Hemispheric Affairs*, June 28. Available at www.coha.org/the-state-department-human-trafficking-report-raw-ideology-rather-than-bona-fide-research, accessed January 2011.

Geddes, Andrew. 2003. *The Politics of Migration and Immigration in Europe*. London: Sage.

Geddes, Andrew, Sam Scott, and Katrine Bang Nielsen. 2007. *Gangmaster Licensing Evaluation Study: Baseline Report*. Nottingham: GLA.

Geggus, David. 1982. *Slavery, War, and Revolution: The British Occupation of Saint Domingue, 1793–1798*. Oxford: Clarendon Press.

———. 2006. "The Arming of the Slaves in the Haitian Revolution." In *Arming Slaves: From Classical Times to the Modern Age*, ed. Christopher Brown and Philip Morgan, 209–32. New Haven, Conn.: Yale University Press.

Gershoni, Yekutiel. 1997. "War Without End and an End to a War: The Prolonged Wars in Liberia and Sierra Leone." *African Studies Review* 40(3): 55–76.

Getz, Trevor. 2004. *Slavery and Reform in West Africa*. Athens: Ohio University Press.

Gibbs, Jack. 1989. *Control: Sociology's Central Notion*. Urbana-Champagne: University of Illinois Press.

Gilens, Martin. 1999. *Why Americans Hate Welfare: Race, Media, and the Politics of Antipoverty Policy*. Chicago: University of Chicago Press.

Gill, Amardeep Kaur. 2007. "Today's Slavery." *Canadian Dimension* 41(3): 19–22.

Gilligan, Michael, and Stephen John Stedman. 2003. "Where Do the Peacekeepers Go?" *International Studies Review* 5(4): 37–54.

Global Alliance Against Traffic in Women (GAATW). 2007. *Collateral Damage: The Impact of Anti-Trafficking Measures on Human Rights Around the World.* Bangkok: Global Alliance Against Traffic in Women.

———. 2008. "Letter to the Honorable Dr. Condoleeza Rice Re: Trafficking in Persons Report June 2008." July 15. Available at www.gaatw.org/statements/TIP_Letter_FINAL.pdf, accessed January 2011.

Global Alliance Against Traffic in Women (GAATW), Anti-Slavery International, La Strada International, Buhay Foundation, Philippines, LSCW, Cambodia, and Sodireitos, Brazil. 2009. "Statement on a Monitoring Mechanism for the United Nations Convention Against Transnational Organized Crime and Each of the Protocols Thereto with Specific Attention to the Protocol to Prevent, Suppress and Punish Trafficking in Persons (the Human Trafficking Protocol)." October 13. Available at www.gaatw.org/statements/Statement_on_a_Monitoring_Mechanism-COPS08.pdf, accessed January 2011.

Goldstein, Joshua. 2001. *War and Gender.* New York: Cambridge University Press.

Gong, Gerrit. 1984. *The Standard of "Civilization" in International Society.* Oxford: Clarendon Press.

Government of Mauritius. 2009. "Trafficking in Persons Report 2009 Ranks Mauritius in Topmost Category." June 18. Available at www.gov.mu/portal/site/Mainhomepage/menuitem.a42b24128104d9845dabddd154508a0c/?content_id=0ad81c562e2f1210VgnVCM1000000a04a8c0RCRD, accessed January 2011.

Graber, Doris A. 2010. *Mass Media and American Politics,* 8th ed. Washington, D.C.: Congressional Quarterly Press.

Grant, Kevin. 2004. *A Civilised Savagery: Britain and the New Slaveries in Africa, 1884–1926.* New York: Routledge.

Graycar, Adam. 1999. "Trafficking in Human Beings." Speech delivered at the International Conference on Migration, Culture and Crime, Israel, July 7.

Group of 77 Plus China. 2009. "Statement of the G77 and China at the Eighteenth Session of the Commission on Crime Prevention and Criminal Justice." April 16–24. Available at www.g77.org/vienna/UNODCCCPCJ18th.htm, accessed January 2011.

Guinn, David E., and Elissa Steglich, eds. 2003. *In Modern Bondage: Sex Trafficking in the Americas.* Ardsley, N.Y.: Transnational.

Hafner-Burton, Emilie, and Alexander Montgomery. 2008. "Power or Plenty: How Do International Trade Institutions Affect Economic Sanctions?" *Journal of Conflict Resolution.* 52(2): 213–42.

Hahn, Steven. 2009. *The Political Worlds of Slavery and Freedom.* Cambridge, Mass.: Harvard University Press.

Hallin, Daniel C., and Paolo Mancini. 2004. *Comparing Media Systems: Three Models of Media and Politics.* New York: Cambridge University Press.

Hansen, Holley E., Sara McLaughlin Mitchell, and Stephen Nemeth. 2008. "IO Mediation of Interstate Conflicts: Moving Beyond the Global Versus Regional Dichotomy." *Journal of Conflict Resolution* 52(2): 295–325.

Haque, Md. Shahidul. 2006. "Ambiguities and Confusions in Migration—Trafficking Nexus: A Development Challenge." In *Trafficking and the Global Sex Industry*, ed. Karen Beeks and Delila Amir, 3–19. New York: Lexington Books.

Hawkins, Mike. 1997. *Social Darwinism in European and American Thought.* Cambridge: Cambridge University Press.

Haynes, Dina Francesca. 2004. "Used, Abused, Arrested and Deported: Extending Immigration Benefits to Protect the Victims of Trafficking and to Secure the Prosecution of Traffickers." *Human Rights Quarterly* 26(May): 221–72.

Hertzke, Allen D. 2004. *Freeing God's Children: The Unlikely Alliance for Global Human Rights.* Oxford: Rowman and Littlefield.

Hill, Clifford. 2005. *The Wilberforce Connection: William Wilberforce and His Friends Transformed a Nation: How Can We Transform Society Today?* Oxford: Monarch Books.

Hochschild, Adam. 1998. *King Leopold's Ghost: A Story of Greed, Terror, and Heroism in Colonial Africa.* Boston: Houghton Mifflin.

Horowitz, Michael. 2010. "2010 TIP Report: 'Profoundly Troubling'" and "2010 TIP Report: 'Follow-up Email.'" Unpublished correspondence, June 19.

Howard-Hassmann, Rhoda. 2008. *Reparations to Africa.* Philadelphia: University of Pennsylvania Press.

Hughes, Donna. 2002. "The 2002 Trafficking in Persons Report: Lost Opportunity for Progress." Speech delivered before the U.S. Congress, House International Relations Committee, June 19.

Human Rights Watch. 2001a. "Haiti: Political Violence Condemned." December 17.

———. 2001b. "Sexual Violence Within the Sierra Leone Conflict." February 26.

———. 2002. "2002 World Report: Events of 2001." Available at www.hrw.org/wr2k2/, accessed January 2011.

———. 2003a. "Trapped by Inequality." August 24.

———. 2003b. "We'll Kill You if You Cry: Sexual Violence in the Sierra Leone Conflict." 15(1): (A).

———. 2004. "Haiti: Security Vacuum in the North; Numerous Journalists and Government Officials in Hiding." March 21.

———. 2006. *Swept Under the Rug: Abuses Against Domestic Workers Worldwide.* Available at www.hrw.org/en/reports/2006/07/27/swept-under-rug, accessed July 14, 2009.

———. 2008. *As If I Am Not Human: Abuses Against Asian Domestic Workers in Saudi Arabia.* July 7. Available at www.hrw.org/en/reports/2008/07/07/if-i-am-not-human-0, accessed January 2011.

———. 2009. *No Refuge: Migrants in Greece.* November 2. New York: Human Rights Watch.

HumanTrafficking.org. 2006. "News and Updates: Human Trafficking Activities Undertaken in Payao, Thailand." March 25. Available at www.humantrafficking.org/
updates/165) accessed January 2011.

Hunt, Lynn. 2007. *Inventing Human Rights: A History*. New York: W.W. Norton.

Huysmans, Jef. 2006. *The Politics of Insecurity: Fear, Migration and Asylum in the EU*.
London:
Routledge, Taylor & Francis Group.

Inter Press Service News Agency. 2007. "Sri Lanka: Timeline." November 7. Available at
psnews.net/srilanka/timeline.shtml, accessed January 2011.

Inter-American Commission on Human Rights. 2008. "Observations of the Inter-
American Commission on Human Rights Upon Conclusion of Its April 2007
Visit to Haiti." OEA/Ser.L/7. 131 doc. 36, March 2.

Inter-American Commission on Women Assembly of Delegates. 2002. "Fighting the
Crime of Trafficking in Persons, Especially Women, Adolescents and Children."
CIM/RES.225 (31–O/02), October 31.

International Human Rights Law Institute. 2002. "In Modern Bondage: Sex Trafficking in the Americas, Central America and the Caribbean." October. Available at
www.oas.org/atip/reports/in%20modern%20bondage.pdf, accessed January 2011.

———. 2005. *In Modern Bondage: Sex Trafficking in the Americas*, 2d rev. ed. Chicago:
DePaul University College of Law. Available at www.law.depaul.edu/centers_
institutes/ihrli/publications/, accessed July 2009.

International Labor Organization. 2001. *Stopping Forced Labor: Global Report Under
the Follow-up to the ILO Declaration on Fundamental Principles and Rights at
Work*. International Labor Conference, 89th Session.

———. 2011. Home page, www.ilo.org, accessed January 2011.

International Organization for Migration. 2000–2005. "Return and Reintegration
Project: Situation Report." Kosovo Counter Trafficking Unit. February.

———. 2006a. "Report of the Mission for Research on the Status of Trafficking and
Trafficking in Persons in Haiti." September.

———. 2006b. "Counter Trafficking Seminar." Press briefing, August 30. Available at
www.iom.int/jahia/Jahia/media/press-briefing-notes/pbnAM/cache/offonce/
lang/en?entryId=6647, accessed January 2011.

———.2011. Home page, www.iom.int, accessed January 2011.

Ishay, Micheline. 2008. *The History of Human Rights: From Ancient Times to the Globalization Era*, 2d ed. Berkeley: University of California Press.

Iyengar, Shanto. 1991. *Is Anyone Responsible? How Television Frames Political Issues*.
Chicago: University of Chicago Press.

Jacobs, Lawrence R., and Robert Y. Shapiro. 2000. *Politicians Don't Pander: Political
Manipulation and the Loss of Democratic Responsiveness*. Chicago: University of
Chicago Press.

Johnson, Robert. 2003. *British Imperialism*. New York: Palgrave.

Jok, Jok Madut. 2007. "Slavery and Slave Redemption and Slave Redemption in the Sudan." In *Buying Freedom: The Ethics and Economics of Slave Redemption*, ed. Kwame Anthony Appiah and Martin Bunzl, 143–57. Princeton, N.J.: Princeton University Press.

Jones, Bryan D., and Frank R. Baumgartner. 2005. *The Politics of Attention: How Government Prioritizes Problems.* Chicago: University of Chicago Press.

Jones, Maggie. 2003. "Thailand's Brothel Busters." *Mother Jones*, November/December.

Jordan, Anne. 2002. "Human Rights or Wrongs: The Struggle for a Rights Based Response to Trafficking in Human Beings." In *Gender, Trafficking and Slavery*, ed. Rachel Masika, 28–37. Oxford: Oxfam Publications.

Jordan, Bill and Franck Düvell. 2002. *Irregular Migration: The Dilemmas of Transnational Mobility.* Cheltenham: Edward Elgar.

Kane, June. 1998. *Sold for Sex.* Aldershot: Ashgate.

Kane, Tim. 2006. "Global U.S. Troop Deployment, 1950–2003." Data set. *Center for Data Analysis Report*, 06–02, May 24. Available at www.heritage.org/research/reports/2004/10/global-us-troop-deployment-1950-2003, accessed January 2011.

Kangaspunta, Kristiina. 2003. "Mapping the Inhuman Trade: Preliminary Findings of the Database on Trafficking in Human Beings." *Forum on Crime and Society* 3(1/2): 81–103.

Kapstein, Ethan B. 2006. "The New Global Slave Trade." *Foreign Affairs* 85(6): 103–15.

Kapur, Ratna. 2005. "Cross-Border Movements and the Law: Renegotiating the Boundaries of Difference." In *Trafficking and Prostitution Reconsidered*, ed. Kamala Kempadoo, 25–41. Boulder, Colo.: Paradigm.

Kara, Siddharth Ashok. 2009. *Sex Trafficking: Inside the Business of Modern Slavery.* New York: Columbia University Press.

Karakatsanis, Neovi M., and Jonathan Swarts. 2003. "Migrant Women, Domestic Work and Sex Trade in Greece: A Snapshot of Migrant Policy in the Making." In *Gender and International Migration: Focus on Greece*, ed. Evangelia Tastsoglou and Laura Maratou-Alipranti, 239–70. Athens: Greek Review of Social Research, National Centre for Social Research.

Katzenstein, Peter J. 2005. *A World of Regions: Asia and Europe in the American Imperium.* London: Cornell University Press.

Kaye, Mike. 2003. *The Migration-Trafficking Nexus: Combating Trafficking Through the Protection of Migrants' Human Rights.* London: Anti-Slavery International/Trocaire.

Keck, Margaret, and Kathryn Sikkink. 1998. *Activists Beyond Borders: Advocacy Networks in International Politics.* Ithaca, N.Y.: Cornell University Press.

Keene, Edward. 2002. *Beyond the Anarchical Society: Grotius, Colonialism and Order in World Politics.* Cambridge: Cambridge University Press.

Kempadoo, Kamala, ed. 2005. *Trafficking and Prostitution Reconsidered: New Perspectives on Migration, Sex Work, and Human Rights*. Boulder, Colo.: Paradigm.

Kempadoo, Kamala, and Jo Doezema, eds. 1998. *Global Sex Workers: Rights, Resistance, and Redefinition*. New York: Routledge.

Kerwin, Donald. 2005. "The Use and Misuse of 'National Security' Rationale in Crafting U.S. Refugee and Immigration Policies." *International Journal of Refugee Law* 17(4): 749–63.

Khosravi, Shahram. 2010a. "An Ethnography of Migrant 'Illegality' in Sweden: Included yet Excepted?" *Journal of International Political Theory* 6(1): 95–116.

———. 2010b. *'Illegal' Traveler: An Auto-Ethnography of Borders*. New York and Basingstoke: Palgrave Macmillan.

Killingray, David. 1989. "Labor Exploitation for Military Campaigns in British Colonial Africa." *Journal of Contemporary History* 24(3): 483–501.

Killingray, David, and James Mathews. 1979. "Beasts of Burden: British West African Carriers in the First World War." *Canadian Journal of African Studies* 13(1/2): 5–23.

King, Gary, Robert O. Keohane, and Sidney Verba. 1994. *Designing Social Inquiry: Scientific Inference in Qualitative Research*. Princeton, N.J.: Princeton University Press.

King, Gilbert. 2004. *Woman, Child for Sale: The New Slave Trade in the 21st Century*. London: Penguin.

Kingdon, John W. 2003. *Agendas, Alternatives, and Public Policies*, 2d ed. New York: Longman.

Kinney, Edith C. M. 2006. "Appropriations for the Abolitionists: Undermining Effects of the U.S. Mandatory Anti-Prostitution Pledge in the Fight Against Human Trafficking and HIV/AIDS." *Berkeley Journal of Gender, Law & Justice* 21: 158–95.

Klein, Martin. 2009. "Slave Descent and Social Status in Sahara and Sudan." In *Reconfiguring Slavery: West African Trajectories*, ed. Benedetta Rossi, 26–44. Liverpool: University of Liverpool Press.

———. 1998. *Slavery and Colonial Rule in French West Africa*. Cambridge: Cambridge University Press.

Kligman, Gail, and Stephanie Limoncelli. 2005. "Trafficking Women After Socialism: To, Through, and From Eastern Europe." *Social Politics: International Studies in Gender, State and Society* 12(1): 118–40.

Klinenberg, Eric. 2003. *Heat Wave: A Social Autopsy of Disaster in Chicago*. Chicago: University of Chicago Press.

Klopcic, Alja. 2004. "Trafficking in Human Beings in Transition and Post-Conflict Countries." *Human Security Perspectives* 1(1): 7–12.

Klotz, Audie. 2002. "Transnational Activism and Global Transformations: The Anti-Apartheid and Abolitionist Experiences." *European Journal of International Relations* 8(1): 49–76.

Krasner, Stephen D. 2001. *Problematic Sovereignty: Contested Rules and Political Possibilities.* New York: Columbia University Press.

Krasniewski, Mariusz. 2005. "*Tro* Adherents in West Africa: Tradition and Slavery." *Hemispheres* 20: 141–50.

Krieger, Heike, ed. 1997. *East Timor and the International Community: Basic Documents.* Cambridge: Cambridge University Press.

Kuo, Lenore. (2002) *Prostitution Policy: Revolutionizing Practice Through a Gendered Perspective.* New York: New York University Press.

Kyle, David, and Ray Koslowski, eds. 2001. *Global Human Smuggling: Comparative Perspectives.* Baltimore: Johns Hopkins University Press.

Laczko, Frank. 2002. "Human Trafficking: The Need for Better Data." *Migration Information Source*, November.

Laczko, Frank, and Elzbieta M. Gozdziak, eds. 2005. *Data and Research on Human Trafficking: A Global Survey.* New York: United Nations Press.

Laczko, Frank, and June J. H. Lee. 2003. "Developing Better Indicators of Human Trafficking for Asia." Paper presented at the Expert Group Meeting on Prevention of International Trafficking. Seoul, Korea, September 22–23.

Landesman, Peter. 2004. "The Girls Next Door." *New York Times Magazine*, January 25.

Langberg, Laura. 2005. "A Review of Recent OAS Research on Human Trafficking in the Latin American and Caribbean Region." *International Migration* 43(1–2): 129–39.

Langum, David J. 2007. *Crossing Over the Line: Legislating Morality and the Mann Act.* Chicago: University of Chicago Press.

LaPalombara, Joseph. 1965. "Italy: Fragmentation, Isolation, Alienation." In *Political Culture and Political Development*, ed. Lucian W. Pye and Sidney Verba, 282–329. Princeton, N.J.: Princeton University Press.

Larson, Stephanie Greco. 2006. *Media & Minorities: The Politics of Race in News and Entertainment.* Lanham, Md.: Rowman & Littlefield.

La Strada International. 2008. *Violation of Women's Rights: A Cause and Consequence of Trafficking in Women.* Amsterdam. March 8. Available at www.humantrafficking.org/uploads/publications/lastrada_08_rights_0708.pdf, accessed January 2011.

Lauren, Paul. 2003. *The Evolution of Human Rights: Visions Seen.* Philadelphia: University of Pennsylvania Press.

Law, Lisa. 2000. *Sex Work in Southeast Asia: The Place of Desire in a Time of AIDS.* New York: Routledge.

Lee, June J. H. 2005. "Human Trafficking in East Asia: Current Trends, Data Collection and Knowledge Gaps." In *Data and Research on Human Trafficking: A Global Survey*, ed. Frank Laczko and Elzbieta Gozdziak, 165–202. New York: United Nations Press.

Lee, Maggie, ed. 2007. *Human Trafficking.* Cullompton: Willan.

Lee, Na Young. 2007. "The Construction of Military Prostitution in South Korea During the U.S. Military Rule, 1945–1948." *Feminist Studies* 33(3): 453–81.

Lobasz, Jennifer. 2009. "Beyond Border Security: Feminist Approaches to Human Trafficking." *Security Studies* 18(2): 319–44.

Lovejoy, Paul. 2005. *Slavery, Commerce and Production in the Sokoto Caliphate of West Africa.* Trenton, N.J.: Africa World Press.

———. 2000. *Transformations in Slavery: A History of Slavery in Africa.* Cambridge: Cambridge University Press.

Lovejoy, Paul, and Jan Hogendorn. 1993. *Slow Death for Slavery: The Course of Abolition in Northern Nigeria, 1897–1936.* Cambridge: Cambridge University Press.

Lovejoy, Paul, and David Richardson. 1995. "The Initial 'Crisis of Adaptation': The Impact of British Abolition on the Atlantic Slave Trade in West Africa, 1808–1820." In *From Slave Trade to "Legitimate" Commerce: The Commercial Transition in Nineteenth Century West Africa,* ed. Robin Law, 32–56. Cambridge: Cambridge University Press.

Lowry, Robert. 1996. *The Armed Forces of Indonesia.* Sydney: Melbourne University Press.

Lukes, Steven. 2004. *Power: A Radical View,* 2nd ed. New York: Palgrave Macmillan.

Macwan, Martin, Christian Davenport, David Armstrong, Monika Kalra Varma, Amanda Klasing, Allan Stam, and Manjula Pradeep. 2010. *Understanding Untouchability: A Comprehensive Study of Practices and Conditions in 1589 Villages.* Gujarat, India, and Washington, D.C.: Navsarjan Trust and Robert F. Kennedy Center for Human Rights.

Mai, Nick. n.d. "Migrant Workers in the UK Sex Industry." *Institute for the Study of European Transformations.* Available at www.londonmet.ac.uk/fms/MRSite/Research/iset/Migrant%20Workers%20in%20the%20UK%20Sex%20Industry%20Policy-Relevant%20Findings2.pdf, accessed January 2011.

"Malaysia 'Immune' to U.S. Criticism of Human Trafficking." 2009. *China Post,* June 18. Available at www.chinapost.com.tw/asia/malaysia/2009/06/18/212649/Malaysia-immune.htm, accessed January 2011.

Malone, John, Kenneth Hyams, Richard Hawkins, Trueman Sharp, and Fredric Danielle. 1993. "Risk Factors for Sexually Transmitted Diseases Among Deployed Military Personnel." *Sexually Transmitted Diseases* (5): 294–98.

Manning, Patrick. 1990. *Slavery and African Life: Occidental, Oriental, and African Slave Trades.* Cambridge: Cambridge University Press.

Manokha, Ivan. 2004. "Modern Slavery and Fair Trade Products: Buy One and Set Someone Free." In *The Political Economy of New Slavery,* ed. Christien van den Anker, 217–34. Basingstoke: Palgrave.

Marchetti, Raffaele. 2008. *Global Democracy: For and Against.* New York and London: Routledge.

Maroukis, Thanos. 2009. "Clandestino Country Report: Greece. Undocumented Migration: Counting the Uncountable. Data and Trends Across Europe." Available at http://clandestino.eliamep.gr/wp-content/uploads/2009/02/greece.pdf,. accessed January 2011.

Martin, Michael, and Marilyn Yaquinto, eds. 2007. *Redress for Historical Injustices in the United States: On Reparations for Slavery, Jim Crow, and their Legacies.* Durham, N.C.: Duke University Press.

Masci, David. 2004. "Human Trafficking and Slavery." *CQ Researcher,* March 26: 273–96.

Mbodji, Mohamed. 1993. "The Abolition of Slavery in Senegal, 1820–1890: Crisis of the Rise of a New Entrepreneurial Class?" In *Breaking the Chains: Slavery, Bondage, and Emancipation in Modern Africa and Asia,* ed. Martin Klein, 197–214. Madison: University of Wisconsin Press.

McAdam, Doug. 1999. *Political Process and the Development of Black Insurgency, 1930–1970,* 2d ed. Chicago: University of Chicago Press.

McCoubrey, Hillaire. 1999. "Kosovo, NATO, and International Law." *International Relations* 14(5): 14–29.

McDowell, Christopher. 1996. *A Tamil Asylum Diaspora: Sri Lankan Migration, Settlement and Politics in Switzerland.* Providence, R.I.: Berghahn Books.

McGill, Craig. 2003. *Human Traffic: Sex, Slaves, and Immigration.* London: Vision Paperbacks.

McKay, Susan, and Dyan Mazurana. 2004. *Where Are the Girls? Girls Fighting Forces, Northern Uganda, Sierra Leone, and Mozambique, Their Lives After War.* Montreal: Canada International Center for Human Rights and Democratic Development.

Mearsheimer, John. 1994/1995. "The False Promise of International Institutions." *International Security* 19(3): 5–26.

Meillassoux, Claude. 1991. *The Anthropology of Slavery: The Womb of Iron and Gold.* London: Athlone Press.

Mendelson, Sarah Elizabeth. 2005. *Barracks and Brothels: Peacekeepers and Human Trafficking in the Balkans.* Washington, D.C.: Center for Strategic & International Studies.

Mermin, Jonathan. 1999. *Debating War and Peace: Media Coverage of U.S. Intervention in the Post-Vietnam Era.* Princeton, NJ.: Princeton University Press.

Miers, Suzanne. 1975. *Britain and the Ending of the Slave Trade.* New York: Africana.

———. 2003. *Slavery in the Twentieth Century.* Walnut Creek, Calif.: Altamira Press.

Miers, Suzanne, and Igor Kopytoff, eds. 1977. *Slavery in Africa: Historical and Anthropological Perspectives.* Madison: University of Wisconsin Press.

Miers, Suzanne, and Richard Roberts. 1988. "The End of Slavery in Africa." In *The End of Slavery in Africa,* ed. Suzanne Miers and Richard Roberts, 3–69. Madison: University of Wisconsin Press.

Migrant Rights Centre Ireland (MRCI). 2006. *No Way Forward. No Going Back. Identifying the Problem of Forced Labor in Ireland.* Dublin: MRCI.

Miko, Francis T. 2004. *Trafficking in Women and Children: The U.S. and International Response.* Washington, D.C.: Congressional Research Service.

Miller, David. 2007. *National Responsibility and Global Justice.* Oxford: Oxford University Press.

Miller, Joseph. 1999a. *Slavery and Slaving in World History: A Bibliography,* Vol. 1, *1900–1991.* New York: M.E. Sharpe.

———. 1999b. *Slavery and Slaving in World History: A Bibliography,* Vol. 2, *1992–1996.* New York: M.E. Sharpe.

Miller, Mark J. 2001. "The Sanctioning of Unauthorized Migration and Alien Employment." In *Global Human Smuggling: Comparative Perspectives,* eds. David Kyle and Ray Koslowski, 318–36. Baltimore: John Hopkins University Press.

———. 2006. "Trafficking and Slavery (T/S) Systems and the European Union: A First Cut." Paper presented at the Conference on Criminal Trafficking and Slavery: The Dark Side of Globalization. University of Illinois, Champaign-Urbana, February 23–25.

Miller, Mark J., and Christina Gabriel. 2008. "The U.S.-Mexico Migration Honeymoon of 2001: A Retrospective." In *Governing International Labor Migration: Current Issues, Challenges and Dilemmas,* ed. Christina Gabriel and Helene Pellerin, 147–62. London: Routledge.

Minderhoud, Paul. 2004. "Coping with Irregular Migration: The Dutch Experience." In *Irregular Migration and Human Rights: Theoretical, European and International Perspectives,* ed. Barbara Bogusz, 387–406. Boston and Leiden: Martinus Nijhoff.

Mirzai, Behnaz, Ismael Musah Montana, and Paul Lovejoy, eds. 2009. *Slavery, Islam and Diaspora.* Trenton, N.J.: Africa World Press.

Moellendorf, Darrel. 2009. *Global Inequality Matters.* New York and Basingstoke: Palgrave Macmillan.

Moghalu, Kingsley Chiedu. 2006. *Global Justice: The Politics of War Crimes Trials.* Westport, Conn.: Praeger.

Moon, Katherine. 1997. *Sex Among Allies: Military Prostitution in U.S.-Korea Relations.* New York: Columbia University Press.

Morecambe Victims Trust Fund. 2009. "Ghosts—The Morecambe Victims Fund." Available at www.ghosts.uk.com/press.html, accessed January 2011.

Nathan, Debbie. 2005. "Oversexed." *The Nation,* August 29, 2005. http://www.thenation.com/doc/20050829/nathan.

National Association of the American People. n.d. "Ending Human Trafficking." City Limits Radio. Available at www.citylimitsradio.com/?p=192, accessed in January 2011, and originally available at thenaap.org.

Naureckas, Him. 1999. "Rescued from the Memory Hole: The Forgotten Background of the Serb/Albanian Conflict." Fairness and Accuracy in Reporting (FAIR). Available at www.fair.org/extra/9905/kosovo.html, accessed January 2011.

Nieuwenhuys, Céline, and Antoine Pécoud. 2007. "Human Trafficking, Information Campaigns, and Strategies of Migration Control." *American Behavioral Scientist* 50(12): 1674–94.

Northrup, David. 1976. "The Compatibility of the Slave and Palm Oil Trades in the Bight of Biafra." *Journal of African History* 17(3): 353–64.

Nye, Joseph P. 2004. *Soft Power: The Means to Success in World Politics.* New York: Public Affairs.

Obokata, Tom. 2006. *Trafficking of Human Beings from a Human Rights Perspective.* Leiden, Netherlands: Brill.

Office of the Press Secretary. 2003. "Trafficking in Persons National Security Presidential Directive." February 25. Available at www.fas.org/irp/offdocs/nspd/trafpers. html, accessed January 2011.

———. 2006. "President Signs H.R. 972: Trafficking Victims Protection Reauthorization Act." White House Press Release, January 10.

———. 2007. "Presidential Determination with Respect to Foreign Governments' Efforts Regarding Trafficking in Persons (Presidential Determination No. 2008–4)." White House Press Release, October 18. Available at http://goliath.ecnext.com/ coms2/gi_0199-7706569/Presidential-Determination-with-Respect-to.html, accessed January 2011.

O'Hear, Ann. 1997. *Power Relations in Nigeria: Ilorin Slaves and Their Successors.* New York: University of Rochester Press.

Oishi, Nana. 2005. *Women in Motion: Globalization, State Policies, and Labor Migration in Asia.* Stanford, Calif.: Stanford University Press.

Opare-Akurang, Kwabena. 1999. "The Administration of the Abolition Laws, African Responses, and Post-Proclamation Slavery in the Gold Coast, 1874–1940." In *Slavery and Colonial Rule in Africa,* ed. Suzanne Miers and Martin A. Klein, 149–66. London: Frank Cass.

Organization of American States. 2004. "Memorandum of Understanding Between the United Nations and the General Secretariat of the Organization of American States Concerning Electoral Assistance to Haiti." OEA/Ser.G/CP/INF. 5104/04, November 18.

———. 2005. *Rapid Assessment Report: Trafficking in Persons from the Latin American and Caribbean (LAC) Region to Japan.* November.

Organization of American States General Assembly. 1991. "The Santiago Commitment to Democracy and the Renewal of the Inter-American System."

———. 2001. "Report of the Secretary General on the OAS Mission and of the Joint OAS/CARICOM Mission to Haiti." AG/INF.264/01, June 3.

———. 2003. "Fighting the Crime of Trafficking in Persons, Especially Women, Adolescents and Children." AG/RES.1948 (33–O/03, June 10.

———. 2004. "Fighting the Crime of Trafficking Persons, Especially Women, Adolescents and Children." AG/RES. 2019 (34–O/04), June 8.

Organization of American States Inter-American Commission on Human Rights. 2005. "Haiti: Failed Justice or the Rule of Law? Challenges Ahead for the International Community." OAS/Ser/L/V/II. 123 Doc.6 Rev.1, October 26.

Othman, Zarina. 2006. "Human In(security): Human Trafficking and Security in Malaysia." In *Trafficking and the Global Sex Industry*, ed. Karen Beeks and Delila Amir, 47–60. Lanham, Md.: Lexington Books.

Ould, David. 2004. "Trafficking and International Law." In *The Political Economy of New Slavery*, ed. Christien van den Anker, 55–74. Basingstoke: Palgrave.

Ould, David, Clair Jordan, Rebecca Reynolds, and Lacey Loftin, eds. 2005. *The Cocoa Industry in West Africa: A History of Exploitation*. London: Anti-Slavery International.

Outshoorn, Joyce. 2005. "The Political Debates on Prostitution and Trafficking of Women." *Social Politics: International Studies in Gender, State and Society*. 12(Spring): 141–55.

Outshoorn, Joyce, ed. 2004. *The Politics of Prostitution: Women's Movements, Democratic States and the Globalisation of Sex Commerce*. Cambridge: Cambridge University Press.

Papanicolaou, Georgios. 2008. "The Sex Industry, Human Trafficking and the Global Prohibition Regime: A Cautionary Tale from Greece." *Trends in Organized Crime* 11(4): 379–409.

Parish, Randall, and Mark Peceny. 2002. "Kantian Liberalism and the Defense of Democracy in Latin America." *Journal of Peace Research* 39(2): 229–50.

Patterson, Thomas. 2008. "Political Roles of the Journalist." In *The Politics of News*, ed. Doris Graber, Dennis McQuail, and Pippa Norris, 23–37. Washington, D.C.: CQ Press.

Pécoud, Antoine, and Paul de Guchteneire. 2006. "International Migration, Border Controls, and Human Rights: Assessing the Relevance of the Right to Mobility." *Journal of Border Studies* 21(1): 69–86.

Peebles, Patrick. 2006. *The History of Sri Lanka*. Westport, Conn.: Greenwood Press.

Perrin, Benjamin. 2010. "Just Passing Through? International Legal Obligations and Policies of Transit Countries in Combating Trafficking in Persons." *European Journal of Criminology* 7(1): 11–28.

Peterson, V. Spike, ed. 1992. *Gendered States: Feminist (Re)visions of International Relations Theory*. Boulder, Colo.: Lynne Rienner.

Pevehouse, Jon, and Bruce Russett. 2006. "Democratic International Governmental Organizations Promote Peace." *International Organization* 60(4): 969–1000.

Pew Research Center. 2009. "On Obama's Desk: Economy, Jobs Trump All Other Policy Priorities." *Pew Research Center for the People & the Press*, January 22.

Phillips, Nicolla. 2009. "Migration as Development Strategy? The New Political Economy of Dispossession and Inequality in the Americas." *Review of International Political Economy* 16(2): 231–59.

PICUM. 2007. *Undocumented Migrants Have Rights: An Overview of the International Human Rights Framework*. Brussels: PICUM.

Piper, Nicole. 2005. "A Problem by a Different Name? A Review of Research on Trafficking in South-East Asia and Oceania." *International Migration* 43: 203–33.

Pisani, Elizabeth. 2008. *The Wisdom of Whores: Bureaucrats, Brothels, and the Business of AIDS*. New York: W.W. Norton.

Platt, Leah. 2001. "Regulating the Global Brothel." *American Prospect*, July 16, 10–14.

Pogge, Thomas. 2008. *World Poverty and Human Rights*, 2d expanded ed. Cambridge: Polity Press.

Posen, Barry R. 2000. "The War for Kosovo: Serbia's Political-Military Strategy." *International Security* 24(4): 39–84.

Powell, Charles. 1996. "International Aspects of Democratization: The Case of Spain." In *The International Dimensions of Democratization: Europe and the Americas*, ed. Laurence Whitehead, 285–314. Oxford: Oxford University Press.

Power, Samantha. 2002. *"A Problem from Hell": America and the Age of Genocide*. New York: Harper Perennial.

Prakesh, Gyan. 1990. *Bonded Histories: Genealogies of Labor Servitude in Colonial India*. Cambridge: Cambridge University Press.

Pro Asyl and Group of Lawyers for the Rights of Refugees and Migrants in Athens. 2007. *The Truth May Be Bitter, but It Must Be Told: The Situation of Refugees in the Aegean and the Practices of the Greek Coast Guard*. Frankfurt: Pro Asyl.

Project for Excellence in Journalism. 1998. "Framing the News: The Triggers, Frames, and Messages in Newspaper Coverage." Pew Project for Excellence in Journalism, July 13.

Quirk, Joel F. 2006. "The Anti-Slavery Project: Linking the Historical and Contemporary." *Human Rights Quarterly* 28(3): 565–89.

———. 2007. "Trafficked into Slavery." *Journal of Human Rights* 6(2): 181–207.

———. 2008. "Historical Methods." In *Oxford Handbook of International Relations*, ed. Duncan Snidal and Christian Reus-Smit, 518–36. Oxford: Oxford University Press.

———. 2009. *Unfinished Business: A Comparative Survey of Historical and Contemporary Slavery*. Paris: UNESCO.

———. 2010. "Wartime Enslavement and Forced Marriage in Sub-Saharan Africa: Linking Historical Slave Systems and Modern Problems?" Manuscript presented at workshop on Forced Marriage in Conflict Situations, Harriet Tubman Institute, York University. On file with author.

———. 2011. *The Anti-Slavery Project: Bridging the Historical and Contemporary*. Philadelphia: University of Pennsylvania Press.

———. Forthcoming. "Modern Slavery." In *The Routledge History of Slavery*, ed. Trevor Bernard and Gad Heuman. London: Routledge.

Quirk, Joel F., and David Richardson. 2008. "Anti-Slavery, European Identity and International Society: A Macro-Historical Perspective." *Journal of Modern European History* 7(1): 70–94.

———. 2010. "Religion, Urbanization and Anti-Slavery Mobilization in Britain, 1788–1833." *European Journal of English Studies* 14(3). 263–79.

Ramet, Sabrina. 2001a. "The Third Yugoslavia: 1992–2001." East European Studies Center Working Paper Series, Woodrow Wilson Center. Available at www.wilsoncenter.org/topics/pubs/ACF430.pdf#50, accessed January 2011.

———. 2001b. "KFOR's Record in Kosovo." In *NATO Enlargement and Peacekeeping: Journeys to Where?*, ed. Sabrina Ramet, 33–36. Washington, D.C.: East European Studies, Woodrow Wilson International Center for Scholars.

Rashid, Ismail. 1999. "'Do Dady Nor Lef Me Make Dem Carry Me': Slave Resistance and Emancipation in Sierra Leone, 1894–1928." In *Slavery and Colonial Rule in Africa*, ed. Suzanne Miers and Martin Klein, 208–31. London: Frank Cass.

Rasnake, Mark, Nicholas Conger, Kenneth Mcallister, King Holmes, and Edmond Tramont. 2005. "History of U.S. Military Contributions to the Study of Sexually Transmitted Diseases." *Military Medicine* 170(4): 61–65.

Raustiala, Kal, and Anne-Marie Slaughter. 2002. "International Law, International Relations and Compliance." In *The Handbook of International Relations*, ed. Walter Carlnaes, Thomas Risse, and Beth Simmons, 538–58. Thousand Oaks, Calif.: Sage.

Ray, James Lee. 1989. "The Abolition of Slavery and the End of International War." *International Organization* 43(3): 405–39.

Raymond, Janice G., and Donna M. Hughes. 2001. *Sex Trafficking of Women in the United States: International and Domestic Trends.* Kingston, R.I.: Coalition Against Trafficking of Women.

Razack, Sherene. 2004. *Dark Threats & White Knights: The Somalia Affair, Peacekeeping, and the New Imperialism.* Toronto: University of Toronto Press.

Regan, Patrick. 2002. "Third-Party Interventions and the Duration of Intrastate Conflicts." *Journal of Conflict Resolution* 46(1): 55–73.

Ribando, Clare M. 2007. *Congressional Research Service Report for Congress: Trafficking in Persons in Latin America and the Caribbean.* Washington, D.C.: Congressional Research Service.

Ricchiardi, Sherry. 2008. "Covering the World American." *American Journalism Review* (December/January).

Rieger, April. 2007. "Missing the Mark: Why the Trafficking Victims Protection Act Fails to Protect Sex Trafficking Victims in the United States." *Harvard Journal of Law & Gender* 30: 231–56.

Ringquist, Evan, and Tatiana Kostadinova. 2005. "Assessing the Effectiveness of International Environmental Agreements: The Case of the 1985 Helsinki Protocol." *American Journal of Political Science* 49(1): 86–102.

Robinson, Piers. 2002. *The CNN Effect: The Myth of News, Foreign Policy and Intervention.* London: Routledge.

Rocha, J. 2009. "I Am Not Much of Ducking My Head: How Irregular Migrant Workers in Madrid and Amsterdam Deal with Precarious Working Conditions." MA thesis, ISHSS, University of Amsterdam.

Roessingh, Martijn. 2009–10. Series on Human Trafficking in the Dutch newspaper *Trouw*. Available at www.trouw.nl/achtergrond/Dossiers/article1956341.ece, accessed January 2011.

Rossi, Benedetta. 2009. "Introduction: Rethinking Slavery in West Africa." In *Reconfiguring Slavery: West African Trajectories*, ed. Benedetta Rossi, 1–25. Liverpool: University of Liverpool Press.

Ruggiero, Vincenzo. 1997. "Trafficking in Human Beings: Slaves in Contemporary Europe." *International Journal of Sociology of Law* 25: 231–44.

Saba, Behrouz. 2003. "An Iranian Prostitute's Electronic Plea for Help." *Salam World-Wide*. Available at www.salamworldwide.com/issues11th.html, accessed January 2011.

Sachs, Jeffrey. 2005. *The End of Poverty*. New York: Penguin.

Sage, Jesse, and Liora Kasten, eds. 2006. *Enslaved: True Stories of Modern Day Slavery*. New York: Palgrave Macmillan.

Sage Project. n.d. "Issue Paper: The Effects of Systems of Prostitution and CSE in the United States and Worldwide." Available at www.sagesf.org/html/info_briefs_effects.htm, accessed July 2009.

Saito, Kaori. 2007. "International Protection for Trafficked Persons and Those Who Fear Being Trafficked." UNHCR Research Paper 149. Available at www.unhcr.org/research/RESEARCH/476652742.pdf, accessed January 2011.

Salt, John. 2000. "Trafficking and Human Smuggling: A European Perspective." *International Migration* 38(1): 32–56.

Salt, John, and Jeremy Stein. 1997. "Migration as a Business: The Case of Trafficking." *International Migration* 35(4): 467–94.

Samarasinghe, Vidyamali. 2007. *Female Sex Trafficking in Asia: The Resilience of Patriarchy in a Changing World*. New York: Routledge.

Savona, Erneto, and Sonia Stefanizzi, eds. 2007. *Measuring Human Trafficking: Complexities and Pitfalls*. New York: Springer.

Schafer, Jack. 2005. "Sex Slaves Revisted," *Slate.com*, June 7, 2005. http://www.slate.com/id/2120331.

Schloenhardt, Andreas. 1999. "Organized Crime and the Business of Migrant Trafficking: An Economic Analysis." *Crime, Law and Social Change* 32: 203–33.

Schudson, Mark. 1980. *Discovering the News*. New York: Basic Books.

Scott, James C. 1987. *Weapons of the Weak: Everyday Forms of Peasant Resistance*. New Haven, Conn.: Princeton University Press.

———. 1990. *Domination and the Arts of Resistance: Hidden Transcripts*. New Haven, Conn.: Yale University Press.

Seabrook, Jeremy. 2009. *The Refuge and the Fortress: Britain and the Flight from Tyranny*. Basingstoke: Palgrave Macmillan.

Searing, James. 1993. *West African Slavery and Atlantic Commerce*. Cambridge: Cambridge University Press.

Seddon, David. 2000. "Unfinished Business: Slavery in Saharan Africa." In *After Slavery: Emancipation and Its Discontents*, ed. Howard Temperley, 208–36. London: Frank Cass.

Shamsie, Yasmine. 2004. "Building 'Low-Intensity' Democracy in Haiti: The OAS Contribution." *Third World Quarterly* 25(6): 1097–1115.

Shannon, Sarah. 1999. "Prostitution and the Mafia: The Involvement of Organized Crime in the Global Economy." In *Illegal Immigration and Commercial Sex: The New Slave Trade*, ed. Phil Williams, 119–44. London: Frank Cass.

Shauer, Edward, and Elizabeth Wheaton. 2006. "Sex Trafficking into the United States: A Literature Review." *Criminal Justice Review* 31(2): 146–69.

Shelley, Louise. 2010. *Human Trafficking: A Global Perspective*. Cambridge: Cambridge University Press.

Shepherd, Laura. 2007. "'Victims, Perpetrators and Actors' Revisited: Exploring the Potential for a Feminist Reconceptualization of (International) Security and (Gender) Violence." *British Journal of Politics* 9: 239–56.

Singapore Ministry of Foreign Affairs (MFA) (2010). "Singapore's Detailed Response to the Allegations in the 2010 U.S. State Department's Trafficking in Persons Report." Available at www.news.gov.sg/public/sgpc/en/media_releases/agencies/mica/press_release/P-20100703-1/AttachmentPar/0/file/Detailed%20Reponse%20TIP%20report%202010%20(Final).pdf, accessed January 2011.

Singh, J.P., and Shilpa Hart. 2007. "Sex Workers and Cultural Policy: Mapping the Issues and Actors in Thailand." *Review of Policy Research* 24(March): 155–73.

Singh, Sunit, and Rama Charan Tripathi. 2010. "Why Do the Bonded Fear Freedom? Some Lessons from the Field." *Psychology and Developing Societies* 22(2): 249–297.

Skeldon, Ronald. 2000. "Trafficking: A Perspective from Asia." *International Migration* 38 (Supplement 1): 7–30.

Skinner, Benjamin E. 2009. *A Crime So Monstrous: Face-to-Face with Modern-Day Slavery*. New York: Simon and Schuster.

Slavers (Kate), The. 1864. *The Supreme Court*, 1864. 69 US 350, 364.

Smith, Charles Anthony, and Heather M. Smith. Forthcoming. "The Unintended Effects of UN Intervention." *International Political Science Review*.

Smith, Rep. Chris. 2006. Statement before the U.S. House Military Personnel Subcommittee of the Committee on Armed Services, meeting jointly with Africa, Global Human Rights, and International Operations Subcommittee of the Committee on International Relations. *Trafficking in Persons* hearing, June 21. Available at http://democrats.foreignaffairs.house.gov/archives/109/33587.PDF, accessed January 2011.

Smith, Danny. 2007. "The Transatlantic Slave Trade and How it Ended." In *Slavery: Now and Then*, ed. Danny Smith, 133–209. Eastbourne: Kingsway.

Smith, Michael, and Moreen Dee. 2003. *Peacekeeping in East Timor: The Path to Independence.* Boulder, Colo.: Lynne Rienner.

Smith, Robert B. 2009. "Global Human Development: Accounting for Its Regional Disparities." *Quality and Quantity* 43(1): 1–34.

Soderlund, Gretchen. 2005. "Running from the Rescuers: New U.S. Crusades Against Sex Trafficking and the Rhetoric of Abolition." *National Women's Studies Association Journal* 17(3): 54–87.

Sotiropoulos, Dimitri A., and Evika Karamagioli. 2006. "Greek Civil Society: The Long Road to Maturity. Civicus Civil Society Index Shortened Assessment Tool: Report for the Case of Greece." Available at www.civicus.org/new/media/CSI _Greece_Executive_Summary.pdf, accessed January 2011.

Soto, Jorene. 2007. "'We're Here to Protect Democracy. We're Not Here to Practice It': The U.S. Military's Involvement in Trafficking in Persons and Suggestions for the Future." *Cardozo Journal of Law & Gender* 13: 560–77.

Spaulding, Jay, and Stephanie Beswick, eds. 2010. *African Systems of Slavery.* Trenton, N.J.: Africa World Press.

Stetson, Chuck. 2007. "The Birth of Issue Campaigning." In *Creating the Better Hour: Lessons from William Wilberforce,* ed. Chuck Stetson, 87–104. Macon, Ga.: Stroud & Hall.

Stockholm International Peace Research Institute. 2010. Multilateral Peace Operations Database. Available at www.sipri.org/databases/pko/, accessed January 2011.

Stojanovic, Dusan. 1998. "Unrest Among Ethnic Albanians Raises Fear of War in Yugoslavia." Associated Press: International News, March 2.

Stolz, Barbara. 2005. "Educating Policymakers and Setting the Criminal Justice Policymaking Agenda: Interest Groups and the 'Victims of Trafficking and Violence Act of 2000.'" *Criminal Justice* 5(4): 407–30.

———. 2007. "Interpreting the U.S. Human Trafficking Debate Through the Lens of Symbolic Politics." *Law & Policy* 29 (July): 311–38.

Strecker, Sally and Louise Shelley. 2004. *Human Traffic and Transnational Crime: Eurasian and American Perspectives.* Lanham, MD: Rowman and Littlefield.

Sturcke, James. 2007. "Key Events in Sri Lanka's Tamil Separatist War." *Guardian,* November 2.

Sturdevant, Sandra Pollock, and Brenda Stoltzfus. 1992. *Let the Good Times Roll: Prostitution and the U.S. Military in Asia.* New York: New Press.

Sun, Sue. 2004. "Where the Girls Are: The Management of Venereal Disease by United States Military Forces in Vietnam." *Literature and Medicine* 23(1): 66–87.

Szulecka, M. forthcoming. "The Right To Be Exploited?" In *Human Rights and Migration,* ed. Christien van den Anker and Ilse van Liempt. New York and Basingstoke: Palgrave Macmillan.

Teitz, Susan. 1999. "America's Best Newspapers." *Columbia Journalism Review* (November/December).

Temperley, Howard. 1972. *British Anti-Slavery 1833–1870*. London: Longman.

Thrupkaew, Noy. 2009. "The Crusade Against Sex Trafficking." *The Nation*, October 5, and "Beyond Rescue," *The Nation*, October 26. Available at www.theinvestigative fund.org/reporters/noythrupkaew/, accessed January 2011.

Tickner, J. Ann. 1992. *Gender in International Relations: Feminist Perspectives on Achieving Global Security*. New York: Columbia University Press.

Tiefenbrun, Susan W. 2006–2007. "Updating the Domestic and International Impact of the U.S. Victims of Trafficking and Protection Act of 2000: Does Law Deter Crime?" *Case Western Reserve Journal of International Law* 38(2): 249–80.

Toledano, Ehud. 2007. *As if Silent and Absent: Bonds of Enslavement in the Islamic Middle East*. New Haven, Conn.: Yale University Press.

Tong-hyung, Kim. 2006. "Illegal Sex Trade Dying Hard." *Korea Times*, September 18.

Trafficking Victims Protection Reauthorization Act (TVPA). 2005. Pub. L. 109–164, H.R. 972.

———. 2003. Pub. L. No. 108–193, H.R. 2620.

Transatlantic Trends. 2009. *Transatlantic Trends: Immigration—Key Findings 2009*. Washington, D.C.: Transatlantic Trends. Available at www.gmfus.org/trends/ immigration/doc/TTI_2009_Key.pdf, accessed January 2011.

Tritaki, Panagiota. 2003. *Peacekeepers and Sex Trafficking: Supply and Demand in the Aftermath of the Kosovo Conflict*. Unpublished thesis, Faculty of the Fletcher School of Law and Diplomacy, Tufts University.

Truong, Thanh-Dam. 1990. *Sex, Money, and Morality: Prostitution and Tourism in Southeast Asia*. London: Zed Books.

Tuchman, Gaye. 1978. *Making News: A Study in the Construction of Reality*. New York: Free Press.

Turner, Rick.1994. "HIV Infection Rate, Use of Prostitutes Are Both High Among Young Military Recruits in Northern Thailand." *International Family Planning Perspectives* 20(1): 35–36.

Uçarer, Emek M. 1999. "Trafficking in Women: Alternate Migration or Modern Slave Trade?" In *Gender Politics in Global Governance*, ed. Mary K. Meyer and Elizabeth Prügl, 230–44. Boulder, Colo.: Rowman & Littlefield.

UK Border Agency. 2011. "Worker Registration Scheme." Available at www.ukba. homeoffice.gov.uk/workingintheuk/eea/wrs/workers/, accessed January 2011.

United Nations Conference of the Parties to the United Nations Convention Against Transnational Organized Crime (UNCOP). 2009. "Report on the Meeting of Experts on Possible Mechanisms to Review Implementation of the United Nations Convention Against Transnational Organized Crime held in Vienna on 30 September 2009." UN Doc. CTOC/COP/WG.1/2009/3.

United Nations Convention Against Transnational Organized Crime (UNCTOC). 2000. G.A. Res. 55/25, adopted November 15, 2000, and entered into force September 29, 2003.

United Nations Department of Peacekeeping Operations. 2010. "Fact Sheet: United Nations Peacekeeping." DPI/2429/Rev.7, March.

United Nations General Assembly. 1948. *Universal Declaration of Human Rights*. December 10.

United Nations High Commissioner for Refugees. 2002. "Note for Implementing and Operational Partners by UNHCR and Save the Children–UK on Sexual Violence and Exploitation." February 26.

United Nations Mission in Sierra Leone. 2002. "Statement by Acting-Special Representative of the Secretary-General Mr. Behrooz Sadry, in Reaction to the UNHCR–Save the Children Report." Press release, February 28.

United Nations News Centre. 2007. "Haiti: Over 100 Sri Lankan Blue Helmets Repatriated on Disciplinary Grounds—UN." November 2. Available at www .un.org/apps/news/story.asp?NewsID=24514&Cr=sri&Cr1=haiti, accessed January 2011.

United Nations Office on Drugs and Crime (UNODC). 2004. *United Nations Convention Against Transnational Organized Crime and the Protocols Thereto*. New York: United Nations.

———. 2006. *Trafficking in Persons: Global Patterns*. United Nations Office on Drugs and Crime.

———. 2009. "Global Report on Trafficking in Persons." Available at www.unodc.org/ documents/Global_Report_on_TIP.pdf, accessed 2011.

United Nations High Commissioner for Human Rights (UNHCHR), Office of. 2009. "UN Expert on Slavery Expresses Concern About 'Restavek' System in Haiti." Press release, June 10.

———. 2006. *Frequently Asked Questions on a Human Rights-Based Approach to International Development Cooperation*. UN Sales No. HR/PUB/06/8.

United Nations Protocol to Prevent, Suppress and Punish Trafficking in Persons, Especially Women and Children, supplementing the United Nations Convention Against Transnational Organized Crime (UN Trafficking Protocol). 2000. G.A. Res. 55/25, Annex II, UN GAOR, 55th Session, Supplement No. 49, at 60, UN Doc. A/45/49 (Vol. 1), 2001. Adopted Nov. 15, 2000, entered into force Dec. 25, 2003.

United Nations Security Council. 2004. *Resolution 1549*. S/RES/1549/2004, February 29.

United Nations Special Rapporteur on Trafficking in Persons. 2009. "Report Submitted by the Special Rapporteur on Trafficking in Persons, Especially Women and Children, Joy Ngozi Ezeilo." UN Doc. A/HRC/10/16, February 20.

United Nations Special Rapporteur on Violence Against Women, 2000. "Report of the Special Rapporteur, Ms. Radhika Coomaraswamy, on Violence Against Women, Its Causes and Consequences, on Trafficking in Women, Women's Migration and Violence against Women." UN Doc. E/CN.4/2000/68, February 29.

United Nations Stabilization Mission in Haiti (MINUSTAH). 2011. "MINUSTAH Background." Available at www.un.org/Depts/dpko/missions/minustah/background .html, accessed January 2011.

"UN Ousts Peacekeepers in Sex Case." 2007. *New York Times*, November 3.

U.S. Attorney General. 2006. *Attorney General's Annual Report to Congress on U.S. Government Activities to Combat Trafficking in Persons, FiscalYear 2005*. Available at www.usdoj.gov/ag/annualreports/tr2005/agreporthumantrafficing2005 .pdf, accessed July 2009.

———. 2007. *Attorney General's Annual Report to Congress and Assessment of the U.S. Government Activities to Combat Trafficking in Persons, Fiscal Year 2006*. Available at www.usdoj.gov/ag/annualreports/tr2006/agreporthumantrafficing2006 .pdf, accessed July 1, 2009.

———. 2008. *Attorney General's Annual Report to Congress and Assessment of the U.S. Government Activities to Combat Trafficking in Persons, Fiscal Year 2007*. Available at www.usdoj.gov/ag/annualreports/tr2007/agreporthumantrafficing2007 .pdf, accessed July 2009.

———. 2009. *Attorney General's Annual Report to Congress and Assessment of the U.S. Government Activities to Combat Trafficking in Persons, Fiscal Year 2008*. Available at www.state.gov/g/tip/rls/reports/2009/125631.htm, accessed January 2011.

U.S. Constitution. §§ 1581–1594.

U.S. Department of Justice. 2002. "Department of Justice Issues T Visa to Protect Women, Children and All Victims of Human Trafficking." Press release, January 24. Available at www.usdoj.gov/opa/pr/2002/January/02_crt_038.htm, accessed January 2011.

———. 2006. "Attorney General's Annual Report to Congress on U.S. Government Activities to Combat Trafficking in Persons Fiscal Year 2005." June. Available at www.justice.gov/archive/ag/annualreports/tr2005/agreporthumantrafficing2005 .pdf), accessed January 2011.

U.S. Department of Labor. 2009. "List of Goods Produced by Child Labor or Forced Labor." Available atwww.dol.gov/ilab/programs/ocft/pdf/2009tvpra.pdf), accessed January 2011.

U.S. Department of State. 1977–2010. *Country Reports on Human Rights Practices*, Washington, D.C.: U.S. Department of State.

———. 2001a. *Haiti: Country Reports on Human Rights Practices*. February, 23. Washington, D.C.: U.S. Department of State.

———. 2001b. *Trafficking in Persons Report*. Washington, D.C.: Office to Monitor and Combat Trafficking in Persons.

———. 2002. *Trafficking in Persons Report*. Washington, D.C.: Office to Monitor and Combat Trafficking in Persons.

———. 2003. *Trafficking in Persons Report*. Washington, D.C.: Office to Monitor and Combat Trafficking in Persons.

———. 2004a. "The Link Between Prostitution and Sex Trafficking." Bureau of Public Affairs, November 24.

——. 2004b. *Trafficking in Persons Report.* Washington, D.C.: Office to Monitor and Combat Trafficking in Persons.

——. 2005. *Trafficking in Persons Report.* Washington, D.C.: Office to Monitor and Combat Trafficking in Persons.

——. 2006. *Trafficking in Persons Report.* Washington, D.C.: Office to Monitor and Combat Trafficking in Persons.

——. 2007a. *Trafficking in Persons Report.* Washington, D.C.: Office to Monitor and Combat Trafficking in Persons.

——. 2007b. "U.S. Efforts to End Modern-Day Slavery." *States News Service,* May 9.

——. 2008. *Trafficking in Persons Report.* Washington, D.C.: Office to Monitor and Combat Trafficking in Persons.

——. 2009. *Trafficking in Persons Report.* Washington, D.C.: Office to Monitor and Combat Trafficking in Persons.

——. 2010a. *Trafficking in Persons Report.* Washington, D.C.: Office to Monitor and Combat Trafficking in Persons.

——. 2010b. *2010 International Narcotics Control Strategy Report.* Washington, D.C.: U.S. Department of State.

U.S. Government Accountability Office (USGAO). 2006. *Report to the Chairman, Committee on the Judiciary, and the Chairman, Committee on International Relations, House of Representatives: Human Trafficking: Better Data, Strategy, and Reporting Needed to Enhance U.S. Antitrafficking Efforts Abroad.* GAO-06–825. Washington, D.C.: U.S. Government Accountability Office.

——. 2007. *Human Trafficking: Monitoring and Evaluation of International Antitrafficking Projects Are Limited, but Experts Suggest Improvements.* GAO-07–1034. Washington, D.C.: U.S. Government Accountability Office.

U.S. House of Representatives. 2002. *Foreign Complicity in Human Trafficking: A Review of the State Department's "2002 Trafficking in Persons Report."* Committee on International Relations hearing, June 19.

——. 2004. "U.S. Command in Korea Gets Tough on Demand Side of Prostitution." Armed Services Committee and the Commission on Security and Cooperation in Europe statement, September 21. Available at www.america.gov/st/washfile-english/2004/September/20040923172445AJesroM0.8452722.html, accessed January 2011.

——. 2006. Military Personnel Subcommittee of the Committee on Armed Services, meeting jointly with Africa, Global Human Rights, and International Operations Subcommittee of the Committee on International Relations, *Trafficking in Persons* hearing, June 21. Available at http://democrats.foreignaffairs.house.gov/archives/109/33587.PDF, accessed January 2011.

U.S. President. 2005. "Executive Order 13387–2005, Amendments to the Manual for Courts-Martial, United States." *Federal Register* 70, no. 200. October 18.

U.S. Senate. 2000. *Trafficking Victims Protection Act of 2000.* 106th Congress, Public Law 106–386.

————. 2003. *Trafficking Victims Protection Reauthorization Act of 2003*. 108th Congress, Public Law 108–193.

Van Bueren, Geraldine. 2004. "Slavery as Piracy: The Legal Case for Reparations for the Slave Trade." In *The Political Economy of New Slavery*, ed. Christien van den Anker, 235–47. Basingstoke: Palgrave.

van Dam, Marcel. 2009. *Niemandsland: Biografie van een ideaal*. Amsterdam: De Bezige Bij.

van den Anker, Christien. 2002. "Global Justice, Global Institutions and Global Citizenship." In *Global Citizenship*, ed. Nigel Dower and John Williams, 158–68. Edinburgh: Edinburgh University Press.

————, ed. 2004. *The Political Economy of New Slavery*. Basingstoke: Palgrave.

————. 2005. "Cosmopolitanism and Human Rights." In *The Essentials of Human Rights*, ed. Rhona Smith and Christien van den Anker, 67–69. Oxford: Hodder Arnold.

————. 2006. "Trafficking and Women's Rights: Beyond the Sex Industry to Other Industries." *Journal of Global Ethics*, Special Issue: Women's Rights in Europe 3(1): 161–80.

————. 2007. "Contemporary Slavery and Global Ethics." *Global Social Policy* (April): 7–10.

————. 2008. "Cosmopolitanism and Trafficking in Human Beings for Forced Labor." In *Sex as Crime?* ed. Gayle Letherby, Kate Williams, Philip Birch, and Maureen E. Cain, 137–55. Cullompton: Willan.

————. 2010. "Transnationalism and Cosmopolitanism: Towards Global Citizenship?" *Journal of International Political Theory* 6(1): 73–94.

van den Anker, Christien, and Anti-Slavery International. 2006. *Trafficking for Forced Labor in Europe*. London: Antislavery International.

van den Anker, Christien, and Joroen Doomernik, eds. 2006. *Trafficking and Women's Rights*. New York and Basingstoke: Palgrave Macmillan.

Van der Leun, Joanne. 2010. "The Netherlands: Assessing the Irregular Population in a Restrictive Setting." In *Irregular Migration in Europe: Myths and Realities*, ed. Anna Triandafyllidou, 187–206. Farnham: Ashgate.

van Liempt, Ilse. 2007. *Navigating Borders*. Amsterdam: Amsterdam University Press.

————. 2010. "Different Geographies and Experiences of 'Assisted' Types of Migration: A Gendered Critique on the Distinction Between Trafficking and Smuggling." *Gender, Place and Culture* 18(2).

Van Walsum, Sarah, and Thomas Spijkerboer. 2007. Introduction. In *Women and Immigration Law: New Variation on Classical Feminist Themes*, ed. Sarah Van Walsum and Thomas Spijkerboer, 1–11. New York: Routledge-Cavendish.

Vandenberg, Martina. 2002. *Hopes Betrayed: Trafficking of Women and Girls to Post-Conflict Bosnia and Herzegovina for Forced Prostitution*, 14:9. New York: Human Rights Watch.

Verlinden, An. 2010. "On the Liberal Impasse in Coping with the Immigration Dilemma." *Journal of International Political Theory* 6(1): 51–72.

Victims of Trafficking and Violence Protection Act (TVPA). 2000. Pub. L. No. 106–386.

Vollmer, Bastian. 2010. "Dichotomized Discourses and Changing Landscapes: Counting the Uncountable in the UK." In *Irregular Migration in Europe: Myths and Realities*, ed. Anna Triandafyllidou, 267–90. Farnham: Ashgate.

Vreeland, James. 2008. "The Effect of Political Regime on Civil War: Unpacking Anocracy." *Journal of Conflict Resolution* 52(3): 401–25.

Waever, Ole, Barry Buzan, Morten Kelstrup, and Pierre Lemaitre. 1993. *Identity, Migration and the New Security Agenda in Europe*. New York: St. Martin's Press.

Warren, Kay. 2010. "The Illusiveness of Counting 'Victims' and the Concreteness of Ranking Counties: Trafficking in Persons from Colombia to Japan." In *Sex, Drugs and Body Counts: The Politics of Numbers in Global Crime and Conflict*, ed. Peter Andreas and Kelly M. Greenhill. Ithaca, N.Y.: Cornell University Press.

Waugh, Louisa. 2006. *Selling Olga: Stories of Human Trafficking and Resistance*. London: Phoenix.

Weissbrodt, David. 2008. *The Rights of Non-Citizens*. Oxford: Oxford University Press.

Weitzer, Ronald. 2007. "The Social Construction of Sex Trafficking: Ideology and Institutionalization of a Moral Crusade." *Politics & Society* 35(3): 447–75.

Welch, Claude. 2009. "Defining Contemporary Forms of Slavery: Updating a Venerable NGO." *Human Rights Quarterly* 31(1): 70–129.

Whelan, Daniel. 2010. *Indivisible Human Rights: A History*. Philadelphia: University of Pennsylvania Press.

Wickramasinghe, Nira. 2006. *Sri Lanka in the Modern Age: A History of Contested Identities*. New Delhi: Foundation Books.

Wilkenfield, Jonathan, and Michael Brecher. 1984. "International Crisis, 1945–1975: The UN Dimension." *International Studies Quarterly* 28(1): 45–67.

William Wilberforce Trafficking Victims Protection Reauthorization Act (TVPA). 2008. Pub. L. 110–457, H.R. 7311.

Williams, Carol. 2007. "UN Confronts Another Sex Scandal." *Los Angeles Times*, December 15.

Wolff, Tobias Barrington. 2002. "The Thirteenth Amendment and Slavery in the Global Economy." *Columbia Law Review* 102: 973–1050.

The Women Outside: Korean Women and the U.S. Military. 1995. Produced and directed by J.T. Takagi and Hye Jung Park. Third World Newsreel. Videocassette. 52 min.

Wood, Elisabeth Jean. 2006. "Variation in Sexual Violence During War." *Politics & Society* 34(3): 307–42.

Wright, Marcia. 1993. *Strategies of Slaves & Women: Life Stories from East/Central Africa*. London: James Currey.

Wyler, Liana Sun, and Alison Siskin. 2010. "Trafficking in Persons: U.S. Policy and Issues for Congress." Congressional Research Service. Available at www.fpc.state.gov/documents/organization/139278.pdf, accessed January 2011.

Wyler, Liana Sun, Alison Siskin, and Clare Ribando Seelke. 2009. "Trafficking in Persons: U.S. Policy and Issues for Congress (July 2)." Washington, D.C.: Congressional Research Service.

Wylie, Gillian, and Penelope McRedmond. 2010. *Human Trafficking in Europe: Character, Causes and Consequences.* New York and Basingstoke: Palgrave Macmillan.

Zhang, Sheldon X. 2007. *Smuggling and Trafficking in Human Beings.* Westport, Conn.: Praeger.

Zimelis, Andris. 2009. "Human Rights, the Sex Industry and Foreign Troops." *Cooperation and Conflict* 44(1): 51–71.

Zimmerman, Yvonne C. 2005. "Situating the Ninety-Nine: A Critique of the Trafficking Victims Protection Act." *Journal of Religion & Abuse* 7(3): 37–56.

List of Contributors

Kevin Bales, Professor of Modern Slavery, Wilberforce Institute for the Study of Slavery and Emancipation, University of Hull, and President of Free the Slaves.

Alison Brysk, Mellichamp Professor, Global and International Studies Program, University of California, Santa Barbara.

Austin Choi-Fitzpatrick, PhD Candidate in Sociology and Assistant Director at the Center for the Study of Social Movements, University of Notre Dame.

Anne Gallagher, Independent Scholar, Bangkok, Thailand.

Jeff Gulati, Associate Professor, Political Science, Bentley University.

Laura Hebert, Associate Professor, Department of Diplomacy and World Affairs, Occidental College.

Mark J. Miller, Emma Smith Morris Professor, Department of Political Science and International Relations, University of Delaware.

Joel Quirk, Deputy Director of the Wilberforce Institute for the Study of Slavery and Emancipation, and RCUK Fellow in Law, Culture, and Human Rights at the University of Hull.

Charles Anthony Smith, Assistant Professor, Political Science, University of California at Irvine.

Heather T. Smith, Assistant Professor, Department of International Affairs, Lewis and Clark College.

Christien van den Anker, Reader in the Department of History, Politics, and Philosophy at the University of West England, Bristol.

Gabriela Wasileski, PhD Candidate, Department of Sociology and Criminology, University of Delaware.

Index

Acknowledgments

This project is the fruition of several cross-cutting dialogues. Alison Brysk is grateful to Austin Choi-Fitzpatrick, for laying the initial foundation through a series of conference panels, and Joel Quirk for his editorial role in that early phase. Tony Smith has also played a special collaborative role in bringing additional contributions and authors from his own co-edited journal issue into this dialogue, along with Heather Smith. We thank *Human Rights Review* and Springer Publications for allowing this project to publish revised versions of the chapters by Anne Gallagher, Tony Smith, Wasileski and Miller, and Alison Brysk that previously appeared in other forms in that journal. We appreciate the efforts of Peter Agree and the University of Pennsylvania Press to give the project a home in the Pennsylvania Studies in Human Rights series, and the editorial assistance of Josh Dinsman.

Alison Brysk's research on all aspects of international human rights has been generously supported by the Duncan and Suzanne Mellichamp Chair in Global Governance of the University of California at Santa Barbara. She has also received timely research assistance from UC Irvine doctoral student Madeline Baer, and useful academic reflections from professor Gershon Shafir of the University of California San Diego. Above all, she is grateful for the support of her family, friends, and fellow travelers in the struggle for human dignity, especially Miriam and Ana Brysk Freeman—who each in their own way embody the spirit of rethinking and emancipation of this volume.

Austin would like to thank the volume's contributors, all of whom were a pleasure to work with. Many thanks to my co-editor, Alison Brysk, for believing in this project and for giving it the fuel it needed, and also to Kevin Bales, for agreeing to collaborate on an essay developing the conclusions planted in his 2007 book. With Alison I share a deep appreciation of Peter Agree at Penn, who recognized the project's potential and provided crucial support. This volume's origins lie in a brainstorm with Laura Hebert at a long-ago International Studies Association meeting and were developed further with Joel

Quirk. Along the way the ideas here have been nurtured and refined through conversations and debates with friends, colleagues, and mentors: Joshua MacIvor-Andersen, Beth Dunlap, Sophia Javed, and Kathryn MacIvor-Andersen; Kevin Bales, Peggy Callahan, and Jolene Smith; Jacqueline Bearman, Grace Chang, Rich Fineman, Joel Quirk, and Chris Sullivan; Kraig Beyerlein, Alison Brysk, Christian Davenport, Rory McVeigh, Dan Myers, Jackie Smith, and Ernesto Verdeja; Diane West, Jim Norton, Tom Jimison, Chris Harris, David Levine, Peter Van Arsdale, Erika Summers-Effler and Christian Smith. Thanks as well to members of the Politics and Movements Working Group at Notre Dame, who provided early and challenging encouragement when this project was in the earliest stages.

This project benefited from the research assistance of Anna Nanigian and Neva Lundy (facilitated by the financial support of the Institute for the Study of Liberal Arts) as well as the keen editorial sensibilities of Josh Dinsman. Financial support for my work has come in various forms over the life of the project. Particular thanks to Mary Beckman, at the Center for Social Concerns (Notre Dame), and Dean Greg Sterling for early funding of the optimistic sort, and to the fine folks at the Kellogg Institute for International Studies (Notre Dame) for a subsequent and sensible Graduate Seed Grant. I owe a hearty thanks to everyone mentioned, and heartfelt apologies to anyone I have inadvertently overlooked. A final nod goes to Jack Donnelly, whose wise counsel in a graduate seminar long ago, "always turn dichotomies into continuum," has remained with me to this day.

On a personal note I am greatly appreciative of my parents, David Fitzpatrick and Peggy Yoder, who have modeled for their children a life of inquiry and awe, and to their parents, from whom they learned these foundational attributes. A deep debt of happy gratitude to my two daughters, Aila Pax and Eden Justice. They are testimony to the fact that the world has everything to gain from powerful, persistent, and creative women. A final thanks to my life partner, Jenny Choi, whose leadership and life work gives daughters around the world the opportunities they deserve.

CPSIA information can be obtained
at www.ICGtesting.com
Printed in the USA
JSHW012001201119
2570JS00001B/120